WE WANT YOUR OPINION!

The lilaguide is written exclusively *by* parents *for* parents.

We collect thousands of surveys from parents to create these unique word-of-mouth guides for new and expectant parents.

To participate in our survey please go to:

www.lilaguide.com

the lila guide

by PARENTS *for* PARENTS

THE WORD-OF-MOUTH SURVIVAL GUIDE FOR
NEW AND EXPECTANT PARENTS

SAN FRANCISCO & BAY AREA

2003

PUBLISHED & DISTRIBUTED BY OAM SOLUTIONS, INC.
SAN FRANCISCO, CA   WWW.LILAGUIDE.COM

THE LILAGUIDE – BY PARENTS, FOR PARENTS
SAN FRANCISCO & BAY AREA 2003

Published by:
OAM Solutions, Inc.
139 Saturn Street
San Francisco, CA 94114, USA
orders@lilaguide.com
www.lilaguide.com

table of contents

No, for the last time, the baby does not come with a handbook. And even if there were a handbook, you wouldn't read it. You'd fill out the warranty card, throw out the box, and start playing right away. Until a few hours passed and you were hit with the epiphany of, "Jeeze honey, what in the wide, wide world of childcare are we doing here?"

Relax. We had that panicked thought when we had our daughter Delilah. And so did all the parents we talked to when they had their children. And while we all knew there was no handbook, there was, we found, a whole lot of word-of-mouth information. Everyone we talked to had some bit of child rearing advice about what baby gear store is the most helpful. Some nugget of parenting wisdom about which restaurant tolerates strained carrots on the floor. It all really seemed to help. Someone, we thought, should write this down.

And that's when, please pardon the pun, the lilaguide was born. The book you're holding now is a guide written by Bay Area parents for Bay Area parents. It's what happens when someone actually does write it down (and organizes it, calculates it, and presents it in an easy-to-use format).

Over 6,000 surveys have produced the 2003 edition of the San Francisco & Bay Area lilaguide. It provides a truly unique insider's view of over 1,200 "parent-friendly" stores, restaurants, service providers, and activities that are about to become a very big part of your life. And while this guide won't tell you how to change a diaper or how to get by on little or no sleep (that's what grandparents are for), it will tell you what other local parents have learned about the amazing things the Bay Area has to offer.

So there you have it. Now go make some phone calls, clean up the house, take a nap, or do something on your list before the baby arrives.

Enjoy!

Oli Mittermaier & Elysa Marco, MD

We'd like to take a moment to offer a heart-felt thank you to all the **parents** who **participated in the survey** and took the time to share their thoughts and opinions. Without your participation, we would never have been able to create this unique guide.

Special thanks to **Felicity John Odell** for leading the editorial charge, **Satoko Furuta** for her beautiful sense of design and **Lane Foard** for making the words yell.

Additional thanks also to **Mindy Ariowitsch, Cullen Curtiss, Kristin Lamson**, and **Mary Steele** for hours spent proofreading and making sure all the pieces fit together. And, of course, thank you to **Paul Smith, Ken Miles** and **T. Jackson** for their creativity, support and encouragement.

And last, but certainly not least, a big thank you to **our parents** for their unconditional support in this and all our other endeavors.

disclaimer

This book is designed to share parents' opinions regarding baby-related products, services and activities. It is sold with the understanding that the information contained in the book does not represent the publisher's opinion or recommendations.

The reviews contained in this guide are based on public opinion surveys and are therefore subjective in nature. The publisher shall have neither liability nor responsibility to any person or entity with respect to any loss or damage caused, or alleged to have been caused, directly or indirectly, by the information contained in this book.

If you do not wish to be bound by the above, you may return this book (in resalable condition) to the publisher for a full refund.

Please remember that this guide is **not intended to be a comprehensive directory** since it does not contain every baby store or activity in the Bay Area. Rather, it is intended to provide a short-list of places that parents **deemed exciting and noteworthy**. If a place or business is not included in the guide it simply means that nobody rated or submitted information about it to us. **Please let us know** about providers you think should be included in the guide via our website at **www.lilaguide.com**.

listings & ratings

Most listings have stars and numbers as part of their write-up. These symbols mean the following:

❺ / ★★★★★	extraordinary
❹ / ★★★★	very good
❸ / ★★★	good
❷ / ★★	fair
❶ / ★	poor
✓	available
✗	not available/applicable

If a ☆ is listed instead of ★, it means that the rating is less reliable because a small number of parents surveyed the listing. Furthermore, if a listing has **no stars** or **criteria ratings**, it means that although the listing was rated, the number of surveys submitted was so low that we did not feel it justified an actual rating.

The **quotes** are taken directly from surveys submitted to the lilaguide. Other than spelling and minor grammatical changes, they come to you as they came to us. Quotes were selected based on how well they appeared to represent the collective opinions of the surveys submitted.

We have contacted the businesses listed to verify their address and phone number, as well as to inquire about their hours, class schedules and web site information. Since some of this information may change after this guide has been printed we appreciate you letting us know of any errors/omissions by notifying us via email at lila@lilaguide.com.

Parent picks were selected based on a combination of their **overall rating** and the **number of surveys** submitted. In other words, those places that received the highest ratings from the most parents were selected.

maternity clothing

DAYONE	san francisco	p.19
DRESS	san francisco	p.19
JAPANESE WEEKEND MATERNITY	san francisco	p.20
MIMI MATERNITY	multiple locations	
MOM'S THE WORD	multiple locations	
MOTHERHOOD MATERNITY	multiple locations	
TARGET	multiple locations	

nursery furnishings

BABIES R US	multiple locations	
CARTAN'S	san ramon	p.52
CITIKIDS	san francisco	p.36
GOODNIGHT ROOM	berkeley	p.54
HELLER'S FOR CHILDREN	san rafael	p.71
JONATHAN KAYE BABY	san francisco	p.40
LULLABY LANE	san bruno	p.84

baby clothing

BABIES R US	multiple locations	
BABYGAP/GAPKIDS	multiple locations	
LULLABY LANE	san bruno	p.84
OLD NAVY	san francisco	p.45
SWEET POTATOES	albany	p.63
THE CHILDREN'S PLACE	multiple locations	

baby & toddler shoes

toys & books

used baby items

breast pump sales & rentals

parenting resources & classes

nanny referrals & baby sitters

exercise programs

haircuts

children's photographers

activities & play groups

playgrounds & parks

child-friendly restaurants

While there may be days when you'd enjoy having someone paint a big logo on your naked belly and float you over a major sporting event, more often than not you'll want to be dressed.

And that's where maternity shops come in. But think about it. How great is this? You get to shop for an entirely new wardrobe. In doing so, of course, you could end up spending much of your unborn's college savings on clothes you'll wear only a few times. For that very reason, mothers insist it's important to find a store with an experienced and knowledgeable staff (and a good return policy) who can steer you toward the right styles that can be worn for several months (and perhaps even a few years later when you have baby number two).

San Francisco

A Pea In The Pod ★★★

www.apeainthepod.com
SAN FRANCISCO - 290 SUTTER ST (AT GRANT AVE)
TEL: 415.391.1400 HOURS: M-SA 10-6; SU 11-5
Parking: garage on Stockton

❝...although this store can be pricey, the clothing is of good quality and will last you throughout your pregnancy...best to catch their sales where you can find some great buys...great for career oriented clothing...they have dressier clothes than most other stores, but they also have a higher price tag...their bathing suit selection was the best I have seen anywhere... **❞**

Product Selection

		Criteria	
Casual attire	✓	$$$$	Prices
Business wear	✓	❹	Product availability
Intimate apparel	✓	❹	Staff knowledge
Nursing accessories	✓	❹	Customer service
Used items available	✗	❹	Decor

DayOne ★★★★

www.dayonecenter.com
SAN FRANCISCO - 3490 CALIFORNIA ST, STE 203 (AT LOCUST ST)
TEL: 415.440.3291 HOURS: M-F 9:30-6; SA 11-6; SU 11-5
Parking: garage on Locust St

❝...a great moms store with a decent selection of maternity clothing...the staff is a great resource for all things related to parenting and they are very helpful in determining what size and style of nursing bras to use...good sales... **❞**

Product Selection

		Criteria	
Casual attire	✓	$$$	Prices
Business wear	✗	❹	Product availability
Intimate apparel	✓	❹	Staff knowledge
Nursing accessories	✓	❺	Customer service
Used items available	✗	❹	Decor

Dress ★★★★

SAN FRANCISCO - 2271 CHESTNUT ST (AT SCOTT ST)
TEL: 415.440.3737 HOURS: M-SA 10:30-6:30; SU 12-5
Parking: street parking

❝...if you need something special for a big event or just want to treat yourself - this is the place to go...many stylish finds for moms-to-be who are ardently anti-frump and looking for non-chain-retailer clothing...chic maternity wear at very chic prices...who knew that maternity clothes could be so sexy... **❞**

Product Selection

		Criteria	
Casual attire	✓	$$$$	Prices
Business wear	✓	❹	Product availability
Intimate apparel	✓	❹	Staff knowledge
Nursing accessories	✓	❺	Customer service
Used items available	✗	❹	Decor

Japanese Weekend Maternity ★★★★

SAN FRANCISCO - 500 SUTTER ST (AT POWELL ST)
TEL: 415.989.6667 HOURS: M-SA 10-6; SU 11-5
Parking: garage on Stockton St

❝...great styles and the fit is great...fabulous selection of very trendy, formfitting clothes...love their comfy, under-the-belly pants...good sales...plenty to choose from - business wear to casual...changing area is a bit weird and public...website is great as well, you can make website returns in the store...excellent mid-priced maternity wear... ❞

Product Selection

		Criteria	
Casual attire	✓	$$$	Prices
Business wear	✓	❺	Product availability
Intimate apparel	✓	❹	Staff knowledge
Nursing accessories	✓	❺	Customer service
Used items available	✗	❹	Decor

Minis-Kids & Maternity

SAN FRANCISCO - 2278 UNION ST (AT FILLMORE ST)
TEL: 415.567.9537 HOURS: M-SA 10:30-6:30; SU 11-5
Parking: street parking

Mom's The Word ★★★★

www.momstheword.com
SAN FRANCISCO - 3385 SACRAMENTO ST (AT WALNUT ST)
TEL: 415.441.8261 HOURS: M-SA 10-6; SU 12-5
Parking: street parking

❝...you can get a trendy outfit for everyday, a special occasion dress, a stylish swimsuit and cute workout clothes - total one-stop maternity shopping...finally a store that has normal clothes to get you through your pregnancy without looking like a big pumpkin...a bit pricey but the clothes are beautiful...the staff is very helpful - they'll take your number and call you when an item comes in from a manufacturer...they carry XS sizes too... ❞

Product Selection

		Criteria	
Casual attire	✓	$$$$	Prices
Business wear	✓	❹	Product availability
Intimate apparel	✓	❹	Staff knowledge
Nursing accessories	✓	❺	Customer service
Used items available	✗	❹	Decor

Natural Resources ★★★

www.naturalresourcesonline.com

SAN FRANCISCO - 1307 CASTRO ST (AT 24TH ST)
TEL: 415.550.2611 HOURS: M-F 10:30-6; SA 11-5; SU 12-4
Parking: street parking

❝...more of a community resource place than a retail shop...a limited selection of maternity clothes, but their staff is great...good selection of nursing accessories...the styles are not the hippest, but very practical...street parking can be tough around there... ❞

Product Selection

			Criteria
Casual attire	✓	$$$	Prices
Business wear	✓	❸	Product availability
Intimate apparel	✓	❹	Staff knowledge
Nursing accessories	✓	❹	Customer service
Used items available	✓	❷	Decor

Newborn Connections ★★★★

www.cpmc.org/newbornconnections

SAN FRANCISCO - 3698 CALIFORNIA ST, 1ST FL (AT MAPLE ST)
TEL: 415.600.2229 HOURS: M T TH F 9-5; W 9-6; SA 10-2
Parking: garage on Locust St

❝...this is a great place for nursing wear and intimate apparel...not an enormous selection of maternity clothing, but you will find something cute...comfortable environment and very helpful staff...parking's always lousy in the area... ❞

Product Selection

			Criteria
Casual attire	✗	$$$	Prices
Business wear	✗	❸	Product availability
Intimate apparel	✓	❹	Staff knowledge
Nursing accessories	✓	❹	Customer service
Used items available	✗	❷	Decor

Nordstrom ★★★

www.nordstrom.com

SAN FRANCISCO - 865 MARKET ST # 500 (AT 5TH ST)
TEL: 415.243.8500 HOURS: M-SA 9:30-9; SU 10-7
Parking: garage on Mission St btwn 4th & 5th Sts

❝...one of the few stores that seems to carry the unbelievably comfortable and stylish belly basics line of maternity clothing...limited selection, but always an easy store to shop in...prices are higher than they should be... ❞

Product Selection

Casual attire .... ✓
Business wear......................... ✗
Intimate apparel .... ✓
Nursing accessories................. ✗
Used items available .... ✗

Criteria

$$$ .... Prices
❸ .... Product availability
❸ .... Staff knowledge
❹ .... Customer service
❹ .... Decor

Old Navy   ★ ★ ★ ★

www.oldnavy.com

SAN FRANCISCO - 801 MARKET ST (AT 4TH ST)
TEL: 415.344.0375 HOURS: M-SA 9:30-9; SU 11-8
Parking: garage on Mission St btwn 4th & 5th Sts

❝...you get a nice casual wardrobe for not a lot of money...they also have a good online ordering system and you can return online orders in the store...don't expect expert too much sales help - you're on your own...the selection of stretchy T's is great...won't feel guilty if you get rid of your maternity clothes after the pregnancy because the prices are so reasonable...❞

Product Selection

Casual attire .... ✓
Business wear......................... ✗
Intimate apparel .... ✗
Nursing accessories................. ✗
Used items available .... ✗

Criteria

$$.. Prices
❹ .... Product availability
❸ .... Staff knowledge
❸ .... Customer service
❸ .... Decor

Ross Dress For Less   ☆ ☆

www.rossstores.com

SAN FRANCISCO - 1545 SLOAT BLVD (BTWN RIVERTON & SPRINGFIELD DRS)
TEL: 415.661.0481 HOURS: M-SA 9:30-9:30; SU 11-7
Parking: lot in front of store

SAN FRANCISCO - 2300 16TH ST # 265 (AT POTRERO AVE)
TEL: 415.554.1901 HOURS: M-SA 9:30-9:30; SU 11-7
Parking: lot in front of store

SAN FRANCISCO - 5200 GEARY BLVD (AT 16TH AVE)
TEL: 415.386.7677 HOURS: M-SA 9:30-9:30; SU 11-7
Parking: lot in front of store

❝...go early in your pregnancy while you have the stamina for digging around and standing in a slow line...the shopping experience is not wonderful...you have to get lucky at Ross since availability of good brand names is minimal...the prices are rock bottom...❞

Product Selection

Casual attire .... ✓
Business wear......................... ✗
Intimate apparel .... ✗
Nursing accessories................. ✗
Used items available .... ✗

Criteria

$ .... Prices
❷ .... Product availability
❷ .... Staff knowledge
❷ .... Customer service
❶ .... Decor

East Bay

1 2 Just Like New

ALAMEDA - 1203 PARK ST (AT SAN JOSE AVE)
TEL: 510.523.6506   HOURS: M-SA 10:30-5; SU BY APPT
Parking: street parking

Birth & Bonding Family Ctr

www.birthbonding.org

ALBANY - 1126 SOLANO AVE (AT SAN PABLO AVE)
TEL: 510.527.2121 HOURS: M-SA 10-5
Parking: street parking

Product Selection		Criteria	
Casual attire	✓	$$$$	Prices
Business wear	✓	❸	Product availability
Intimate apparel	✓	❺	Staff knowledge
Nursing accessories	✓	❺	Customer service
Used items available	✗	❸	Decor

Child's Play   ☆ ☆ ☆ ☆

OAKLAND - 5858 COLLEGE AVE (AT CHABOT RD)
TEL: 510.653.3989 HOURS: TU-F 10-5:30; SA 11-5; SU 12-5
Parking: lot behind store

"...really friendly...a nice place to get good prices on new and used items...it is hit-or-miss as is any other second-hand place...they have a gated play area for children... **"**

Product Selection		Criteria	
Casual attire	✓	$$	Prices
Business wear	✓	❹	Product availability
Intimate apparel	✓	❺	Staff knowledge
Nursing accessories	✗	❹	Customer service
Used items available	✓	❸	Decor

Cotton & Co   ★ ★ ★ ★

LAFAYETTE - 3535 MT DIABLO BLVD (AT MORAGA RD)
TEL: 925.299.9356 HOURS: M-SA 10-6; SU 12-5
Parking: street parking

OAKLAND - 5901 COLLEGE AVE (AT CHABOT RD)
TEL: 510.653.8058 HOURS: M-SA 10-6; SU 12-5
Parking: lot behind store

"...the best place to go for nursing bras...do an excellent job of fitting you, they even know to ask if you are 'full' or not...Claudette, the owner, is terrific and knowledgeable - she will take one look at you, and know exactly the right size for you, and fit you out so you walk out more comfortable than ever...a bit on the pricey side... **"**

Product Selection

Casual attire .... ✓
Business wear........................... ✓
Intimate apparel .... ✓
Nursing accessories.................. ✓
Used items available .... ✗

Criteria

$$$$ .... Prices
❸ .... Product availability
❹ .... Staff knowledge
❹ .... Customer service
❹ .... Decor

Crackerjacks

OAKLAND - 14 GLEN AVE (AT PIEDMONT AVE)
TEL: 510.654.8844 HOURS: M-F 10-5:30; SA 10-5
Parking: street parking

Fashion After Passion   ★ ★ ★ ★

www.fashionafterpassion.com
ALAMEDA - 1521 WEBSTER ST (AT HAIGHT AVE)
TEL: 510.769.6667 HOURS: TU-SA 10-5:30
Parking: street parking

❝...supposedly they have thousands of nursing bras in stock...friendly staff...a great place to trade in maternity clothes...the owner is very up-to-date about products...a bit on the chilly side, literally...could be more organized... ❞

Product Selection

Casual attire .... ✓
Business wear........................... ✗
Intimate apparel .... ✓
Nursing accessories.................. ✓
Used items available .... ✗

Criteria

$$ .... Prices
❹ .... Product availability
❹ .... Staff knowledge
❺ .... Customer service
❷ .... Decor

JCPenney   ☆ ☆ ☆

www.jcpenney.com
CONCORD - 484 SUN VALLEY MALLTEL: 925.687.6000 HOURS: M-SA 10-9; SU 11-7
Parking: mall has a lot

PLEASANTON - 1500 STONERIDGE MALL RD (AT STONERIDGE DR)
TEL: 925.463.9780 HOURS: M-SA 10-9; SU 11-7
Parking: mall has a lot

❝...too many old-fashioned-type maternity clothes that made me feel like I was an old lady...I was able to find work attire and casual clothes without having to spend a fortune...although their stores do not carry large sizes, the catalog has a great selection... ❞

Product Selection

Casual attire .... ✓
Business wear........................... ✗
Intimate apparel .... ✓
Nursing accessories.................. ✗
Used items available .... ✗

Criteria

$$ .... Prices
❸ .... Product availability
❸ .... Staff knowledge
❸ .... Customer service
❷ .... Decor

Kids Again

DUBLIN - 6891 VILLAGE PKWY (AT LEWIS AVE)
TEL: 925.828.7334 HOURS: M-SA 10-5
Parking: lot behind store

Lauren's Closet

ALAMEDA - 1420 PARK ST (BTWN SANTA CLARA & CENTRAL AVES)
TEL: 510.865.2219 HOURS: M W F SA 10-5:30; TU & TH 11-5:30; SU 12-4
Parking: lot behind store

Mimi Maternity

www.mimimaternity.com

WALNUT CREEK - 2 BROADWAY LN (AT S MAIN ST)
TEL: 925.932.8863 HOURS: M-F 10-9; SA 10-7; SU 11-6
Parking: garage behind store

❝*...if you're still working, it's worth buying a few good pieces here for business attire...a solid selection of cute casual stuff too....good deals to be found on the sales rack...clothing seems to run small with not a lot of size variety...you won't look like Rachel on Friends, but you can get the basics here...* **❞**

Product Selection

		Criteria
Casual attire	✓	$$$ .... Prices
Business wear	✓	❹ .... Product availability
Intimate apparel	✓	❹ .... Staff knowledge
Nursing accessories	✓	❹ .... Customer service
Used items available	✗	❹ .... Decor

Mom's The Word

www.momstheword.com

WALNUT CREEK - 1628 NORTH MAIN ST (BTWN LINCOLN AVE & CIVIC DR)
TEL: 925.937.6818 HOURS: M-SA 10-6; SU 11-5
Parking: lot behind store

Motherhood Maternity

www.motherhood.com

CONCORD - 274 SUN VALLEY MALL
TEL: 925.609.8965 HOURS: M-SA 10-9; SU 11-6
Parking: mall has a big lot

NEWARK - 1074 NEWPARK MALL (AT MOWRY AVE)
TEL: 510.794.9616 HOURS: M-SA 10-9; SU 11-6
Parking: mall has lot

PLEASANTON - 2337 STONERIDGE MALL RD (AT LAUREL CREEK)
TEL: 925.463.8700 HOURS: M-SA 10-9; SU 11-6
Parking: mall has lot

RICHMOND - 1312 HILLTOP MALL RD (OFF BLUME DR)
TEL: 510.243.0902 HOURS: M-SA 10-9; SU 11-6
Parking: mall has a lot

WALNUT CREEK - 1551 BOTELHO DR (AT S CALIFORNIA BLVD)
TEL: 925.934.8694 HOURS: M-SA 10-9; SU 11-6
Parking: lot in front of store

❝...inexpensive and good for everyday-around-the-house wear...not necessarily the most stylish clothes, but they certainly cover all the basics...they could use a better selection of nursing bras in a greater range of sizes...highly recommended for those who don't want to spend a fortune on maternity clothes...overall, great value for the money...**❞**

Product Selection		Criteria	
Casual attire	✓	$$	Prices
Business wear	✓	❹	Product availability
Intimate apparel	✓	❹	Staff knowledge
Nursing accessories	✓	❹	Customer service
Used items available	✗	❸	Decor

Nurture Ctr

www.nurturecenter.com

LAFAYETTE - 3399 MT DIABLO BLVD (AT BROWN AVE)
TEL: 925.283.1346 HOURS: M-W & F-SA 10-5; TH 10-8
Parking: lot in front & back of store

❝...great selection of maternity and nursing wear...very helpful and very knowledgeable staff...pleasant environment...lots of resources...locally owned business...**❞**

Product Selection		Criteria	
Casual attire	✓	$$	Prices
Business wear	✗	❹	Product availability
Intimate apparel	✓	❺	Staff knowledge
Nursing accessories	✓	❺	Customer service
Used items available	✗	❹	Decor

Ross Dress For Less

www.rossstores.com

BERKELEY - 2190 SHATTUCK AVE (AT ALLSTON WY)
TEL: 510.549.9761 HOURS: M-SA 9:30-8; SU 11:30-8:30
Parking: lot in front of store

www.rossstores.com

WALNUT CREEK - 1295 S MAIN ST (AT BROADWAY LN)
TEL: 925.934.1900 HOURS: M-SA 9:30-9:30; SU 11-7
Parking: lot in front of store

❝...go early in your pregnancy while you have the stamina for digging around and standing in a slow line...the shopping experience is not wonderful...you have to get lucky at Ross since availability of good brand names is minimal...the prices are rock bottom...**❞**

Product Selection

Casual attire .... ✓
Business wear........................... ✗
Intimate apparel .... ✗
Nursing accessories................. ✗
Used items available .... ✗

Criteria

$ .... Prices
❷ .... Product availability
❷ .... Staff knowledge
❷ .... Customer service
❷ .... Decor

Target

★ ★ ★ ★

www.target.com

SAN RAMON - 2610 BISHOP DR (AT BOLLINGER CANYON RD)
TEL: 925.277.0202 HOURS: M-SA 8-10; SU 8-9
Parking: lot in front of store

WALNUT CREEK - 1871 N MAIN ST (AT YGNACIO VALLEY RD)
TEL: 925.979.0083 HOURS: M-SA 8-10; SU 8-9
Parking: lot in front of store

"...casual wear and intimate apparel for a great price...you don't have to go out of your way to go maternity clothes shopping...a very convenient place to fill your wardrobe at very low prices...solid on the basics as well as some fashionable seasonal pieces...not the greatest customer service, because you can never find anyone to help you...overall worth checking out... "

Product Selection

Casual attire .... ✓
Business wear........................... ✗
Intimate apparel .... ✗
Nursing accessories................. ✗
Used items available .... ✗

Criteria

$ .... Prices
❹ .... Product availability
❷ .... Staff knowledge
❸ .... Customer service
❸ .... Decor

North Bay

Glow Girl

www.glowgirlmaternity.com

MILL VALLEY - 7 THROCKMORTON AVE (AT E BLITHEDALE AVE)
TEL: 415.383.4141 HOURS: M-SA 10:30-6; SU 12-5
Parking: street parking

"*...Sooooooo cute...the style is flirty, hip and downright non-maternity...the things you buy here are items you'll want to wear after your baby is born...the most enjoyable shopping experience you can have trying on maternity clothes...clothing ranges from reasonably priced to more high end...***"**

Product Selection		Criteria
Casual attire .... ✓	$$$ .... Prices
Business wear.......................... ✓	❸ .... Product availability
Intimate apparel .... ✓	❹ .... Staff knowledge
Nursing accessories.................. ✓	❹ .... Customer service
Used items available .... ✗	❹ .... Decor

Mimi Maternity

www.mimimaternity.com

CORTE MADERA - 1514 REDWOOD HWY (AT TAMALPAIS DR)
TEL: 415.945.3275 HOURS: M-F 10-9; SA 10-7:30; SU 11-6
Parking: mall has a lot

"*...if you're still working, it's worth buying a few good pieces here for business attire...a solid selection of cute casual stuff too....good deals to be found on the sales rack...clothing seems to run small with not a lot of size variety...you won't look like Rachel on Friends, but you can get the basics here...***"**

Product Selection		Criteria
Casual attire .... ✓	$$$ .... Prices
Business wear.......................... ✓	❹ .... Product availability
Intimate apparel .... ✓	❹ .... Staff knowledge
Nursing accessories.................. ✓	❹ .... Customer service
Used items available .... ✗	❸ .... Decor

Motherhood Maternity

www.motherhood.com

NOVATO - 104 VINTAGE WY # A7 (AT ROWLAND BLVD)
TEL: 415.209.9755 HOURS: M-SA 10-9; SU 11-6
Parking: mall has lot

PETALUMA - 2200 PETALUMA BLVD N # 1115 (AT SKILLMAN LN)
TEL: 707.763.3261 HOURS: M-SA 10-8; SU 11-6
Parking: lot in front of store

VACAVILLE - 311 NUT TREE RD # H (AT ORANGE DR)
TEL: 707.446.4792 HOURS: M-SA 10-9; SU 11-6
Parking: lot in front of store

"...*inexpensive and good for everyday-around-the-house wear...not necessarily the most stylish clothes, but they certainly cover all the basics...they could use a better selection of nursing bras in a greater range of sizes...highly recommended for those who don't want to spend a fortune on maternity clothes...overall, great value for the money...* **"**

Product Selection

			Criteria	
Casual attire	✓	$$	....	Prices
Business wear	✓	❹	....	Product availability
Intimate apparel	✓	❹	....	Staff knowledge
Nursing accessories	✓	❹	....	Customer service
Used items available	✗	❸	....	Decor

Target   ★ ★ ★

www.target.com

NAPA - 205 SOSCOL AVE (AT IMOLA AVE)
TEL: 707.224.1058 HOURS: M-SA 8-10; SU 8-9
Parking: lot in front of store

NOVATO - 200 VINTAGE WY (AT ROWLAND BLVD)
TEL: 415.892.3313 HOURS: M-SA 8-10; SU 8-9
Parking: lot in front of store

ROHNERT PARK - 475 ROHNERT PARK EXPY W (AT LABATH AVE)
TEL: 707.586.2901 HOURS: M-SA 8-10; SU 8-9
Parking: lot in front of store

"...*casual wear and intimate apparel for a great price...you don't have to go out of your way to go maternity clothes shopping...a very convenient place to fill your wardrobe at very low prices...solid on the basics as well as some fashionable seasonal pieces...not the greatest customer service, because you can never find anyone to help you...overall worth checking out...* **"**

Product Selection

			Criteria	
Casual attire	✓	$$	....	Prices
Business wear	✗	❸	....	Product availability
Intimate apparel	✗	❷	....	Staff knowledge
Nursing accessories	✗	❷	....	Customer service
Used items available	✗	❷	....	Decor

Peninsula

A Pea In The Pod

www.apeainthepod.com

MENLO PARK - 180 EL CAMINO REAL # 155 (AT CAMBRIDGE AVE)
TEL: 650.321.0752 HOURS: M-F 10-6; SA 10-7; SU 11-6
Parking: lot in front of store

PALO ALTO - 180 STANFORD SHOPPING CTR # 74 (AT UNIVERISTY AVE)
TEL: 650.321.0752 HOURS: M-F 10-9; SA 10-7; SU 11-6
Parking: mall has a lot

❝...although this store can be pricey, the clothing is of quality and will last you throughout your pregnancy...best to catch their sales where you can find some great buys...great for career oriented clothing...they have dressier clothes than most other stores, but they also have a higher price tag...their bathing suit selection was the best I have seen anywhere...❞

Product Selection		Criteria	
Casual attire	✓	$$$$	Prices
Business wear	✓	❹	Product availability
Intimate apparel	✓	❹	Staff knowledge
Nursing accessories	✓	❹	Customer service
Used items available	✗	❹	Decor

JCPenney

www.jcpenney.com

SAN BRUNO - 1122 EL CAMINO REAL (AT SNEATH LN)
TEL: 650.873.4100 HOURS: M-SA 10-9; SU 11-7
Parking: mall has a lot

Motherhood Maternity

www.motherhood.com

DALY CITY - 37 SERRAMONTE CTR (AT SERRAMONTE BLVD)
TEL: 650.992.1673 HOURS: M-SA 10-9; SU 11-6
Parking: mall has a big lot

MILPITAS - 266 GREAT MALL DR (AT ESCORT DR)
TEL: 408.262.0950 HOURS: M-SA 10-9; SU 11-6
Parking: mall has a lot

SAN JOSE - 114 OAKRIDGE MALL # 501 (AT SANTA TERESA BLVD)
TEL: 408.972.8969 HOURS: M-SA 10-9; SU 11-6
Parking: mall has a lot

SAN MATEO - 3400 S EL CAMINO REAL # 233 (AT HILLSDALE BLVD)
TEL: 650.358.9628 HOURS: M-SA 10-9; SU 11-6
Parking: lot in front of store

❝...inexpensive and good for everyday-around-the-house wear...not necessarily the most stylish clothes, but they certainly cover all the basics...they could use a better selection of nursing *bras in a greater range of sizes...highly recommended for those who don't want to spend a fortune on maternity clothes...overall, great value for the money...* **"**

Product Selection

Casual attire	....	✓
Business wear	....	✓
Intimate apparel	....	✓
Nursing accessories	....	✓
Used items available	....	✗

Criteria

$$	....	Prices
❹	....	Product availability
❹	....	Staff knowledge
❹	....	Customer service
❸	....	Decor

Target

★ ★ ★ ★

www.target.com

DALY CITY - 5001 JUNIPERO SERRA BLVD (AT SERRAMONTE BLVD)
TEL: 650.992.8433 HOURS: M-SA 8-10; SU 8-9
Parking: lot in front of store

SAN BRUNO - 1150 EL CAMINO REAL (AT SNEATH LN)
TEL: 650.827.0171 HOURS: M-SA 8-10; SU 8-9

"*...casual wear and intimate apparel for a great price...you don't have to go out of your way to go maternity clothes shopping...a very convenient place to fill your wardrobe at very low prices...solid on the basics as well as some fashionable seasonal pieces...not the greatest customer service, because you can never find anyone to help you...overall worth checking out...* **"**

Product Selection

Casual attire	....	✓
Business wear	....	✗
Intimate apparel	....	✗
Nursing accessories	....	✗
Used items available	....	✗

Criteria

$$	....	Prices
❹	....	Product availability
❷	....	Staff knowledge
❸	....	Customer service
❸	....	Decor

Online

Babystyle ★ ★ ★ ★

www.babystyle.com

"...great selection of maternity clothes...good prices...watch for free shipping offers...items generally ship quickly..."

Product Selection

Casual attire .... ✓

Business wear........................... ✓

Intimate apparel .... ✓

Nursing accessories .... ✓

Used items available .... ✗

Criteria

$$$ .... Prices

 .... Product availability

GapMaternity ★ ★ ★ ★

www.gap.com

"...great for wardrobe builders at pretty good prices...the site does a good job of explaining fits...quality is pretty good and this is a great place to stock up on your casual clothing...very hip and cool maternity clothes that fit great and are very comfortable..."

Product Selection

Casual attire .... ✓

Business wear........................... ✗

Intimate apparel .... ✗

Nursing accessories .... ✗

Used items available .... ✗

Criteria

$$ .... Prices

 .... Product availability

Old Navy ★ ★ ★ ★

www.oldnavy.com

"...so easy and convenient...they have free shipping if you need to exchange for a differnet size..."

Product Selection

Casual attire .... ✓

Business wear........................... ✗

Intimate apparel .... ✗

Nursing accessories .... ✗

Used items available .... ✗

Criteria

$$ .... Prices

 .... Product availability

As we all strive to be as perfect and happy as the family pictured on the box the car seat came in, we have to remember that those people are models and have had their sleep deprivation and absolute confusion airbrushed out. Nonetheless you will have to buy your share of baby accessories and look at these people's faces. So don't let it get to you.

Anyway, "baby basics" is a catch-all term for everything ranging from baby clothing and nursery furnishings to outing equipment and toys. There is a vast choice of products and brands for you to spend money on and equally a large selection of sources from which you can buy these products. The stores listed in this section range from little boutiques to large baby super stores. Some provide convenient parking which is worth investigating, especially since many stores will offer to help load items into your car and will even install a car seat for you. Stores also vary from ones that are cute and fun to shop in, to larger mall-like shops whose primary focus is price and product selection. Finding a store with staff that is both knowledgeable and willing to help is advisable since you will probably have lots of questions that will need to be answered.

San Francisco

Ambassador Toys ★★★★

SAN FRANCISCO - 186 W PORTAL AVE (BTWN 14TH & SANTA CLARA AVES)
TEL: 415.759.8697 HOURS: M-SA 9-7; SU 9-5
Parking: street parking

SAN FRANCISCO - 1981 UNION ST (AT BUCHANAN ST)
TEL: 415.345.8697 HOURS: DAILY 10-7
Parking: street parking

"...great toy store...huge variety of unique items for all ages...nice stuff, but overpriced...knowledgeable and friendly staff...when you're done shopping at the store, there are lots of cafes and other shops nearby for grown-ups...... **"**

Product Selection

			Criteria
Nursery furnishings	✗	$$$	Prices
Baby clothing	✗	❹	Product availability
Baby/toddler shoes	✗	❹	Staff knowledge
Feeding supplies	✗	❹	Customer service
Diapers & toiletries	✗	❹	Decor
Outing equipment	✗		
Toys & books	✓		
Used items available	✗		

Ark Toys Books & Crafts ★★★★

SAN FRANCISCO - 3845 24TH ST (AT SANCHEZ ST)
TEL: 415.821.1257 HOURS: M-TH & SA 10-6; F 10-7; SU 10-5
Parking: street parking

"...good selection of whimsical, well-crafted toys...very inviting window display...nice, but not cheap...this tiny store is chock-full, so the staff is helpful when you need a hand navigating the packed shelves and aisles...the focus is on learning and imagination toys and activities, rather than licensed characters or the usual plastics...great selection of wooden toys... **"**

Product Selection

			Criteria
Nursery furnishings	✗	$$$	Prices
Baby clothing	✗	❹	Product availability
Baby/toddler shoes	✗	❹	Staff knowledge
Feeding supplies	✗	❹	Customer service
Diapers & toiletries	✗	❹	Decor
Outing equipment	✗		
Toys & books	✓		
Used items available	✗		

BabyGap/GapKids

★ ★ ★ ★

www.gap.com

SAN FRANCISCO - 100 POST ST (AT KEARNY ST)
TEL: 415.421.2314 HOURS: M-SA 9:30-8; SU 11-7
Parking: street parking

SAN FRANCISCO - 2169 CHESTNUT ST (AT SCOTT ST)
TEL: 415.771.9316 HOURS: M-SA 10-8; SU 11-6
Parking: street parking

SAN FRANCISCO - 3251 20TH AVE # 113-17 (AT STONESTOWN GALLERIA)
TEL: 415.564.7137 HOURS: M-SA 10-9; SU 11-6
Parking: mall has a lot

SAN FRANCISCO - 3491 CALIFORNIA ST (AT LOCUST ST)
TEL: 415.386.7517 HOURS: M-SA 9:30-7; SU 11-6
Parking: garage on Locust St

SAN FRANCISCO - 890 MARKET ST (AT POWELL ST)
TEL: 415.788.4648 HOURS: M-SA 9:30-9; SU 10-7
Parking: garage on Mission St btwn 4th & 5th Sts

❝...cute, hip and fun baby and kids clothes that are practical and affordable...check out the sale rack for the best bargains around...they are a little light on the boy clothes but who isn't...nursing station and bathroom in most stores...products are generally available and if not, they will find what you're looking for in a nearby store...staff is usually very knowledgeable and available to help...the only problem with BabyGap is that almost none of the clothes for 12 months and over have snaps on the legs, which doesn't make changing easy...good return policy, which is great for gifts ❞

Product Selection

Nursery furnishings .... ✗
Baby clothing .... ✓
Baby/toddler shoes .... ✗
Feeding supplies .... ✗
Diapers & toiletries .... ✗
Outing equipment .... ✗
Toys & books........................... ✗
Used items available .... ✗

Criteria

$$$ .... Prices
❹ .... Product availability
❹ .... Staff knowledge
❹ .... Customer service
❹ .... Decor

Citikids

★ ★ ★ ★ ★

www.citikids.com

SAN FRANCISCO - 152 CLEMENT ST (BTWN 2ND & 3RD AVES)
TEL: 415.752.3837 HOURS: M-SA 10-6; SU 11-5
Parking: small lot in front of store

❝...one of the few independent children's stores left...very well run store located in the heart of SF...they have almost everything you need, especially the big ticket items like car seats, highchairs, strollers, furniture...it is a delight to shop there because they are so friendly and the store is clean and bright....they will also install your car seat for you for free...certainly not the cheapest store, but a nice one-stop shop...service, service, service - they'll even carry things to your car for you...Clement Street parking is generally rough and parking in the store's small lot is hit-or-miss... **"**

Product Selection

			Criteria
Nursery furnishings	✓	$$$	Prices
Baby clothing	✓	❹	Product availability
Baby/toddler shoes	✓	❹	Staff knowledge
Feeding supplies	✓	❺	Customer service
Diapers & toiletries	✗	❸	Decor
Outing equipment	✓		
Toys & books	✓		
Used items available	✗		

Costco Wholesale ★ ★ ★

www.costco.com

SAN FRANCISCO - 450 10TH ST (AT HARRISON ST)
TEL: 415.626.4288 HOURS: M-F 11-8:30; SA 9:30-6; SU 10-6
Parking: garage on site

"...Costco is great for diapers, wipes and formula all in bulk at unbeatable prices...lots of great children's books and some toys at discount prices...limited selection of baby clothing...gets really crowded and can be a real pain with a baby...easy parking... **"**

Product Selection

			Criteria
Nursery furnishings	✓	$	Prices
Baby clothing	✓	❸	Product availability
Baby/toddler shoes	✗	❷	Staff knowledge
Feeding supplies	✓	❸	Customer service
Diapers & toiletries	✓	❷	Decor
Outing equipment	✓		
Toys & books	✓		
Used items available	✗		

DayOne ★ ★ ★ ★

www.dayonecenter.com

SAN FRANCISCO - 3490 CALIFORNIA ST, STE 203 (AT LOCUST ST)
TEL: 415.440.3291 HOURS: M-F 9:30-6; SA 11-6; SU 11-5
Parking: garage on Locust St

"...an amazing resource for Bay Area parents...a welcoming atmosphere makes it a great place to shop for baby essentials...incredible nurses, lactation counselors, classes, toys, books and clothes...parenting references and web access available...a comfy place for nursing and changing makes it a good place to shop if you're in the neighborhood... **"**

Product Selection

Nursery furnishings	✓
Baby clothing	✓
Baby/toddler shoes	✓
Feeding supplies	✓
Diapers & toiletries	✗
Outing equipment	✓
Toys & books	✓
Used items available	✗

Criteria

$$$	Prices
❹	Product availability
❺	Staff knowledge
❺	Customer service
❺	Decor

Dottie Doolittle ★★★

SAN FRANCISCO - 3680 SACRAMENTO ST (AT SPRUCE ST)
TEL: 415.563.3244 HOURS: M-SA 9:30-6; SU 12-5
Parking: street parking

❝...plenty of sweet, hard-to-find-elsewhere fancy clothes here...prices reach the upper margins, so my shopping at Dottie's is limited to special-events attire and big-milestone gifts...superb customer service...baby clothes worth bragging about... ❞

Product Selection

Nursery furnishings	✗
Baby clothing	✓
Baby/toddler shoes	✗
Feeding supplies	✗
Diapers & toiletries	✗
Outing equipment	✗
Toys & books	✓
Used items available	✗

Criteria

$$$$	Prices
❸	Product availability
❹	Staff knowledge
❹	Customer service
❺	Decor

FAO Schwarz ★★★★

www.fao.com

SAN FRANCISCO - 48 STOCKTON ST (BTWN ELLIS & OFARREL STS)
TEL: 415.394.8700 HOURS: M-TH 10-6; F-SA 10-7; SU 11-6
Parking: garage at Ellis & Ofarrel Sts

❝...kid heaven...amazingly fun place to visit but some things are pretty expensive...the store is one big building of eye candy...FAO Schwarz will have everything you're looking for and more...staff is very knowledgeable and eager to please customers...worth the trip, even if only to gawk... ❞

Product Selection

Nursery furnishings	✗
Baby clothing	✗
Baby/toddler shoes	✗
Feeding supplies	✗
Diapers & toiletries	✗
Outing equipment	✗
Toys & books	✓
Used items available	✗

Criteria

$$$$	Prices
❹	Product availability
❹	Staff knowledge
❹	Customer service
❺	Decor

Growing Up

SAN FRANCISCO - 240 W PORTAL AVE (BTWN VICENTE ST & SAN ANSELMO AVE)
TEL: 415.661.6304 HOURS: M-SA 10-6; SU 12-4
Parking: street parking

Gymboree ★★★★

www.gymboree.com

SAN FRANCISCO - 3407 CALIFORNIA ST (AT LAUREL ST)
TEL: 415.668.1387 HOURS: M-F 9:30-7; SA 9:30-6; SU 11-5
Parking: lot in front of store

SAN FRANCISCO - 865 MARKET ST # 106 (AT 5TH ST)
TEL: 415.543.9488 HOURS: M-SA 9:30-8; SU 11-6
Parking: lot in front of store

❝...great stuff...very cute...expensive but good quality items...staff is always nice...great for sales - you can usually find clothing for 50-75% off, and there is a wide range of sizes in sale items...designs for girls are bright and colorful...boys clothes are slightly conservative but very cute...clothes have a tendency to run slightly smaller then other comparable brands...very durable and make great hand-me-downs... ❞

Product Selection

		Criteria	
Nursery furnishings	✗	$$$	Prices
Baby clothing	✓	❹	Product availability
Baby/toddler shoes	✗	❹	Staff knowledge
Feeding supplies	✗	❹	Customer service
Diapers & toiletries	✗	❹	Decor
Outing equipment	✗		
Toys & books	✗		
Used items available	✗		

Home Remedies

www.homeremediessf.com

SAN FRANCISCO - 1026 VALENCIA ST (AT 21ST ST)
TEL: 415.826.2026 HOURS: T-F 12-7; SA 11-6; SU 12-5
Parking: garage located at 21st & Bartlett

Imaginarium ★★★★

www.imaginarium.com

SAN FRANCISCO - 3535 CALIFORNIA ST (BTWN LOCUST & SPRUCE STS)
TEL: 415.387.9885 HOURS: M-SA 10-7; SU 10-5
Parking: lot behind store

❝...great toys and gifts...layout of store a bit cluttered making it hard to shop and maneuver a stroller...all kinds of toys for various developmental levels and ages...customer service is excellent...quality is exceptional... ❞

Product Selection

Nursery furnishings .... ✗
Baby clothing .... ✗
Baby/toddler shoes .... ✗
Feeding supplies .... ✗
Diapers & toiletries .... ✗
Outing equipment .... ✗
Toys & books........................... ✓
Used items available .... ✗

Criteria

$$ .... Prices
❹ .... Product availability
❸ .... Staff knowledge
❸ .... Customer service
❹ .... Decor

Jean Et Marie ★★★★

www.jeanetmarie.com
SAN FRANCISCO - 100 CLEMENT ST (AT 2ND AVE)
TEL: 415.379.1111 HOURS: M-SA 10-6; SU 12-5
Parking: street parking

❝...owned by a delightful French woman who clearly takes pride in her inventory...a wonderful selection of French baby and children's clothing...cute selection of soft toys...unless you have a few extra dollars to spend, this is probably not the best place for buying wardrobe basics...unlike any other store in San Francisco...perfect place to buy special gifts...parking is not the best... ❞

Product Selection

Nursery furnishings .... ✗
Baby clothing .... ✓
Baby/toddler shoes .... ✗
Feeding supplies .... ✗
Diapers & toiletries .... ✗
Outing equipment .... ✗
Toys & books........................... ✓
Used items available .... ✗

Criteria

$$$ .... Prices
❺ .... Product availability
❹ .... Staff knowledge
❹ .... Customer service
❹ .... Decor

Jonathan Kaye Baby ★★★★

www.jonathankaye.com
SAN FRANCISCO - 3615 SACRAMENTO ST (AT LOCUST ST)
TEL: 415.922.3233 HOURS: M-F 10-6; SA 10-5:30
Parking: street parking

❝...top-notch furnishings displayed in a welcoming, fun atmosphere...a complete A to Z, upscale baby furniture store...definitely not the cheapest, but if you want gorgeous stuff this is the place to get it...their clothing selection can be limited in choice and size...metered and 2-hour neighborhood street parking is easiest to find on weekdays... ❞

Product Selection

Nursery furnishings .... ✓
Baby clothing .... ✓
Baby/toddler shoes .... ✗
Feeding supplies .... ✗
Diapers & toiletries .... ✗
Outing equipment .... ✗
Toys & books......................... ✓
Used items available .... ✗

Criteria

$$$$ .... Prices
❸ .... Product availability
❹ .... Staff knowledge
❸ .... Customer service
❺ .... Decor

Junior Boot Shop

SAN FRANCISCO - 3555 CALIFORNIA ST (AT LOCUST & SPRUCE STS)
TEL: 415.751.5444 HOURS: M-SA 9:30-6
Parking: garage on Locust St

❝*...this is the kind of shoe store that measures your baby's foot and keeps a size chart on file for you in case you forget...staff very knowledgeable and helpful...happy place to be...they send reminder cards based upon when they think your child will need his next pair of shoes...* ❞

Product Selection

Nursery furnishings .... ✗
Baby clothing .... ✗
Baby/toddler shoes .... ✓
Feeding supplies .... ✗
Diapers & toiletries .... ✗
Outing equipment .... ✗
Toys & books......................... ✗
Used items available .... ✗

Criteria

$$$ .... Prices
❹ .... Product availability
❹ .... Staff knowledge
❹ .... Customer service
❸ .... Decor

Just For Fun-Scribble Doodles

www.justforfun.invitations.com

SAN FRANCISCO - 3982 24TH ST (AT NOE ST)
TEL: 415.285.4068 HOURS: M-F 9-8; SA 9-7; SU 10-6
Parking: street parking

❝*...amazing what they cram into this tiny store...a well-edited selection of gifts and things...the best place for custom invitations and announcements...fabulous displays...gifts for all ages and lots of arts/crafts too...* ❞

Product Selection

Nursery furnishings .... ✗
Baby clothing .... ✗
Baby/toddler shoes .... ✗
Feeding supplies .... ✗
Diapers & toiletries .... ✗
Outing equipment .... ✗
Toys & books......................... ✓
Used items available .... ✗

Criteria

$$$ .... Prices
❹ .... Product availability
❹ .... Staff knowledge
❹ .... Customer service
❺ .... Decor

K-B Toys

★ ★ ★

www.kbtoys.com

SAN FRANCISCO - 3251 20TH AVE # 173 (AT STONESTOWN GALLERIA)
TEL: 415.665.5254 HOURS: M-SA 10-9; SU 11-7
Parking: mall has a lot

"...a big toy super store...very good prices and convenient parking...lots of store specials...not the place if you're looking for unique toys...their best attribute is their willy-nilly mark down procedure - sometimes over 75 percent off...a lot of plastic...recommended for staples such as Play-doh or Fisher-Price baby toys..."

Product Selection		Criteria	
Nursery furnishings	✗	$$	Prices
Baby clothing	✗	❸	Product availability
Baby/toddler shoes	✗	❸	Staff knowledge
Feeding supplies	✗	❸	Customer service
Diapers & toiletries	✗	❷	Decor
Outing equipment	✗		
Toys & books	✓		
Used items available	✗		

Kidiniki

☆ ☆ ☆ ☆

SAN FRANCISCO - 2 EMBARCADERO CTR (AT DRUMM ST)
TEL: 415.986.5437 HOURS: M-F 10-7; SA 10-5; SU 12-5
Parking: garage in the Embarcadero Ctr

"...great place for specialty clothing for kids...especially good if you need a unique gift or a special occasion outfit...prices are a bit steep, but you definitely get what you pay for..."

Product Selection		Criteria	
Nursery furnishings	✗	$$$$	Prices
Baby clothing	✓	❸	Product availability
Baby/toddler shoes	✓	❸	Staff knowledge
Feeding supplies	✗	❸	Customer service
Diapers & toiletries	✗	❹	Decor
Outing equipment	✗		
Toys & books	✓		
Used items available	✗		

Kids Only

☆ ☆ ☆ ☆

SAN FRANCISCO - 1608 HAIGHT ST (AT CLAYTON ST)
TEL: 415.552.5445 Parking: street parking

"...the funkiest fashions in town - from tie-dyed onesies to fur-lined satin jackets...this is a gem of a store...a friendly-faced shop owner who runs a Haight Street classic...parking is rough..."

Product Selection

Nursery furnishings .... ✗
Baby clothing .... ✓
Baby/toddler shoes .... ✓
Feeding supplies .... ✗
Diapers & toiletries .... ✗
Outing equipment .... ✗
Toys & books.......................... ✓
Used items available .... ✗

Criteria

$$$$ .... Prices
 .... Product availability
❹ .... Staff knowledge
❺ .... Customer service
❹ .... Decor

Kinder Sport Junior Ski & Sport

www.kindersport.com

SAN FRANCISCO - 3566 SACRAMENTO ST (AT LOCUST ST)
TEL: 415.563.7778 HOURS: M-F 10-6; SA 10-5SU 12-5
Parking: garage on Locust St

Maison De Belles Choses ☆☆☆☆☆

SAN FRANCISCO - 3263 SACRAMENTO ST # A (AT PRESIDIO AVE)
TEL: 415.345.1797 HOURS: M-SA 10-6; SU 11-5
Parking: street parking

❝...lots of beautiful French clothes from basic cotton pajamas to occasion clothes...cute store...great place for baby gifts...she not only carries baby items but also other things which mom might like for herself... ❞

Product Selection

Nursery furnishings .... ✗
Baby clothing .... ✓
Baby/toddler shoes .... ✗
Feeding supplies .... ✗
Diapers & toiletries .... ✗
Outing equipment .... ✗
Toys & books.......................... ✓
Used items available .... ✗

Criteria

$$ .... Prices
 .... Product availability
❺ .... Staff knowledge
❺ .... Customer service
❺ .... Decor

Mervyn's ★★★★

www.mervyns.com

SAN FRANCISCO - 2675 GEARY BLVD (AT MASONIC AVE)
TEL: 415.921.0888 HOURS: DAILY 9-10
Parking: lot on site

❝...you don't go for service, you go for prices...when you hit, you hit big at Mervyns...lots to choose from...great prices for basics...essentials are often on sale too...you can get other family shopping done too... ❞

Product Selection

Nursery furnishings	✗
Baby clothing	✓
Baby/toddler shoes	✗
Feeding supplies	✗
Diapers & toiletries	✗
Outing equipment	✗
Toys & books	✗
Used items available	✗

Criteria

$	Prices
❹	Product availability
❸	Staff knowledge
❸	Customer service
❷	Decor

Mudpie ★★★

SAN FRANCISCO - 1694 UNION ST (AT GOUGH ST)
TEL: 415.771.9262   HOURS: M-SA 10-6; SU 11-5
Parking: street parking

❝...the clothes are darling...makes a mom drool, but so expensive that you wouldn't want baby to drool...beautiful selection of adorable items...best for fancy party dresses...aloof staff that can be unbearably snooty...good place for gifts or special occasion items...pray for good parking karma because it can be a pain to park around Union Street...**❞**

Product Selection

Nursery furnishings	✓
Baby clothing	✓
Baby/toddler shoes	✗
Feeding supplies	✗
Diapers & toiletries	✗
Outing equipment	✗
Toys & books	✗
Used items available	✗

Criteria

$$$$	Prices
❸	Product availability
❹	Staff knowledge
❸	Customer service
❺	Decor

Mudpie Homeworks ★★★

SAN FRANCISCO - 1750 UNION ST (BTWN OCTAVIA & GOUGH STS)
TEL: 415.673.8060   HOURS: M-SA 11-5; SU 12-5
Parking: street parking

❝...small, special selection of nursery furnishings...best suited to larger budgets...if custom and high end is what you want then this is the place to buy...**❞**

Product Selection

Nursery furnishings	✓
Baby clothing	✗
Baby/toddler shoes	✗
Feeding supplies	✗
Diapers & toiletries	✗
Outing equipment	✗
Toys & books	✗
Used items available	✗

Criteria

$$$$	Prices
❸	Product availability
❹	Staff knowledge
❸	Customer service
❺	Decor

Natural Resources

www.naturalresourcesonline.com

SAN FRANCISCO - 1307 CASTRO ST (AT 24TH ST)
TEL: 415.550.2611 HOURS: M-F 10:30-6; SA 11-5; SU 12-4
Parking: street parking

Nordstrom ★★★★

www.nordstrom.com

SAN FRANCISCO - 865 MARKET ST # 500 (AT 5TH ST)
TEL: 415.243.8500 HOURS: M-SA 9:30-9; SU 10-7
Parking: garage on Mission St btwn 4th & 5th Sts

"...if you have the money it's definitely worth shopping at Nordstrom...the quality is beyond compare...their liberal return policy makes it convenient to shop there...excellent customer service...good selection of high quality formal outfits for all seasons and both genders... **"**

Product Selection

			Criteria
Nursery furnishings	✗	$$$	Prices
Baby clothing	✓	❹	Product availability
Baby/toddler shoes	✓	❹	Staff knowledge
Feeding supplies	✗	❺	Customer service
Diapers & toiletries	✗	❹	Decor
Outing equipment	✗		
Toys & books	✗		
Used items available	✗		

Old Navy ★★★★

www.oldnavy.com

SAN FRANCISCO - 801 MARKET ST (AT 4TH ST)
TEL: 415.344.0375 HOURS: M-SA 9:30-9; SU 11-8
Parking: garage on Mission St btwn 4th & 5th Sts

"...cheap, cheap, cheap...this place rocks...Old Navy should definitely be on every new parent's rounds...great play clothes...prices are excellent and the quality is solid...if you see something you like, buy it - it probably won't be there next week...so much stuff and so many people that the experience can be overwhelming...very friendly, but sometimes scarce staff... **"**

Product Selection

			Criteria
Nursery furnishings	✗	$	Prices
Baby clothing	✓	❹	Product availability
Baby/toddler shoes	✗	❸	Staff knowledge
Feeding supplies	✗	❹	Customer service
Diapers & toiletries	✗	❸	Decor
Outing equipment	✗		
Toys & books	✗		
Used items available	✗		

Peek-A-Bootique

SAN FRANCISCO - 1306 CASTRO ST (AT 24TH ST)
TEL: 415.641.6192 HOURS: M-SA 10:30-6; SU 12-5
Parking: street parking

"...this is one of the best places in town to get used baby clothes, especially newborn...the staff is usually pretty busy and stretched for time, but don't let that put you off...everything is at least half of what you would pay to get it new...it's worth looking through their well organized racks...easy parking and a friendly neighborhood makes this store a regular place to stop and check out ... **"**

Product Selection

Nursery furnishings	✓
Baby clothing	✓
Baby/toddler shoes	✓
Feeding supplies	✗
Diapers & toiletries	✓
Outing equipment	✓
Toys & books	✓
Used items available	✓

Criteria

$$	Prices
❸	Product availability
❸	Staff knowledge
❸	Customer service
❸	Decor

Right Start

www.rightstart.com
SAN FRANCISCO - 3435 SACRAMENTO ST (BTWN WALNUT & LAUREL STS)
TEL: 415.202.1901 HOURS: M-SA 10-6; SU 11-5
Parking: street parking

"...love, love, love the Right Start...so many wonderful developmentally appropriate toys, books, videos and equipment...only carries top of the line infant carriers, strollers, and joggers, which is very comforting...perfect place to register if you're having a baby shower...store appears to be stocked with carefully selected, high quality products...wish there were more discounts on big ticket items to be found...the store charges full retail, but well worth it... **"**

Product Selection

Nursery furnishings	✗
Baby clothing	✗
Baby/toddler shoes	✗
Feeding supplies	✓
Diapers & toiletries	✗
Outing equipment	✓
Toys & books	✓
Used items available	✗

Criteria

$$$	Prices
❹	Product availability
❺	Staff knowledge
❹	Customer service
❹	Decor

Small Frys ★★★★

www.smallfrys.com

SAN FRANCISCO - 4066 24TH ST (AT CASTRO ST)
TEL: 415.648.3954 HOURS: M-TH & SA 10-6; F 10-7; SU 11-5:30
Parking: small lot across the street

"...a charming boutique with a delightful clothing, educational toy and infant shoe selection...mix of traditional styles and hip clothes...very friendly and knowledgeable staff...you're even welcome to nurse in the fitting rooms...great bulletin board with helpful postings for baby sitters, preschools, daycare, and parent/child classes...toy table to keep children busy while you shop...**"**

Product Selection

		Criteria	
Nursery furnishings	✗	$$$$	Prices
Baby clothing	✓	❸	Product availability
Baby/toddler shoes	✓	❹	Staff knowledge
Feeding supplies	✗	❹	Customer service
Diapers & toiletries	✗	❹	Decor
Outing equipment	✗		
Toys & books	✓		
Used items available	✗		

The Children's Place ★★★★

www.childrensplace.com

SAN FRANCISCO - 180 SUTTER ST (AT KEARNY ST)
TEL: 415.434.4737 HOURS: M-SA 9:30-8; SU 12-5
Parking: garage on Sutter at Kearny

SAN FRANCISCO - 3251 20TH AVE, STE 120/122 (AT STONESTOWN GALLERIA)
TEL: 415.682.9404 HOURS: M-SA 10-9; SU 11-6
Parking: mall has a lot

"...you can't beat them for quality combined with low prices...decent selection for boys...they always have good sales...most of their clothes coordinate with each other, so you can buy a lot of different things and not worry if they will match the other clothes you already have...the staff is friendly and the environment is low-key...a fun, convenient place to shop...**"**

Product Selection

		Criteria	
Nursery furnishings	✗	$$	Prices
Baby clothing	✓	❹	Product availability
Baby/toddler shoes	✗	❹	Staff knowledge
Feeding supplies	✗	❹	Customer service
Diapers & toiletries	✗	❹	Decor
Outing equipment	✗		
Toys & books	✗		
Used items available	✗		

Thrift Town

☆ ☆ ☆ ☆

SAN FRANCISCO - 2101 MISSION ST (AT 17TH ST)
TEL: 415.861.1132 HOURS: M-F 9-8; SA 11-6
Parking: street parking

❝...if you are looking for used items - here you go!!...this is a place worth looking at periodically, as long as you don't absolutely need something in particular, since the stock varies greatly...if you like bargain hunting and flea markets and are willing to sort through racks of less than great items in search of that one great piece that you might find, this is the place for you... ❞

Product Selection

Nursery furnishings	✓
Baby clothing	✓
Baby/toddler shoes	✓
Feeding supplies	✗
Diapers & toiletries	✗
Outing equipment	✓
Toys & books	✓
Used items available	✓

Criteria

$	Prices
❷	Product availability
❸	Staff knowledge
❸	Customer service
❷	Decor

Toys R US

★ ★ ★

www.toysrus.com

SAN FRANCISCO - 2675 GEARY BLVD (AT MASONIC AVE)
TEL: 415.931.8896 HOURS: M-SA 9:30-9:30; SU 10-7
Parking: lot in front of store

❝...I was shocked at how much baby stuff I could purchase, for so little money...feeding supplies were not only available, but discounted...good selection of toys, games and clothes...okay selection of nursery furnishings, strollers, high chairs...not the greatest customer service...do your research before you go, staff is usually not very knowledgeable...convenient parking...a good one-stop shop that doesn't offer the most original or unusual fare... ❞

Product Selection

Nursery furnishings	✓
Baby clothing	✓
Baby/toddler shoes	✓
Feeding supplies	✓
Diapers & toiletries	✓
Outing equipment	✓
Toys & books	✓
Used items available	✗

Criteria

$$	Prices
❹	Product availability
❷	Staff knowledge
❷	Customer service
❷	Decor

Tuffy's Hopscotch

★ ★ ★

SAN FRANCISCO - 3307 SACRAMENTO ST (AT PRESIDIO AVE)
TEL: 415.440.7599 HOURS: M-SA 10-5:30
Parking: street parking

"...an absolutely wonderful selection of children's shoes, however the staff could be friendlier...lots of toys for the children to play with and staff that knows how to fit shoes...get the frequent buyer punch card...hit their sales..."

Product Selection

Nursery furnishings	✗
Baby clothing	✓
Baby/toddler shoes	✓
Feeding supplies	✗
Diapers & toiletries	✗
Outing equipment	✗
Toys & books	✗
Used items available	✗

Criteria

$$$$	Prices
❹	Product availability
❹	Staff knowledge
❷	Customer service
❹	Decor

Wavy Footprints

★ ★ ★ ★

www.wavyfootprints.com

SAN FRANCISCO - 3961 24TH ST (BTWN NOE & SANCHEZ STS)
TEL: 415.285.3668 HOURS: DAILY 10-6
Parking: street parking

"...incredible selection of children's shoes...very cute and different children's shoes...tough to get popular sizes in stock...provide great fit and advice...reasonable prices...the owners are fantastic..."

Product Selection

Nursery furnishings	✗
Baby clothing	✗
Baby/toddler shoes	✓
Feeding supplies	✗
Diapers & toiletries	✗
Outing equipment	✗
Toys & books	✓
Used items available	✗

Criteria

$$$	Prices
❹	Product availability
❺	Staff knowledge
❺	Customer service
❹	Decor

Wishbone

www.wishbonesf.com

SAN FRANCISCO - 601 IRVING ST (AT 7TH AVE)
TEL: 415.242.5540 HOURS: DAILY 11:30-7
Parking: street parking

East Bay

1 2 Just Like New

ALAMEDA - 1203 PARK ST (AT SAN JOSE AVE)
TEL: 510.523.6506   HOURS: M-SA 10:30-5; SU BY APPT
Parking: street parking

2nd Avenue

CASTRO VALLEY - 3325 CASTRO VALLEY BLVD (AT REDWOOD RD)
TEL: 510.885.1658 HOURS: M-SA 10-6
Parking: street parking

"...not your ordinary consignment store...the electronic inventory makes this store more professional - unlike the handwritten tags in other stores...toys and clothes are the strong points, although you can often find other items, like strollers, furniture, boppy pillows too...consigning there is an overall good experience... **"**

Product Selection

		Criteria	
Nursery furnishings	✓	$$	Prices
Baby clothing	✓	❹	Product availability
Baby/toddler shoes	✓	❸	Staff knowledge
Feeding supplies	✗	❹	Customer service
Diapers & toiletries	✗	❸	Decor
Outing equipment	✓		
Toys & books	✓		
Used items available	✓		

A Childs Place

BERKELEY - 1898 SOLANO AVE (AT THE ALAMEDA)
TEL: 510.524.3651 HOURS: M-SA 10:30-5:30; SU 11-4
Parking: street parking

"...you can always find gifts here for young children of all ages...reasonable prices...friendly atmosphere...aisles are impossibly cramped and hard to maneuver with a stroller... **"**

Product Selection

		Criteria	
Nursery furnishings	✗	$$$	Prices
Baby clothing	✓	❸	Product availability
Baby/toddler shoes	✓	❸	Staff knowledge
Feeding supplies	✓	❹	Customer service
Diapers & toiletries	✗	❹	Decor
Outing equipment	✓		
Toys & books	✓		
Used items available	✗		

Babies R Us ★★★★

www.babiesrus.com

DUBLIN - 4990 DUBLIN BLVD (AT CENTRAL PKWY)
TEL: 925.875.0350 HOURS: M-SA 9:30-9:30; SU 11-7
Parking: lot in front of store

"...this store has everything you always wanted for baby - and things you never even knew you needed...great deals on the same products and equipment you might find at a boutique or higher-end shops...don't expect to find anything unique, individualized, or creative...service and staff knowledge can be hit-or-miss so you need to take the time yourself to research products and find them on the shelf...the price is right... **"**

Product Selection

			Criteria
Nursery furnishings	✓	$$	Prices
Baby clothing	✓	❹	Product availability
Baby/toddler shoes	✓	❸	Staff knowledge
Feeding supplies	✓	❸	Customer service
Diapers & toiletries	✓	❹	Decor
Outing equipment	✓		
Toys & books	✓		
Used items available	✗		

Baby World ★★★

OAKLAND - 3925 PIEDMONT AVE (AT MONTELL ST)
TEL: 510.547.7040 HOURS: M-SA 10-6; SU 12-5
Parking: street parking

OAKLAND - 6000 COLLEGE AVE (AT OAK GROVE AVE)
TEL: 510.655.2828 HOURS: M-SA 10-6; SU 12-5

"...we bought all my baby's nursery furnishings, car seats, breastfeeding equipment at this family-owned store...good selection of toys, mobiles, clothes, etc...good place for feeding and breastfeeding supplies...I recommend them for their selection, but feel that customer service is sometimes lacking... **"**

Product Selection

			Criteria
Nursery furnishings	✓	$$$	Prices
Baby clothing	✓	❹	Product availability
Baby/toddler shoes	✓	❹	Staff knowledge
Feeding supplies	✓	❸	Customer service
Diapers & toiletries	✓	❸	Decor
Outing equipment	✓		
Toys & books	✓		
Used items available	✗		

BabyGap/GapKids ★★★★

www.gap.com

WALNUT CREEK - 1152 BROADWAY PLZ (AT MT DIABLO BLVD)
TEL: 925.946.0171 HOURS: M-SA 10-9; SU 11-6
Parking: lot in front of store

> **"**...cute, hip and fun baby and kids clothes that are practical and affordable...check out the sale rack for the best bargains around...they are a little light on the boy clothes but who isn't...nursing station and bathroom in most stores...products are generally available and if not, they will find what you're looking for in a nearby store...staff is usually very knowledgeable and available to help...the only problem with BabyGap is that almost none of the clothes for 12 months and over have snaps on the legs, which doesn't make changing easy...good return policy, which is great for gifts **"**

Product Selection

Nursery furnishings	✗
Baby clothing	✓
Baby/toddler shoes	✗
Feeding supplies	✗
Diapers & toiletries	✗
Outing equipment	✗
Toys & books	✗
Used items available	✗

Criteria

$$$	Prices
❹	Product availability
❹	Staff knowledge
❹	Customer service
❹	Decor

Burlington Coat Factory Baby Depot

www.coat.com
DUBLIN - 6900 AMADOR PLAZA RD (AT DUBLIN BLVD)
TEL: 925.875.0712 HOURS: M-SA 10-9:30; SU 11-7
Parking: lot in front of store

Cartan's

SAN RAMON - 2085 SAN RAMON VALLEY BLVD (AT CROW CANYON RD)
TEL: 925.820.3440 HOURS: M-SA 10-6; SU 11-5
Parking: lot in front of store

> **"**...they know their stuff and sell high-quality baby gear, furnishings, clothes, gliders and more...a definite shopping pleasure and a nice break from the crowds and parking hassles at other larger stores...a good place to register for baby showers...customer service was superb...not pushy and very patient in talking to new parents about pros and cons of products... **"**

Product Selection

Nursery furnishings	✓
Baby clothing	✓
Baby/toddler shoes	✓
Feeding supplies	✓
Diapers & toiletries	✓
Outing equipment	✓
Toys & books	✓
Used items available	✗

Criteria

$$$	Prices
❹	Product availability
❺	Staff knowledge
❺	Customer service
❹	Decor

Child's Play ★★★★

OAKLAND - 5858 COLLEGE AVE (AT CHABOT RD)
TEL: 510.653.3989 HOURS: TU-F 10-5:30; SA 11-5; SU 12-5
Parking: lot behind store

"...*good, basic baby stuff...the staff is very friendly and the prices very fair at this used children's store...the store is organized and the selection is fine...they will take your name if you are looking for a particular item and will call when they get it...* **"**

Product Selection

		Criteria	
Nursery furnishings	✓	$$	Prices
Baby clothing	✓	❸	Product availability
Baby/toddler shoes	✗	❹	Staff knowledge
Feeding supplies	✗	❹	Customer service
Diapers & toiletries	✗	❸	Decor
Outing equipment	✓		
Toys & books	✓		
Used items available	✓		

Cotton & Co ★★★★

LAFAYETTE - 3535 MT DIABLO BLVD (AT MORAGA RD)
TEL: 925.299.9356 HOURS: M-SA 10-6; SU 12-5
Parking: street parking

OAKLAND - 5901 COLLEGE AVE (AT CHABOT RD)
TEL: 510.653.8058 HOURS: M-SA 10-6; SU 12-5
Parking: lot behind store

"...*beautiful baby and kids stuff, including fancy European styles such as Miniman and Confetti...lovely displays and holiday outfits that are adorable...super staff that know how to measure feet and what types of shoes are best for kids...although the normal prices are high you can find good deals during sales...* **"**

Product Selection

		Criteria	
Nursery furnishings	✓	$$$	Prices
Baby clothing	✓	❸	Product availability
Baby/toddler shoes	✓	❹	Staff knowledge
Feeding supplies	✓	❹	Customer service
Diapers & toiletries	✓	❹	Decor
Outing equipment	✓		
Toys & books	✓		
Used items available	✗		

Crackerjacks ☆☆☆

OAKLAND - 14 GLEN AVE (AT PIEDMONT AVE)
TEL: 510.654.8844 HOURS: M-F 10-5:30; SA 10-5
Parking: street parking

"...*used stuff at great prices...books, toys, hats, and lots of clothes...you can make a few buys here...best to go in the middle of the week...* **"**

Product Selection		Criteria	
Nursery furnishings	✓	$$	Prices
Baby clothing	✓	❷	Product availability
Baby/toddler shoes	✓	❸	Staff knowledge
Feeding supplies	✗	❸	Customer service
Diapers & toiletries	✗	❷	Decor
Outing equipment	✓		
Toys & books	✓		
Used items available	✓		

Darla's Baby Boutique

EL CERRITO - 10400 SAN PABLO AVE (AT SANTA CRUZ AVE)
TEL: 510.526.5437 HOURS: M-SA 10-6
Parking: street parking

❝...great selection of used clothing for babies...the prices are right and the staff is extremely knowledgeable...some new items too...staff is very helpful and friendly...product availability can vary quite a bit... ❞

Product Selection		Criteria	
Nursery furnishings	✓	$$	Prices
Baby clothing	✓	❸	Product availability
Baby/toddler shoes	✓	❹	Staff knowledge
Feeding supplies	✓	❹	Customer service
Diapers & toiletries	✗	❸	Decor
Outing equipment	✓		
Toys & books	✓		
Used items available	✓		

Fashion After Passion

www.fashionafterpassion.com
ALAMEDA - 1521 WEBSTER ST (AT HAIGHT AVE)
TEL: 510.769.6667 HOURS: TU-SA 10-5:30
Parking: street parking

Goodnight Room

BERKELEY - 1848 4TH ST (AT HEARST AVE)
TEL: 510.548.2108 HOURS: M-SA 10-6; SU 11-5
Parking: street parking

❝...a treasure trove of wonderful wood furniture and linens...fairly high prices seem justified by solid, high-quality construction that's built to last for ages...darling toys and a limited selection of clothing...a not-too-cramped floor plan is stroller-friendly... ❞

Product Selection

Nursery furnishings	✓
Baby clothing	✓
Baby/toddler shoes	✗
Feeding supplies	✗
Diapers & toiletries	✗
Outing equipment	✗
Toys & books	✓
Used items available	✗

Criteria

$$$$	Prices
❸	Product availability
❹	Staff knowledge
❹	Customer service
❺	Decor

Gymboree   ★ ★ ★ ★

www.gymboree.com

NEWARK - 1039 NEWPARK MALL (AT MOWRY AVE)
TEL: 510.742.6842 HOURS: M-F 10-9; SA 10-9; SU 11-6
Parking: lot in front of store

WALNUT CREEK - 1174 BROADWAY PLZ
TEL: 925.935.6820 HOURS: M-F 10-9; SA 10-7; SU 11-6
Parking: lot in front of store

❝*...great stuff...very cute...expensive but good quality items...staff is always nice...great for sales - you can always find clothing for 50-75% off, and there is a wide range of sizes in sale items...designs for girls are bright and colorful...boys clothes are slightly conservative but very cute...clothes have a tendency to run slightly smaller than comparable brands...very durable - great hand-me-downs...*❞

Product Selection

Nursery furnishings	✗
Baby clothing	✓
Baby/toddler shoes	✗
Feeding supplies	✗
Diapers & toiletries	✗
Outing equipment	✗
Toys & books	✗
Used items available	✗

Criteria

$$$	Prices
❹	Product availability
❺	Staff knowledge
❹	Customer service
❹	Decor

Hannah's Children's Resale   ★ ★ ★ ★

BERKELEY - 1871 SOLANO AVE (AT FRESNO AVE)
TEL: 510.525.3488 HOURS: M-SA 10-6; SU 11-4
Parking: street parking

❝*...clothes are clean, in good shape and offered at a very reasonable price...one of the best-used clothing stores for kids in Berkeley...new items tend to be a bit pricey...overall it's a great shop and worth checking out...*❞

Product Selection

Item	
Nursery furnishings	✗
Baby clothing	✓
Baby/toddler shoes	✓
Feeding supplies	✗
Diapers & toiletries	✗
Outing equipment	✗
Toys & books	✓
Used items available	✓

Criteria

Criteria	
Prices	$$
Product availability	❹
Staff knowledge	❹
Customer service	❺
Decor	❸

IKEA

★ ★ ★ ★

www.ikea-usa.com

EMERYVILLE - 4400 SHELLMOUND ST
TEL: 510.420.4532 HOURS: M-F & SU 10-9; SA 9-9
Parking: big lot/garage

"...a great store for furnishings and toys if you can put stuff together well by yourself...fun products that are inexpensive...the child care area is safe, clean and free...you can get so many ideas for decorating from their showroom...**"**

Product Selection

Item	
Nursery furnishings	✓
Baby clothing	✗
Baby/toddler shoes	✗
Feeding supplies	✗
Diapers & toiletries	✗
Outing equipment	✗
Toys & books	✓
Used items available	✗

Criteria

Criteria	
Prices	$
Product availability	❹
Staff knowledge	❸
Customer service	❸
Decor	❹

Imaginarium

☆ ☆ ☆ ☆ ☆

www.imaginarium.com

LAFAYETTE - 3543 MT DIABLO BLVD (AT MORAGA RD)
TEL: 925.962.9100 HOURS: M-SA 10-7; SU 10-5
Parking: lot behind store

"...a great place to find age-appropriate toys...slightly pricey but fun to browse...staff is very helpful and offer suggestions when needed...pleasantly original for a chain store...customer service is excellent...**"**

Product Selection

Item	
Nursery furnishings	✗
Baby clothing	✗
Baby/toddler shoes	✗
Feeding supplies	✗
Diapers & toiletries	✗
Outing equipment	✗
Toys & books	✓
Used items available	✗

Criteria

Criteria	
Prices	$$$
Product availability	❹
Staff knowledge	❺
Customer service	❺
Decor	❹

JCPenney

☆☆☆☆

www.jcpenney.com

PLEASANTON - 1500 STONERIDGE MALL RD (AT STONERIDGE DR)
TEL: 925.463.9780 HOURS: M-SA 10-9; SU 11-7
Parking: mall has a lot

"...a surprisingly good place to buy baby, toddler and kids clothes...great sales - I buy almost all Carter's there and never pay full price... **"**

Product Selection

		Criteria	
Nursery furnishings	✗	$$	Prices
Baby clothing	✓	❹	Product availability
Baby/toddler shoes	✓	❸	Staff knowledge
Feeding supplies	✗	❸	Customer service
Diapers & toiletries	✗	❸	Decor
Outing equipment	✗		
Toys & books	✗		
Used items available	✗		

Just For Kids

HAYWARD - 603 SOUTHLAND MALL
TEL: 510.785.5020 HOURS: M-SA 10-9; SU 11-7
Parking: mall has lot

K-B Toys

☆☆☆

www.kbtoys.com

ALAMEDA - 2221 S SHORE CTR (AT OTIS ST)
TEL: 510.523.8229 HOURS: M-SA 10-9; SU 11-7
Parking: mall has lot

"...a big toy super store...very good prices and convenient parking...lots of store specials...not the place if you're looking for unique toys...their best attribute is their willy-nilly mark down procedure - sometimes over 75 percent off...a lot of plastic...recommended for staples such as Play-doh or Fisher-Price baby toys... **"**

Product Selection

		Criteria	
Nursery furnishings	✗	$$	Prices
Baby clothing	✗	❹	Product availability
Baby/toddler shoes	✗	❸	Staff knowledge
Feeding supplies	✗	❷	Customer service
Diapers & toiletries	✗	❷	Decor
Outing equipment	✗		
Toys & books	✓		
Used items available	✗		

Kids Again ★★★★

DUBLIN - 6891 VILLAGE PKWY (AT AMADOR VALLEY BLVD)
TEL: 925.828.7334 HOURS: M-W & F-SA 10-5; TH 10-7
Parking: lot behind building

"...a baby clothing, accessories and furniture consignment shop...they only accept used items in really good condition - so you're not plowing through a bunch of junk when shopping...you're bound to find some bargains here...you can also order new furniture...worth checking out, especially if you are on a budget... **"**

Product Selection		Criteria	
Nursery furnishings	✓	$$	Prices
Baby clothing	✓	❸	Product availability
Baby/toddler shoes	✓	❹	Staff knowledge
Feeding supplies	✗	❹	Customer service
Diapers & toiletries	✗	❸	Decor
Outing equipment	✓		
Toys & books	✓		
Used items available	✓		

Kids R US

www.kidsrus.com
NEWARK - 5701 MOWRY AVE (AT NEWPARK MALL)
TEL: 510.796.2021 HOURS: M-F 10-9; SA 10-8; SU 10-7
Parking: mall has a lot

Lakeshore Learning Store

www.lakeshorelearning.com
SAN LEANDRO - 1144 MONTAGUE ST (AT TEAGARDEN ST)
TEL: 510.483.9750 HOURS: M-F 9-7; SA 9-6; SU 11-6
Parking: lot in front of store

Lauren's Closet ★★★★

ALAMEDA - 1420 PARK ST (AT SANTA CLARA AVE)
TEL: 510.865.2219 HOURS: M W F SA 10-5:30; TU TH 11-5:30;
SU 12-4
Parking: lot behind store

"...if you are on a budget, but want your to dress your child otherwise, this is a wonderful place to shop...great place to recycle your kid's outgrown items...prices are good, clothes are clean and presented nicely...service is good... **"**

Product Selection

Nursery furnishings .... ✓
Baby clothing .... ✓
Baby/toddler shoes .... ✓
Feeding supplies .... ✗
Diapers & toiletries .... ✗
Outing equipment .... ✓
Toys & books........................... ✓
Used items available .... ✓

Criteria

$$ .... Prices
❹ .... Product availability
❹ .... Staff knowledge
❹ .... Customer service
❹ .... Decor

Leonard's Tot Shop   ☆ ☆ ☆ ☆

www.babyexpressstores.com

CONCORD - 548 CONTRA COSTA BLVD (AT CONCORD AVE)
TEL: 925.682.5888 HOURS: M-SA 10-6; SU 11-5
Parking: lot in front of store

"...a family-owned store that's been around forever...large selection of strollers, gliders, high chairs, cribs, dressers and car seats...a terrific place to get your baby's nursery completely decked-out...the staff is incredibly knowledgeable and outgoing..."

Product Selection

Nursery furnishings .... ✓
Baby clothing .... ✓
Baby/toddler shoes .... ✗
Feeding supplies .... ✓
Diapers & toiletries .... ✗
Outing equipment .... ✓
Toys & books........................... ✓
Used items available .... ✗

Criteria

$$ .... Prices
❹ .... Product availability
❺ .... Staff knowledge
❺ .... Customer service
❹ .... Decor

Lora's Closet   ★ ★ ★ ★

BERKELEY - 2926 COLLEGE AVE (AT RUSSELL ST)
TEL: 510.845.3157 HOURS: M-SA 10-5:30; SU 12-5
Parking: lot behind store

"...all the clothes are in excellent condition and a complete bargain...there are toys for kids to play with while parents browse...they also sell a few new items, like socks and those great flap-happy hats...good also for reselling grown out of clothes..."

Product Selection

Nursery furnishings .... ✗
Baby clothing .... ✓
Baby/toddler shoes .... ✓
Feeding supplies .... ✗
Diapers & toiletries .... ✗
Outing equipment .... ✗
Toys & books........................... ✗
Used items available .... ✓

Criteria

$$ .... Prices
❹ .... Product availability
❹ .... Staff knowledge
❹ .... Customer service
❹ .... Decor

Making Ends Meet

OAKLAND - 3544 FRUITVALE AVE (BTWN MACARTHUR BLVD & COLOMA ST)
TEL: 510.531.1135 HOURS: M-SA 10-5:30
Parking: lot behind store

"...they have great prices on clothes and they are fair when it comes to trading clothes in...small store that is packed with stuff...they have a nice play area enclosed for your kids so that you can actually shop...the staff is friendly and they know a lot about kids stuff..."

Product Selection

Nursery furnishings	✓
Baby clothing	✓
Baby/toddler shoes	✓
Feeding supplies	✗
Diapers & toiletries	✗
Outing equipment	✓
Toys & books	✓
Used items available	✓

Criteria

$$	Prices
❹	Product availability
❹	Staff knowledge
❺	Customer service
❸	Decor

Marino's Second Time Around

SAN LORENZO - 17279 HESPERIAN BLVD (AT VIA RODRIGUEZ)
TEL: 510.276.8705 HOURS: M-SA 10-5
Parking: lot behind store

Mc Caulou's Department Store

LAFAYETTE - 3512 MT DIABLO BLVD (AT MORAGA RD)
TEL: 925.283.3380 HOURS: M-F 9:30-6:30; SA 9:30-6; SU 10-5
Parking: lot in front of store

MORAGA - 1441 MORAGA WY (AT MORAGA RD)
TEL: 925.376.7252 HOURS: M-SA 10-6; SU 11-5
Parking: lot in front of store

OAKLAND - 6211 MEDAU PL (AT MOUNTAIN BLVD)
TEL: 510.339.2210 HOURS: M-SA 10-6; SU 11-5
Parking: lot behind store

ORINDA - 250 VILLAGE SQ (OFF ORINDA WY)
TEL: 925.254.3448 HOURS: M-SA 10-6; SU 11-5
Parking: lot in front of store

"...very good selection of brand name infant clothing...you can always find a present and they have free gift wrap...the best buy is during the season end sales, when you can buy for the next season ..."

Product Selection

		Criteria	
Nursery furnishings	X	$$$	Prices
Baby clothing	✓	❹	Product availability
Baby/toddler shoes	X	❹	Staff knowledge
Feeding supplies	X	❹	Customer service
Diapers & toiletries	X	❸	Decor
Outing equipment	X		
Toys & books	✓		
Used items available	X		

Mr Mopps' Children's Bookshop ★★★★

BERKELEY - 1405 MARTIN LUTHER KING JR WY (AT ROSE ST)
TEL: 510.525.9633 HOURS: TU-SA 9:30-5:25
Parking: street parking

❝...so good to find a place that doesn't sell only brightly colored plastic toys...great selection, although it is almost impossible to get around the store with a stroller...you can find any sort of gift, stocking stuffer, or whatever you might need here...not your average cookie-cutter toy store... **❞**

Product Selection

		Criteria	
Nursery furnishings	X	$$$	Prices
Baby clothing	X	❹	Product availability
Baby/toddler shoes	X	❹	Staff knowledge
Feeding supplies	X	❹	Customer service
Diapers & toiletries	X	❹	Decor
Outing equipment	X		
Toys & books	✓		
Used items available	X		

Nurture Ctr

www.nurturecenter.com

LAFAYETTE - 3399 MT DIABLO BLVD (AT BROWN AVE)
TEL: 925.283.1346 HOURS: M-W & F-SA 10-5; TH 10-8
Parking: lot in front & back of store

Once Upon A Child

NEWARK - 5462 NEWPARK PLZ (AT NEWPARK MALL)
TEL: 510.494.8822 HOURS: M-F 10-7; SA 10-6; SU 12-5
Parking: mall has a lot

SAN RAMON - 21001 SAN RAMON VALLEY BLVD (ALCOSTA BLVD)
TEL: 925.829.8899 HOURS: TU-SA 10-6; SU 12-4
Parking: lot parking

Right Start ★★★

www.rightstart.com

WALNUT CREEK - 1567 BOTELHO DR (AT S CALIFORNIA BLVD)
TEL: 925.974.1590 HOURS: M-SA 10-6; SU 11-5
Parking: lot located in front of store

"...love, love, love the Right Start...so many wonderful developmentally appropriate toys, books, videos and equipment...only carries top-of-the-line infant carriers, strollers, and joggers, which is very comforting...perfect place to register if you're having a baby shower...store appears to be stocked with carefully selected, high quality products...wish there were more discounts on big ticket items to be found...the store charges full retail, but well worth it..."

Product Selection

Nursery furnishings	✗
Baby clothing	✗
Baby/toddler shoes	✗
Feeding supplies	✓
Diapers & toiletries	✗
Outing equipment	✓
Toys & books	✓
Used items available	✗

Criteria

$$$	Prices
④	Product availability
④	Staff knowledge
④	Customer service
④	Decor

Rockridge Kids

★★★★★

OAKLAND - 5511 COLLEGE AVE (AT MANILA AVE)
TEL: 510.601.5437 HOURS: M-F 10-7; SA 10-6; SU 11-5
Parking: street parking

"...a wonderful place to shop for gifts, music, books, and toys that you can't find at toy superstores...the best place to get any sort of baby equipment in the East Bay...the staff at this store is the best I have encountered in terms of knowledge and service - they clearly enjoy their jobs...expect to pay full price, but well-worth it for the great customer service and excellent selection of items to choose from...when I need to purchase something and need help choosing between brands or just need advice about an appropriate or fabulous gift I always head to Rockridge Kids..."

Product Selection

Nursery furnishings	✓
Baby clothing	✓
Baby/toddler shoes	✓
Feeding supplies	✓
Diapers & toiletries	✗
Outing equipment	✓
Toys & books	✓
Used items available	✗

Criteria

$$$	Prices
④	Product availability
⑤	Staff knowledge
⑤	Customer service
④	Decor

Silver Moon

☆☆☆

OAKLAND - 3221 GRAND AVE (AT LAKE PARK WY)
TEL: 510.835.2229 HOURS: TU-SA 11-5
Parking: street parking

"...a great place to find used toys and books...the staff is great...they also sell new toys that are reasonably priced...parking is really tough in this area..."

Product Selection

		Criteria	
Nursery furnishings	✓	$$	Prices
Baby clothing	✓	❸	Product availability
Baby/toddler shoes	✓	❹	Staff knowledge
Feeding supplies	✗	❺	Customer service
Diapers & toiletries	✗	❹	Decor
Outing equipment	✓		
Toys & books	✓		
Used items available	✓		

Sweet Dreams ★★★★

BERKELEY - 2921 COLLEGE AVE (BTWN RUSSEL & ELMWOOD AVE)
TEL: 510.548.8697 HOURS: M-SA 10-6; SU 11:30-5:30
Parking: street parking

ORINDA - 2 THEATRE SQ # 107 (AT MORAGA WY)
TEL: 925.254.6672 HOURS: M-SA 10-6:30; SU 11:30-5
Parking: garage at Theatre Sq

❝...a cute little store with a good selection of baby and children's clothing, costumes and toys...awesome window displays...great for birthday gifts and special toys...the whole place is like a child's dream room...some items are pretty pricey, but it's such a pleasant place to shop... ❞

Product Selection

		Criteria	
Nursery furnishings	✗	$$$	Prices
Baby clothing	✗	❹	Product availability
Baby/toddler shoes	✗	❹	Staff knowledge
Feeding supplies	✗	❹	Customer service
Diapers & toiletries	✗	❹	Decor
Outing equipment	✗		
Toys & books	✓		
Used items available	✗		

Sweet Potatoes ★★★★

ALBANY - 1224 SOLANO AVE (AT TALBOT AVE)
TEL: 510.527.7975 HOURS: M-SA 10-6; SU 11-5
Parking: street parking

BERKELEY - 1799 A 4TH ST (AT VIRGINIA ST)
TEL: 510.524.3058 HOURS: M-SA 10-6; SU 11-5
Parking: street parking

❝...this is a great place to buy children's clothes especially when they are having one of their many sales...if you are shopping for a boy, you will find the selection somewhat limited - however, you will find a lot of beautiful and fun things for girls...prices are fair and the quality and service are great... ❞

Product Selection

			Criteria	
Nursery furnishings	✗	$$	....	Prices
Baby clothing	✓	❹	....	Product availability
Baby/toddler shoes	✗	❹	....	Staff knowledge
Feeding supplies	✗	❹	....	Customer service
Diapers & toiletries	✗	❹	....	Decor
Outing equipment	✗			
Toys & books	✗			
Used items available	✗			

Sweetie Face

www.sweetieface.com

SAN RAMON - 3191 CROW CANYON RD (AT CROW CANYON RD EXIT OFF 680)
TEL: 925.355.0100 HOURS: M-F 10-5:30 (TH TILL 7); SA 10-5; SU 11-4
Parking: lot in front of store

Target   ★ ★ ★ ★

www.target.com

NEWARK - 400 NEWPARK MALL (AT MOWRY AVE & 880)
TEL: 510.744.1790 HOURS: M-SA 8-10; SU 8-9
Parking: mall has lot

PLEASANT HILL - 560 CONTRA COSTA BLVD (AT CONCORD AVE)
TEL: 925.685.6069 HOURS: M-SA 8-10; SU 8-9
Parking: lot in front of store

WALNUT CREEK - 1871 N MAIN ST (AT YGNACIO VALLEY RD)
TEL: 925.979.0083 HOURS: M-SA 8-10; SU 8-9
Parking: lot in front of store

Product Selection

			Criteria	
Nursery furnishings	✗	$$	....	Prices
Baby clothing	✓	❹	....	Product availability
Baby/toddler shoes	✗	❸	....	Staff knowledge
Feeding supplies	✓	❸	....	Customer service
Diapers & toiletries	✓	❸	....	Decor
Outing equipment	✗			
Toys & books	✓			
Used items available	✗			

Teddy's Little Closet

BERKELEY - 2903 COLLEGE AVE (AT RUSSELL ST)
TEL: 510.549.9177 HOURS: M-SA 10-6; SU 11-5
Parking: street parking

The Ark   ☆ ☆ ☆ ☆

BERKELEY - 1812 4TH ST (AT VIRGINIA ST)
TEL: 510.849.1930 HOURS: DAILY 10-6
Parking: street parking

"...a wonderful selection of natural and imaginative toys that you just can't get at the bigger toy stores...they have something for everyone - from babies up to pre-teen...the sales staff are extremely helpful and if they don't have what you are looking for, they will make a heroic effort to find it for you......"

Product Selection

Nursery furnishings ✗
Baby clothing ✗
Baby/toddler shoes ✗
Feeding supplies ✗
Diapers & toiletries ✗
Outing equipment ✗
Toys & books ✓
Used items available ✗

Criteria

$$ .... Prices
 .... Product availability
❹ .... Staff knowledge
❹ .... Customer service
❹ .... Decor

The Children's Place ★★★★

www.childrensplace.com

CONCORD - 464 SUNVALLEY MALL (AT CONTRA COSTA BLVD)
TEL: 925.691.1198 HOURS: M-SA 9:30-8; SU 12-5
Parking: mall has a lot

PLEASANTON - 1248 STONERIDGE MALL RD (AT STONERIDGE DR)
TEL: 925.734.8588 HOURS: M-SA 10-9; SU 11-6
Parking: mall has a lot

"...you can't beat them for quality combined with low prices...decent selection for boys...they always have good sales...most of their clothes coordinate with each other, so you can buy a lot of different things and not worry if they will match the other clothes you already have...the staff is friendly and the environment is low-key...a fun, convenient place to shop..."

Product Selection

Nursery furnishings ✗
Baby clothing ✓
Baby/toddler shoes ✗
Feeding supplies ✗
Diapers & toiletries ✗
Outing equipment ✗
Toys & books ✗
Used items available ✗

Criteria

$$ .... Prices
 .... Product availability
❹ .... Staff knowledge
❹ .... Customer service
❹ .... Decor

They Grow So Fast ☆☆☆☆☆

LAFAYETTE - 3413 MT DIABLO BLVD (AT ALMANOR LN)
TEL: 925.283.8976 HOURS: TU-SA 10-5
Parking: lot next to building

"...a consignment shop with a long tradition of providing a great selection of baby gear...always a great variety in the selection...prices are great...the staff is very nice and they do provide lots of good information about the products in the store..."

Product Selection		Criteria	
Nursery furnishings	✓	$	Prices
Baby clothing	✓	❹	Product availability
Baby/toddler shoes	✓	❺	Staff knowledge
Feeding supplies	✗	❺	Customer service
Diapers & toiletries	✗	❹	Decor
Outing equipment	✓		
Toys & books	✓		
Used items available	✓		

This Little Piggy Wears Cotton ★ ★ ★

www.littlepiggy.com
BERKELEY - 1840 4TH ST (AT VIRGINIA ST)
TEL: 510.981.1411 HOURS: M-SA 10-6; SU 11-6
Parking: lot behind store

❝...lots of gift items and baby apparel...adorable and fashionable stuff - lots of European brands...parking is terrible on 4th street even during off hours...this little piggy costs bucks... ❞

Product Selection		Criteria	
Nursery furnishings	✗	$$$$	Prices
Baby clothing	✓	❹	Product availability
Baby/toddler shoes	✗	❹	Staff knowledge
Feeding supplies	✗	❹	Customer service
Diapers & toiletries	✗	❺	Decor
Outing equipment	✗		
Toys & books	✓		
Used items available	✗		

Time Out For Fun & Games

OAKLAND - 435 JACK LONDON SQ (AT BROADWAY)
TEL: 510.444.4386 HOURS: M-TH 11-7; F 11-8; SA 10-8; SU 10-6
Parking: street parking

Toy Safari

ALAMEDA - 1410 PARK ST (AT CENTRAL AVE)
TEL: 510.522.1723 HOURS: M-TH 10-6; F SA 10-8; SU 11-6
Parking: street parking

Toy-Go-Round ☆ ☆ ☆ ☆

ALBANY - 1361 SOLANO AVE (AT RAMONA AVE)
TEL: 510.527.1363 HOURS: M-SA 10-5; SU 12-5
Parking: street parking

❝...new and gently used items...great prices...it's a bit cramped, so you can't bring a stroller in... ❞

Product Selection

Nursery furnishings	✗
Baby clothing	✗
Baby/toddler shoes	✗
Feeding supplies	✗
Diapers & toiletries	✗
Outing equipment	✗
Toys & books	✓
Used items available	✓

Criteria

$$	Prices
❸	Product availability
❹	Staff knowledge
❺	Customer service
❸	Decor

Toyhouse

OAKLAND - 6115 LA SALLE AVE (AT MOUNTAIN BLVD)
TEL: 510.339.9023 HOURS: M-SA 9:30-6; SU 11-5
Parking: garage on La Salle

Toys R US ★ ★ ★ ★

www.toysrus.com

EMERYVILLE - 3938 HORTON ST (AT 40TH ST)
TEL: 510.597.0435 HOURS: M-SA 9:30-9:30; SU 10-7
Parking: lot in front of store

PINOLE - 1330 FITZGERALD DR (AT APPIAN WY)
TEL: 510.758.8697 HOURS: M-SA 9:30-9:30; SU 10-7
Parking: lot in front of store

PLEASANT HILL - 568 CONTRA COSTA BLVD (AT CONCORD AVE)
TEL: 925.689.9751 HOURS: M-SA 9:30-9:30; SU 10-7
Parking: lot in front of store

❝...I was shocked at how much baby stuff I could purchase, for so little money...feeding supplies were not only available, but discounted...good selection of toys, games and clothes...okay selection of nursery furnishings, strollers, high chairs...not the greatest customer service...do your research before you go, staff is usually not very knowledgeable...convenient parking...a good one-stop shop that doesn't offer the most original or unusual fare... ❞

Product Selection

Nursery furnishings	✓
Baby clothing	✓
Baby/toddler shoes	✓
Feeding supplies	✓
Diapers & toiletries	✓
Outing equipment	✓
Toys & books	✓
Used items available	✗

Criteria

$$	Prices
❹	Product availability
❷	Staff knowledge
❷	Customer service
❸	Decor

Waddle & Swaddle

www.waddleandswaddle.com

BERKELEY - 1677 SHATTUCK AVE (BTWN CEDAR & LINCOLN STS)
TEL: 510.540.7210 HOURS: M-SA 11-6; SU 11-5
Parking: street parking

❝...an adorable store with wonderful gifts and special items...the store is owned by an experienced doula and all the staff is friendly and knowledgeable...in addition to their baby clothes, they have books, slings, some maternity clothes, gifts and toys...the clothes aren't cheap, but they do have pretty good sales... ❞

Product Selection

		Criteria	
Nursery furnishings	✗	$$$	Prices
Baby clothing	✓	❺	Product availability
Baby/toddler shoes	✗	❹	Staff knowledge
Feeding supplies	✓	❺	Customer service
Diapers & toiletries	✓	❺	Decor
Outing equipment	✓		
Toys & books	✓		
Used items available	✗		

Zany Brainy

www.zanybrainy.com

CONCORD - 1975 DIAMOND BLVD # E360 (AT WILLOW PASS RD)
TEL: 925.363.9303 HOURS: M-SA 10-9; SU 11-5
Parking: mall has lot

DUBLIN - 4948 DUBLIN BLVD (AT HACIENDA DR)
TEL: 925.556.9400 HOURS: M-SA 10-9; SU 10-6
Parking: lot in front of store

❝...a fun store filled with cool stuff and unusual toys...a nice collection of equipment and toys...if you're looking for a neat gift, then you're in the right place...items can be a bit pricey, but you'll enjoy shopping here... ❞

Product Selection

		Criteria	
Nursery furnishings	✗	$$$	Prices
Baby clothing	✗	❹	Product availability
Baby/toddler shoes	✗	❸	Staff knowledge
Feeding supplies	✗	❹	Customer service
Diapers & toiletries	✗	❹	Decor
Outing equipment	✗		
Toys & books	✓		
Used items available	✗		

North Bay

Baby News Children's Stores

SANTA ROSA - 1445 SANTA ROSA AVE # A1 (AT FLOWER AVE)
TEL: 707.542.1006 HOURS: M-SA 10-6; SU 11-5
Parking: lot in front of store

BabyGap/GapKids ★★★★

www.gap.com

CORTE MADERA - 1820 REDWOOD HWY (AT TAMALPAIS DR)
TEL: 415.924.4079 HOURS: M-F 10-9; SA 11:30-8:30; SU 11-6
Parking: lot in front of store

"...cute, hip and fun baby and kids clothes that are practical and affordable...check out the sale rack for the best bargains around...they are a little light on the boy clothes but who isn't...nursing station and bathroom in most stores...products are generally available and if not, they will find what you're looking for in a nearby store...staff is usually very knowledgeable and available to help...the only problem with BabyGap is that almost none of the clothes for 12 months and over have snaps on the legs, which doesn't make changing easy...good return policy, which is great for gifts **"**

Product Selection

			Criteria
Nursery furnishings	✗	$$	Prices
Baby clothing	✓	❹	Product availability
Baby/toddler shoes	✗	❸	Staff knowledge
Feeding supplies	✗	❹	Customer service
Diapers & toiletries	✗	❹	Decor
Outing equipment	✗		
Toys & books	✗		
Used items available	✗		

Bug A Boo ★★★★

www.bug-a-boo.com

FAIRFAX - 14 BOLINAS RD (AT BROADWAY BLVD)
TEL: 415.457.2884 HOURS: M-SA 10-6; SU 11-5
Parking: street parking

"...many adorable unique clothes and gifts...the diversity and quality of the selections seems to improve every season...they also have child activities and a play area for children so you can concentrate on your shopping...knowledgeable and friendly owner... **"**

Product Selection

Nursery furnishings .... ✓
Baby clothing .... ✓
Baby/toddler shoes .... ✓
Feeding supplies .... ✗
Diapers & toiletries .... ✗
Outing equipment .... ✓
Toys & books............................ ✓
Used items available .... ✗

Criteria

$$$ .... Prices
❹ .... Product availability
❹ .... Staff knowledge
❹ .... Customer service
❹ .... Decor

Burlington Coat Factory Baby Depot

www.coat.com
ROHNERT PARK - 311 ROHNERT PARK EXPY W (AT REDWOOD DR)
TEL: 707.588.2628 HOURS: M-SA 10-9; SU 11-7
Parking: lot in front

Child's Delight

SAN RAFAEL - 3320 NORTHGATE MALL (AT LAS GALLINAS AVE)
TEL: 415.499.0736 HOURS: M-SA 10-9; SU 11-6
Parking: mall has a lot

Ciao Ragazzi

SAN ANSELMO - 532 SAN ANSELMO AVE (AT SIR FRANCIS DRAKE BLVD)
TEL: 415.454.4844 HOURS: M-SA 10-6; SU 11-5
Parking: street parking

Goodnite Moon

CORTE MADERA - 111 CORTE MADERA TOWN CTR (AT TAMALPAIS DR)
TEL: 415.945.0677 HOURS: M-TU 10-6; W-F 10-6:30; SA 10-6; SU 11-5
Parking: mall has a lot

❝...this is a great store for special gifts and children's room decor...neat selection of high-end items such as wrought iron cribs...the friendly staff make for an overall pleasant shopping experience...the product line is noticeably expanding each season so it is worth checking in every few months to see what they have added to the line... ❞

Product Selection

Nursery furnishings .... ✓
Baby clothing .... ✓
Baby/toddler shoes .... ✗
Feeding supplies .... ✗
Diapers & toiletries .... ✗
Outing equipment .... ✓
Toys & books........................... ✓
Used items available .... ✗

Criteria

$$$ .... Prices
❹ .... Product availability
❹ .... Staff knowledge
❹ .... Customer service
❺ .... Decor

Gymboree

★ ★ ★ ★

www.gymboree.com

CORTE MADERA - 1716 REDWOOD HWY (AT TAMALPAIS DR)
TEL: 415.924.1116 HOURS: M-F 10-9; SA 10-7:30; SU 11-6
Parking: lot in front of store
SAN RAFAEL - 3800 NORTHGATE MALL TEL: 415.491.4496 HOURS:
M-SA 10-9; SU 11-6
Parking: lot in front of store

❝...great stuff...very cute...expensive but good quality
items...staff is always nice...great for sales - you can always find
clothing for 50-75% off, and there is a wide range of sizes in sale
items...designs for girls are bright and colorful...boys clothes are
slightly conservative but very cute...clothes have a tendency to
run slightly smaller then other comparable brands...very durable
and make great hand-me-downs... ❞

Product Selection

Nursery furnishings .... ✗
Baby clothing .... ✓
Baby/toddler shoes .... ✗
Feeding supplies .... ✗
Diapers & toiletries .... ✗
Outing equipment .... ✗
Toys & books........................... ✗
Used items available .... ✗

Criteria

$$$ .... Prices
❹ .... Product availability
❹ .... Staff knowledge
❹ .... Customer service
❹ .... Decor

Heller's For Children

★ ★ ★ ★ ★

SAN RAFAEL - 514 4TH ST (AT GRAND AVE)
TEL: 415.456.5533 HOURS: M-SA 9:30-6; SU 11-5
Parking: lot in front of store

❝...a great supply store for everything from cribs, strollers,
highchairs, gliders to bibs, bottles and nipples...a privately-run
business that has a very family-friendly atmosphere...staff is
helpful, and you can get in and out very quickly...while it's not
the cheapest store in the area, it is THE one-stop baby shop in
Marin...their customer service is the number one reason why we
don't shop anywhere else... ❞

Product Selection

Nursery furnishings .... ✓
Baby clothing .... ✓
Baby/toddler shoes .... ✗
Feeding supplies .... ✓
Diapers & toiletries .... ✓
Outing equipment .... ✓
Toys & books........................... ✓
Used items available .... ✗

Criteria

$$$ .... Prices
❹ .... Product availability
❹ .... Staff knowledge
❺ .... Customer service
❸ .... Decor

Hopscotch Kids

MILL VALLEY - 352 MILLER AVE (AT LOCUST AVE)
TEL: 415.381.9858 HOURS: M-F 9:30-5; SA 10-5; SU 10-3
Parking: lot in front of store

❝...a great selection of toys, especially hard-to-find and unusual ones...a friendly place to shop...prices can be steep and there are better deals to be found elsewhere, but if you are looking for something special it is the place to do...❞

Product Selection

Nursery furnishings .... ✗
Baby clothing .... ✗
Baby/toddler shoes .... ✗
Feeding supplies .... ✗
Diapers & toiletries .... ✗
Outing equipment .... ✓
Toys & books........................... ✓
Used items available .... ✗

Criteria

$$$ .... Prices
❺ .... Product availability
❹ .... Staff knowledge
❹ .... Customer service
❹ .... Decor

K-B Toys

www.kbtoys.com

CORTE MADERA - 327 CORTE MADERA TOWN CTR (AT TAMALPAIS DR)
TEL: 415.924.4288 HOURS: M-SA 10-9; SU 11-7
Parking: mall has a lot

Kid's Exchange

MILL VALLEY - 10 LOCUST AVE (AT MILLER AVE)
TEL: 415.388.9068 HOURS: M-SA 11-5
Parking: street parking

Mill Valley Mercantile

MILL VALLEY - 167 THROCKMORTON AVE (AT MILLER AVE)
TEL: 415.388.9588 HOURS: M-SA 10-5:30; SU 12-5
Parking: street parking

❝...many unique things that I have not seen elsewhere, and usually a few special items on sale...great selection of clothing and nice selection of books and toys too...lots of Petit Bateau,

Zutano, and other designer wear...very kid-friendly staff and environment.... **"**

Product Selection

			Criteria
Nursery furnishings	✗	$$$	Prices
Baby clothing	✓	❹	Product availability
Baby/toddler shoes	✗	❹	Staff knowledge
Feeding supplies	✗	❹	Customer service
Diapers & toiletries	✗	❺	Decor
Outing equipment	✗		
Toys & books	✓		
Used items available	✗		

Noodle Soup

CORTE MADERA - 117 CORTE MADERA TOWN CTR (AT TAMALPAIS DR)
TEL: 415.945.9683 HOURS: M-F 10-6; SU 10-5
Parking: mall has a lot

SAN ANSELMO - 718 SAN ANSELMO AVE (AT TAMALPAIS AVE)
TEL: 415.455.0141 HOURS: M-F 10-6; SA 10-5; SU 11-5
Parking: street parking

"*...some beautiful items...one of those if-only-I-could-win-the lottery kind of places...* **"**

Product Selection

			Criteria
Nursery furnishings	✗	$$$$	Prices
Baby clothing	✓	❹	Product availability
Baby/toddler shoes	✗	❸	Staff knowledge
Feeding supplies	✗	❹	Customer service
Diapers & toiletries	✗	❹	Decor
Outing equipment	✗		
Toys & books	✓		
Used items available	✗		

Outgrown

SAN RAFAEL - 1417 4TH ST (AT D ST)
TEL: 415.457.2219 HOURS: M-SA 10-4

"*...a decent consignment shop...cluttered, but there can be great finds such as close-out jogging strollers...sometimes more expensive than new items...really poor parking...* **"**

Product Selection

			Criteria
Nursery furnishings	✓	$$	Prices
Baby clothing	✓	❸	Product availability
Baby/toddler shoes	✓	❹	Staff knowledge
Feeding supplies	✓	❹	Customer service
Diapers & toiletries	✓	❸	Decor
Outing equipment	✓		
Toys & books	✓		
Used items available	✓		

Play It Again Kids

SAN RAFAEL - 508 4TH ST (AT GRAND AVE)
TEL: 415.485.0304   HOURS: M-SA 10-5; SU 12-4
Parking: lot in front of store

❝...this used store has the greatest variety of products...every staff member I have met seems to know how to operate everything...fun to browse and a great place to get rid of those items your kid has outgrown...you have to work hard to find something clean and well-maintained but if you do you'll get it at a good price... ❞

Product Selection

Nursery furnishings .... ✓
Baby clothing .... ✓
Baby/toddler shoes .... ✓
Feeding supplies .... ✓
Diapers & toiletries .... ✓
Outing equipment .... ✓
Toys & books........................... ✓
Used items available .... ✓

Criteria

$$ .... Prices
❹ .... Product availability
❸ .... Staff knowledge
❸ .... Customer service
❷ .... Decor

Play Mates

MILL VALLEY - 31 SUNNYSIDE AVE (AT E BLITHEDALE AVE)
TEL: 415.381.3047 HOURS: M-SA 10-5:30
Parking: street parking

Pottery Barn Kids

www.potterybarnkids.com

CORTE MADERA - 1640 REDWOOD HWY (AT TAMALPAIS DR)
TEL: 415.927.3558 HOURS: M-F 10-9; SA 10-7:30, SU 11-6
Parking: lot in front of store

❝...beautiful, cute and trendy nursery and bedroom essentials...the store is full of very nice things, but the real deal is to get things on sale...prices can be kind of steep, but you definitely get what you pay for... ❞

Product Selection

Nursery furnishings .... ✓
Baby clothing .... ✗
Baby/toddler shoes .... ✗
Feeding supplies .... ✗
Diapers & toiletries .... ✗
Outing equipment .... ✗
Toys & books........................... ✓
Used items available .... ✗

Criteria

$$$ .... Prices
❹ .... Product availability
❹ .... Staff knowledge
❹ .... Customer service
❺ .... Decor

Right Start

★★★★

www.rightstart.com

CORTE MADERA - 47 TAMAL VISTA BLVD # G (AT MADERA BLVD)
TEL: 415.927.8670   HOURS: M-SA 10-6; SU 11-5
Parking: lot located at The Market Place

"...love, love, love the Right Start...so many wonderful developmentally appropriate toys, books, videos and equipment...only carries top of the line infant carriers, strollers, and joggers, which is very comforting...perfect place to register if you're having a baby shower...store appears to be stocked with carefully selected, high quality products...wish there were more discounts on big ticket items to be found...the store charges full retail but well worth it...**"**

Product Selection

			Criteria
Nursery furnishings	✗	$$$	Prices
Baby clothing	✗	❹	Product availability
Baby/toddler shoes	✗	❹	Staff knowledge
Feeding supplies	✓	❹	Customer service
Diapers & toiletries	✗	❹	Decor
Outing equipment	✓		
Toys & books	✓		
Used items available	✗		

Riley's

☆☆☆☆

MILL VALLEY - 310 STRAWBERRY VLG (AT TAMALPAIS RD)
TEL: 415.388.2446   HOURS: M-SA 10-6; SU 12-5
Parking: mall has a lot

"...I love the little girls clothes here, but can never seem to find anything for my boys...gorgeous but top-dollar clothing...great gifts for infants/kids of all ages...styles are somewhat conservative...**"**

Product Selection

			Criteria
Nursery furnishings	✗	$$$$	Prices
Baby clothing	✓	❹	Product availability
Baby/toddler shoes	✓	❺	Staff knowledge
Feeding supplies	✗	❹	Customer service
Diapers & toiletries	✗	❹	Decor
Outing equipment	✗		
Toys & books	✓		
Used items available	✗		

Rocking Chairs 100 Percent

☆☆☆☆☆

www.rocking-chairs.com

CORTE MADERA - 212 CORTE MADERA TOWN CTR (AT TAMALPAIS DR)
TEL: 415.924.9492   HOURS: M-F 10-7; SA 10-6; SU 11-6
Parking: mall has a lot

"...more rocking chairs than you ever thought existed...they sell just one thing, but they've got that one thing down...relaxed, non-pressured experience...at least 20% - 30% cheaper than most other places I looked...excellent selection and service..."

Product Selection		Criteria	
Nursery furnishings	✓	$$$	Prices
Baby clothing	✗	❺	Product availability
Baby/toddler shoes	✗	❺	Staff knowledge
Feeding supplies	✗	❺	Customer service
Diapers & toiletries	✗	❸	Decor
Outing equipment	✗		
Toys & books	✗		
Used items available	✗		

Second Banana Kid's Shop

MILL VALLEY - 401 MILLER AVE (BTWN MONTFORD & EVERGREEN AVES)
TEL: 415.383.2699 HOURS: T-F 10-5:30; SA 11-5:30
Parking: lot in front of store

"...a nice secondhand store...what you see is what you get - sometimes you can get something great, other times nothing at all...like walking into your grandmother's attic...not for the fainthearted - this place is a mess...there are some special finds if you are willing to dig a little..."

Product Selection		Criteria	
Nursery furnishings	✓	$	Prices
Baby clothing	✓	❷	Product availability
Baby/toddler shoes	✓	❸	Staff knowledge
Feeding supplies	✗	❸	Customer service
Diapers & toiletries	✗	❷	Decor
Outing equipment	✓		
Toys & books	✓		
Used items available	✓		

Shorebirds Kids

BELVEDERE TIBURON - 1550 TIBURON BLVD (AT BOARDWALK PLAZA)
TEL: 415.435.4323 HOURS: M-SA 10-5
Parking: lot in

Tapioca Tiger

ST HELENA - 1234 ADAMS ST (AT MAIN ST)
TEL: 707.967.0608 HOURS: M-SA 10-5:30; SU 10:30-4
Parking: lot behind store

Target

★★★★

www.target.com

NOVATO - 200 VINTAGE WY (AT ROWLAND BLVD)
TEL: 415.892.3313 HOURS: M-SA 8-10; SU 8-9
Parking: lot in front of store

Product Selection

Nursery furnishings	✗
Baby clothing	✓
Baby/toddler shoes	✗
Feeding supplies	✓
Diapers & toiletries	✓
Outing equipment	✗
Toys & books	✓
Used items available	✗

Criteria

$	Prices
❹	Product availability
❷	Staff knowledge
❷	Customer service
❷	Decor

Toys R Us

★★★

www.toysrus.com

SAN RAFAEL - 600 FRANCISCO BLVD (AT MEDWAY RD)
TEL: 415.721.7188 HOURS: M-SA 9:30-9:30; SU 10-7
Parking: lot in front of store

"...I was shocked at how much baby stuff I could purchase, for so little money...feeding supplies were not only available, but discounted...good selection of toys, games and clothes...okay selection of nursery furnishings, strollers, high chairs...not the greatest customer service...do your research before you go, staff is usually not very knowledgeable...convenient parking...a good one-stop shop that doesn't offer the most original or unusual fare...**"**

Product Selection

Nursery furnishings	✓
Baby clothing	✓
Baby/toddler shoes	✓
Feeding supplies	✓
Diapers & toiletries	✓
Outing equipment	✓
Toys & books	✓
Used items available	✗

Criteria

$$	Prices
❸	Product availability
❷	Staff knowledge
❷	Customer service
❸	Decor

White Rabbit

☆☆☆☆

SAN ANSELMO - 601 SAN ANSELMO AVE (AT MAGNOLIA AVE)
TEL: 415.456.1938 HOURS: TU-SA 10:30-5
Parking: lot behind store

"...one of those places where you can find really beautiful children's clothes...good selection of toys and gifts...the owner is usually in the shop and she has years and years of experience and knows her product lines very well...classic clothes that never go out of style...tough parking...**"**

Product Selection

Nursery furnishings .... ✗
Baby clothing .... ✓
Baby/toddler shoes .... ✓
Feeding supplies .... ✗
Diapers & toiletries .... ✗
Outing equipment .... ✗
Toys & books........................... ✓
Used items available .... ✗

Criteria

$$$$ .... Prices
❹ .... Product availability
❹ .... Staff knowledge
❹ .... Customer service
⓬ .... Decor

Peninsula

Babies R Us

★★★★

www.babiesrus.com

SAN JOSE - 865 BLOSSOM HILL RD (AT SANTA TERESA BLVD)
TEL: 408.281.1710 HOURS: M-SA 9:30-9:30; SU 11-7
Parking: lot in front of store

❝...this store has everything you always wanted for baby - and things you never even knew you needed...great deals on the same products and equipment you might find at a boutique or higher-end shops...don't expect to find anything unique, individualized, or creative...service and staff knowledge can be hit-or-miss so you need to take the time yourself to research products and find them on the shelf...the price is right... ❞

Product Selection

Nursery furnishings	✓	
Baby clothing	✓	
Baby/toddler shoes	✓	
Feeding supplies	✓	
Diapers & toiletries	✓	
Outing equipment	✓	
Toys & books	✓	
Used items available	✗	

Criteria

$$	Prices
❹	Product availability
❸	Staff knowledge
❸	Customer service
❸	Decor

Baby Land Furniture

www.babylandfurniture.com

SAN JOSE - 1990 W SAN CARLOS ST (AT S BASCOM AVE)
TEL: 408.293.1515 HOURS: M SA 10-6; T-F 10-6:30; SU 11-5
Parking: lot in front of store

Baby Super & Rocker World

★★★★

SAN JOSE - 1523 PARKMOOR AVE (AT S BASCOM AVE)
TEL: 408.293.0358 HOURS: M-SA 10-6 (TH TILL 8:30); SU 12-5
Parking: lot in front of store

❝...one-stop shopping for putting together your baby's nursery...they were very informative and helpful when I was shopping, plus delivery was fast and easy...best selection of rockers and baby furniture that I have seen - they also have a decent selection of strollers and car seats...prices are very competitive... ❞

Product Selection

Nursery furnishings .... ✓
Baby clothing .... ✓
Baby/toddler shoes .... ✗
Feeding supplies .... ✓
Diapers & toiletries .... ✗
Outing equipment .... ✓
Toys & books........................... ✓
Used items available .... ✗

Criteria

$$ .... Prices
❹ .... Product availability
❹ .... Staff knowledge
❹ .... Customer service
❹ .... Decor

BabyGap/GapKids

www.gap.com

BURLINGAME - 1390 BURLINGAME AVE (AT PRIMROSE RD)
TEL: 650.375.1055 HOURS: M-SA 10-8; SU 11-6
Parking: street parking

SAN JOSE - 181 OAKRIDGE MALL (AT BLOSSOM HILL RD)
TEL: 408.629.5116 HOURS: M-SA 10-9; SU 11-7
Parking: mall has a lot

❝...cute, hip and fun baby and kids clothes that are practical and affordable...check out the sale rack for the best bargains around...they are a little light on the boy clothes but who isn't...nursing station and bathroom in most stores...products are generally available and if not, they will find what you're looking for in a nearby store...staff is usually very knowledgeable and available to help...the only problem with BabyGap is that almost none of the clothes for 12 months and over have snaps on the legs, which doesn't make changing easy...good return policy, which is great for gifts ❞

Product Selection

Nursery furnishings .... ✗
Baby clothing .... ✓
Baby/toddler shoes .... ✗
Feeding supplies .... ✗
Diapers & toiletries .... ✗
Outing equipment .... ✗
Toys & books........................... ✗
Used items available .... ✗

Criteria

$$$ .... Prices
❸ .... Product availability
❹ .... Staff knowledge
❹ .... Customer service
❹ .... Decor

Burlington Coat Factory Baby Depot

www.coat.com

SAN JOSE - 1600 SARATOGA AVE (AT W CAMPBELL AVE)
TEL: 408.378.2628 HOURS: M-SA 10-8; SU 11-7
Parking: lot in front of store

❝...they have a surprisingly good baby section that carries all types of affordable baby gear and clothing...we bought our Medela pump here, because they had the lowest prices around for nursing gear, bottles, and baby health care stuff... ❞

Product Selection

Nursery furnishings .... ✓
Baby clothing .... ✓
Baby/toddler shoes .... ✓
Feeding supplies .... ✓
Diapers & toiletries .... ✗
Outing equipment .... ✓
Toys & books........................... ✓
Used items available .... ✗

Criteria

$$ .... Prices
❸ .... Product availability
❸ .... Staff knowledge
❸ .... Customer service
❸ .... Decor

Carter's Childrens Wear

MILPITAS - 447 GREAT MALL DR (AT S MAIN ST)
TEL: 408.942.6621 HOURS: M-SA 10-9; SU 11-8
Parking: mall has a lot

Cheeky Monkey Toys

www.cheekymonkeytoys.com
MENLO PARK - 714 SANTA CRUZ AVE (AT CHESTNUT ST)
TEL: 650.328.7975 HOURS: M-SA 10-6
Parking: street parking

Gymboree   ★★★★

www.gymboree.com
BURLINGAME - 1202 BURLINGAME AVE (AT LORTON AVE)
TEL: 650.685.0909 HOURS: M-F 10-8; SA 10-7; SU 11-6
Parking: lot in front of store

SAN MATEO - 332 HILLSDALE MALL # 1212 (AT 31ST AVE)
TEL: 650.573.7666 HOURS: M-SA 10-9; SU 11-7
Parking: mall has a lot

"...great stuff...very cute...expensive but good quality items...staff is always nice...great for sales - you can always find clothing for 50-75% off, and there is a wide range of sizes in sale items...designs for girls are bright and colorful...boys clothes are slightly conservative but very cute...clothes have a tendency to run slightly smaller then other comparable brands...very durable and make great hand-me-downs... **"**

Product Selection

Nursery furnishings .... ✗
Baby clothing .... ✓
Baby/toddler shoes .... ✗
Feeding supplies .... ✗
Diapers & toiletries .... ✗
Outing equipment .... ✗
Toys & books........................... ✗
Used items available .... ✗

Criteria

$$$ .... Prices
❹ .... Product availability
❹ .... Staff knowledge
❹ .... Customer service
❹ .... Decor

Howard's Children's Shop

SAN MATEO - 115 E 4TH AVE (AT S SAN MATEO DR)
TEL: 650.343.1518 HOURS: M-SA 10-5:30
Parking: lot behind building

"...*timeless clothing - the kind you can hand down from generation to generation...they also had the biggest selection of baby/toddler shoes...very special and unusual item but pricey...very knowledgeable and helpful...huge selection of baby/toddler shoes...* **"**

Product Selection

Nursery furnishings	✗
Baby clothing	✓
Baby/toddler shoes	✓
Feeding supplies	✗
Diapers & toiletries	✗
Outing equipment	✗
Toys & books	✓
Used items available	✗

Criteria

$$$	Prices
❹	Product availability
❺	Staff knowledge
❺	Customer service
❺	Decor

Jacadi

www.jacadiusa.com

BURLINGAME - 1215 BURLINGAME AVE (AT CALIFORNIA DR)
TEL: 650.558.1122 HOURS: M-SA 10-7:30; SU 11-6
Parking: lot at the back of the store

"...*if you are looking for more European style items, this is the place to go...beautiful baby clothes at prices that I would never pay...* **"**

Product Selection

Nursery furnishings	✓
Baby clothing	✓
Baby/toddler shoes	✓
Feeding supplies	✗
Diapers & toiletries	✗
Outing equipment	✓
Toys & books	✓
Used items available	✗

Criteria

$$$$	Prices
❸	Product availability
❸	Staff knowledge
❸	Customer service
❹	Decor

K-B Toys

www.kbtoys.com

DALY CITY - 126 SERRAMONTE CTR (AT SERRAMONTE BLVD)
TEL: 650.756.3300 HOURS: M-SA 10-9; SU 11-7
Parking: mall has lot

Kiddie World Furniture ★★★

www.kiddieworldfurniture.com

CAMPBELL - 150 N SAN TOMAS AQUINO RD (AT W CAMPBELL AVE)
TEL: 408.370.3550 HOURS: M-W & F 9:30-6; TH 9:30-8; SA 9:30-6; SU 11-5

"...unbeatable selection...huge amount of outdoor children's furniture...staff is pleasant and knowledgeable... **"**

Product Selection

		Criteria
Nursery furnishings	✓	**$$$** .... Prices
Baby clothing	✗	**4** .... Product availability
Baby/toddler shoes	✗	**4** .... Staff knowledge
Feeding supplies	✗	**4** .... Customer service
Diapers & toiletries	✗	**4** .... Decor
Outing equipment	✓	
Toys & books	✗	
Used items available	✗	

Kids Only

LOS ALTOS - 248 MAIN ST (AT FOOTHILL EXPWY)
TEL: 650.947.0699 HOURS: M-SA 10-6; SU 11-5
Parking: street parking

Kids R US

www.kidsrus.com

SUNNYVALE - 154 E EL CAMINO REAL (AT S SUNNYVALE AVE)
TEL: 408.730.5013 HOURS: M-F 10-9; SA 10-8; SU 10-6
Parking: lot in front of store

Little Cousins ★★★★

SAN MATEO - 138 W 25TH AVE (AT HACIENDA ST)
TEL: 650.341.8726 HOURS: M-SA 10-5
Parking: street parking

"...we've gotten some real deals here but it's hit-or-miss since it's mostly used items...everything is nicely displayed and organized...they will put you on a waiting list if you're looking for something specific...I've purchased several items here and always feel that the staff is pleasant and knowledgeable... **"**

Product Selection

		Criteria
Nursery furnishings	✓	**$$** .... Prices
Baby clothing	✓	**3** .... Product availability
Baby/toddler shoes	✓	**4** .... Staff knowledge
Feeding supplies	✗	**4** .... Customer service
Diapers & toiletries	✗	**3** .... Decor
Outing equipment	✓	
Toys & books	✓	
Used items available	✓	

Lullaby Lane

www.lullabylane.com

SAN BRUNO - 556 SAN MATEO AVE (AT SYLVAN AVE)
TEL: 650.588.7644 HOURS: M TU TH F 10-6; W 10-8; SA 9:30-5:30; SU 12-5
Parking: lot behind store

❝...the best selection of quality baby gear and accessories at reasonable prices...you'll find what you need and get great service...go a few doors down and check out the discount store - if you get lucky, you can find furniture, strollers, and other big-ticket items at a real savings...watch for the warehouse sales 1-2 times/year...a must see for would-be parents in the Bay Area...they also have changing tables and breastfeeding areas...they know everything you need to know when it comes to providing a safe and cozy place for your child...**❞**

Product Selection

Nursery furnishings .... ✓
Baby clothing .... ✓
Baby/toddler shoes .... ✓
Feeding supplies .... ✓
Diapers & toiletries .... ✓
Outing equipment .... ✓
Toys & books........................... ✓
Used items available .... ✓

Criteria

$$$ .... Prices
❹ .... Product availability
❹ .... Staff knowledge
❹ .... Customer service
❹ .... Decor

Marshalls

www.marshallsonline.com

COLMA - 65 COLMA BLVD (AT JUNIPERO SERRA BLVD)
TEL: 650.992.5350 HOURS: M-SA 9:30-9:30; SU 11-7
Parking: lot in front of store

P Cottontail & Co

HALF MOON BAY - 527 MAIN ST (AT MIRAMONTES ST)
TEL: 650.726.0200 HOURS: M-SA 10-5:30; SU 11-5
Parking: street parking

Planet Kids

www.planetkidsbabynews.com

MENLO PARK - 1145 EL CAMINO REAL (AT VALAPARISO AVE)
TEL: 650.329.8488 HOURS: M-SA 10-5:30; SU 12-4
Parking: lot behind store

❝...they are responsive and easy to work with...willing to negotiate on large furniture purchases...I really enjoy shopping here, but it's tough on the pocketbook...**❞**

Product Selection

Nursery furnishings	✓
Baby clothing	✓
Baby/toddler shoes	✗
Feeding supplies	✓
Diapers & toiletries	✗
Outing equipment	✓
Toys & books	✓
Used items available	✗

Criteria

$$$$	Prices
❸	Product availability
❹	Staff knowledge
❹	Customer service
❹	Decor

Play Store

www.playstoretoys.com
PALO ALTO - 508 UNIVERSITY AVE (AT COWPER ST)
TEL: 650.326.9070 HOURS: T-SA 10-5:30; SU 1-5
Parking: garage on Cowper St

Pottery Barn Kids

www.potterybarnkids.com
PALO ALTO - 88 STANFORD SHOPPING CTR (AT UNIVERISTY AVE)
TEL: 650.321.2563 HOURS: M-F 10-9; SA 10-7; SU 11-6
Parking: lot in front of store

Right Start   ★ ★ ★

www.rightstart.com
BURLINGAME - 1111 HOWARD AVE (AT BLOOMFIELD RD)
TEL: 650.685.2270 HOURS: M-SA 10-6; SU 11-5
Parking: lot behind store

❝...love, love, love the Right Start...so many wonderful developmentally appropriate toys, books, videos and equipment...only carries top of the line infant carriers, strollers, and joggers, which is very comforting...perfect place to register if you're having a baby shower...store appears to be stocked with carefully selected, high quality products...wish there were more discounts on big ticket items to be found...the store charges full retail but well worth it... ❞

Product Selection

Nursery furnishings	✗
Baby clothing	✗
Baby/toddler shoes	✗
Feeding supplies	✓
Diapers & toiletries	✗
Outing equipment	✓
Toys & books	✓
Used items available	✗

Criteria

$$$	Prices
❹	Product availability
❹	Staff knowledge
❹	Customer service
❸	Decor

Ross Dress For Less

www.rossstores.com
DALY CITY - 311 GELLERT BLVD (AT SERRAMONTE BLVD)
TEL: 650.997.3101 HOURS: M-SA 9:30-9:30; SU 11-7
Parking: lot in front of store

Talbots Toyland

SAN MATEO - 445 S B ST (AT E 4TH AVE)
TEL: 650.342.0126 HOURS: M-SA 9:30-6; SU 11-5
Parking: lot behind building

❝...a wonderful selection of quality toys - much less "junk" than other big toy stores...they let us take car seats out to the parking lot to try them in our car before purchasing...their prices are very competitive and I can easily spend an hour browsing and buying...lots of wooden toys, puzzles, dolls, play structures, sand toys, and some essentials, like feeding supplies, strollers, blankets - I just wish they carried clothes...❞

Product Selection

Nursery furnishings	✗
Baby clothing	✗
Baby/toddler shoes	✗
Feeding supplies	✓
Diapers & toiletries	✗
Outing equipment	✓
Toys & books	✓
Used items available	✗

Criteria

$$	Prices
❹	Product availability
❹	Staff knowledge
❺	Customer service
❸	Decor

Target

www.target.com
CUPERTINO - 20745 STEVENS CREEK BLVD (AT DEANZA BLVD)
TEL: 408.725.2651 HOURS: M-SA 8-10; SU 8-9
Parking: lot in front of store
DALY CITY - 5001 JUNIPERO SERRA BLVD (AT SERRAMONTE BLVD)
TEL: 650.992.8433 HOURS: M-SA 8-10; SU 8-9
Parking: lot in front of store
SAN JOSE - 2155 MORRILL AVE (AT E MONTAGUE EXPWY)
TEL: 408.946.6791 HOURS: M-SA 8-10; SU 8-9
Parking: mall has lot

Product Selection

Nursery furnishings	✗
Baby clothing	✓
Baby/toddler shoes	✗
Feeding supplies	✓
Diapers & toiletries	✓
Outing equipment	✗
Toys & books	✓
Used items available	✗

Criteria

$$	Prices
❹	Product availability
❷	Staff knowledge
❸	Customer service
❸	Decor

The Children's Place ★★★★

www.childrensplace.com

DALY CITY - 117-A SERRAMONTE CTR (AT SERRAMONTE BLVD)
TEL: 650.992.6091 HOURS: M-SA 10-9; SU 11-7
Parking: mall has a lot

SAN JOSE - 190 OAKRIDGE MALL (OFF BLOSSOM HILL RD)
TEL: 408.227.9060 HOURS: M-SA 10-9; SU 11-7
Parking: mall has a lot

SAN MATEO - 394 HILLSDALE SHOPPING CTR (AT 31ST AVE)
TEL: 650.357.1124 HOURS: M-SA 9:30-8; SU 12-5
Parking: mall has a lot

❝...you can't beat them for quality combined with low prices...decent selection for boys...they always have good sales...most of their clothes coordinate with each other, so you can buy a lot of different things and not worry if they will match the other clothes you already have...the staff is friendly and the environment is low-key...a fun, convenient place to shop...❞

Product Selection

Nursery furnishings .... ✗
Baby clothing .... ✓
Baby/toddler shoes .... ✗
Feeding supplies .... ✗
Diapers & toiletries .... ✗
Outing equipment .... ✗
Toys & books........................... ✗
Used items available .... ✗

Criteria

$$ .... Prices
❹ .... Product availability
❹ .... Staff knowledge
❹ .... Customer service
❹ .... Decor

Toys R US ★★★

www.toysrus.com

DALY CITY - 775 SERRAMONTE BLVD (AT JUNIPERO SERRA BLVD)
TEL: 650.755.9000 HOURS: M-SA 9:30-9:30; SU 10-7
Parking: lot in front of store

SAN JOSE - 330 N CAPITOL AVE (AT MKKEE RD)
TEL: 408.259.2211 HOURS: M-SA 9:30-9:30; SU 10-7
Parking: lot in front of store

SAN MATEO - 2270 BRIDGEPOINTE PKWY (AT FASHION ISLAND BLVD EXIT)
TEL: 650.345.4475 HOURS: M-SA 9:30-9:30; SU 10-7
Parking: lot in front of store

❝...I was shocked at how much baby stuff I could purchase, for so little money...feeding supplies were not only available, but discounted...good selection of toys, games and clothes...okay selection of nursery furnishings, strollers, high chairs...not the greatest customer service...do your research before you go, staff is usually not very knowledgeable...convenient parking...a good one-stop shop that doesn't offer the most original or unusual fare...❞

Product Selection

Nursery furnishings .... ✓
Baby clothing .... ✓
Baby/toddler shoes .... ✓
Feeding supplies .... ✓
Diapers & toiletries .... ✓
Outing equipment .... ✓
Toys & books........................... ✓
Used items available .... ✗

Criteria

$$ .... Prices
❸ .... Product availability
❷ .... Staff knowledge
❷ .... Customer service
❷ .... Decor

Young Villagers

LOS ALTOS - 205 MAIN ST (AT 3RD ST)
TEL: 650.948.2856 HOURS: M-SA 10-5:30
Parking: lot behind building

Online

Babies R Us

www.babiesrus.com

★★★★

Product Selection

Nursery furnishings .... ✓
Baby clothing .... ✓
Baby/toddler shoes .... ✓
Feeding supplies .... ✓
Diapers & toiletries .... ✓
Outing equipment .... ✓
Toys & books........................... ✓
Used items available .... ✗

Criteria

$$$ .... Prices
❹ .... Product availability

Baby Bazaar

www.babybazaar.com

Baby Center

www.babycenter.com

☆☆☆☆

"...products and delivery are quite satisfactory, and prices are good...also a good information source on any number or parenting topics...awesome customer service... **"**

Product Selection

Nursery furnishings .... ✓
Baby clothing .... ✓
Baby/toddler shoes .... ✗
Feeding supplies .... ✓
Diapers & toiletries .... ✓
Outing equipment .... ✓
Toys & books........................... ✓
Used items available .... ✗

Criteria

$$.. Prices
❹ .... Product availability

BabyGap/GapKids

www.gap.com

☆☆☆☆

"...cute, hip and fun baby and kids clothes....very practical and affordable...check out the sale rack for the best bargains around...they are a little light on the boy clothes but who isn't...nursing station and bathroom in most stores...jeans last forever (great for hand-me-downs)...products are always available and if not, they will find what you're looking for in a nearby store...staff is usually very knowledgeable...great for gifts, great return policy and good quality...only problem with Baby Gap is that almost none of the clothes for 12 months and over have snaps on the legs, which doesn't make changing easy... **"**

Product Selection

Nursery furnishings .... ✗

Baby clothing .... ✓

Baby/toddler shoes .... ✗

Feeding supplies .... ✗

Diapers & toiletries .... ✗

Outing equipment .... ✗

Toys & books........................... ✗

Used items available .... ✗

Criteria

$$ .... Prices

❹ .... Product availability

Geniusbabies
www.geniusbabies.com

Stroller Depot
www.strollerdepot.com

Strollers4less
www.strollers4less.com

As you will soon find out, breastfeeding while **returning to work** requires some dedicated coordination and planning. Pumping can be irritatingly time-consuming or a welcomed fifteen minute break for you several times a day. Either way finding the right pump is key.

Breast pumps can be **rented** or **purchased** and are available in a wide range of styles, qualities and costs. The myriad of possibilities means you'll have lots of questions about which one is right for you. It also means finding a store with staff who are **patient** and **knowledgeable** of the different models and features is mandatory.

San Francisco

Citikids

www.citikids.com

SAN FRANCISCO - 152 CLEMENT ST (BTWN 2ND & 3RD AVES)
TEL: 415.752.3837 HOURS: M-SA 10-6; SU 11-5
Parking: small lot in front of store

DayOne ★★★★★

www.dayonecenter.com

SAN FRANCISCO - 3490 CALIFORNIA ST, STE 203 (AT LOCUST ST)
TEL: 415.440.3291 HOURS: M-F 9:30-6; SA 11-6; SU 11-5
Parking: garage on Locust St

❝...when it comes to breastfeeding issues and concerns, this is the place to go - they have and know everything...very knowledgeable of all nursing products, books, breast pumps and nursing bras...fabulous lactation consultants - I don't know what I would have done without them...**❞**

Criteria

Rentals available .... ✓
Staff knowledge .... ❺

$$$ .... Prices
❺ .... Customer service

Kaiser San Francisco Breastfeeding Ctr ★★★★

SAN FRANCISCO - 2200 OFARRELL ST (AT DIVISADERO ST)
TEL: 415.833.3236 HOURS: M-F 9-5
Parking: lot next to store

❝...an excellent place for breastfeeding moms with a wonderful support and resource center...the staff is knowledgeable and will assist you in finding the right breastfeeding supplies and accessories...Kaiser members get very good prices for breast pumps...they also have a hotline that can be called with questions...lactation consultants are available and very helpful...**❞**

Criteria

Rentals available .... ✓
Staff knowledge .... ❹

$$ .... Prices
❸ .... Customer service

Natural Resources Childbirth ★★★★

www.naturalresourcesonline.com

SAN FRANCISCO - 1307 CASTRO ST (AT 24TH ST)
TEL: 415.550.2611 HOURS: M-F 10:30-6; SA 11-5; SU 12-4
Parking: street parking

❝...very knowledgeable staff - they always have good advice...good pricing and good selection...they have newer and more powerful models...the rental rates are quite competitive...**❞**

Criteria

Rentals available .... ✓ $$ .... Prices
Staff knowledge .... ❺   ❹ .... Customer service

Newborn Connections

www.cpmc.org/newbornconnections

SAN FRANCISCO - 3698 CALIFORNIA ST, 1ST FL (AT MAPLE ST)
TEL: 415.600.2229 HOURS: M T TH F 9-5; W 9-6; SA 10-2
Parking: garage on Locust St

"...the lactation consultants are wonderful...they specialize in breastfeeding and have all the help you need to get you into a good routine with your baby...you can also attend free breastfeeding forums if you have questions about your pump or breastfeeding in general...in addition to selling breast pumps, nursing attire, nursing bras, baby clothes and other items, they also have a video and book library..."

Criteria

Rentals available .... ✓ $$ .... Prices
Staff knowledge .... ❹   ❹ .... Customer service

UCSF Women's Health Resource Ctr

www.ucsf.edu/whrc

SAN FRANCISCO - 2356 SUTTER ST, 1ST FL (AT DIVISADERO ST)
TEL: 415.353.2668 HOURS: M-W & F 9-5; TH 9-8
Parking: street parking

East Bay

Babies R Us

www.babiesrus.com

UNION CITY - 31250 COURT HOUSE DR (AT ALVARADO NILES RD)
TEL: 510.471.0382 HOURS: M-SA 9:30-9:30; SU 11-7
Parking: lot in front of store

Criteria

Rentals available...................... ✗ $ .... Prices
Staff knowledge .... ❹   ❹ ....Customer service

Birth & Bonding Family Ctr   ★★★★

www.birthbonding.org

ALBANY - 1126 SOLANO AVE (AT SAN PABLO AVE)
TEL: 510.527.2121 HOURS: M-SA 10-5
Parking: street parking

❝...good, friendly place to gather information...I had such a wonderful experience here - anyone needing to rent a pump or wondering what the tradeoffs of renting over buying are, should ask these folks...the parking is tough... ❞

Criteria

Rentals available...................... ✓ $$$ .... Prices
Staff knowledge .... ❹   ❹ ....Customer service

Cotton & Co

LAFAYETTE - 3535 MT DIABLO BLVD (AT MORAGA RD)
TEL: 925.299.9356 HOURS: M-SA 10-6; SU 12-5
Parking: street parking

OAKLAND - 5901 COLLEGE AVE (AT CHABOT RD)
TEL: 510.653.8058 HOURS: M-SA 10-6; SU 12-5
Parking: lot behind store

Fashion After Passion

www.fashionafterpassion.com

ALAMEDA - 1521 WEBSTER ST (AT HAIGHT AVE)
TEL: 510.769.6667 HOURS: TU-SA 10-5:30
Parking: street parking

Janaki Costello

EL CERRITO
TEL: 510.525.1155 HOURS: BY APPOINTMENT ONLY

John Muir Mt Diablo Health System - Womens Health Ctr

www.jmmdhs.com
WALNUT CREEK - 1656 N CALIFORNIA BLVD (AT CIVIC DR)
TEL: 925.941.7900 HOURS: M-TH 9-7; F 9-5
Parking: street parking

Nurture Ctr

www.nurturecenter.com
LAFAYETTE - 3399 MT DIABLO BLVD (AT BROWN AVE)
TEL: 925.283.1346 HOURS: M-W & F-SA 10-5; TH 10-8
Parking: lot in front & back of store

"...super nice, genuinely helpful people...the staff is very knowledgeable in helping customers to select their pump...they have all the accessory parts as well...**"**

Criteria

Rentals available....................✓	$$...Prices	
Staff knowledge ....❺	❺ ....Customer service	

San Ramon Regional Medical Ctr - Breastfeeding Resource Ctr

SAN RAMON - 6001 NORRIS CANYON RD (AT ALCOSTA BLVD)
TEL: 925.275.9200 HOURS: M-F 10-4
Parking: lot parking

UC Berkeley Tang Ctr

www.uhs.berkeley.edu
BERKELEY - 2222 BANCROFT WY (AT FULTON ST)
TEL: 510.643.4646 HOURS: M-F 8-5
Parking: street parking

Valley Care Lactation Ctr

PLEASANTON - 3160 SANTA RITA RD, STE B6 (AT SUTTER GATE AVE)
TEL: 925.846.1452 HOURS: M-F 1-4
Parking: mall has lot

Waddle & Swaddle

www.waddleandswaddle.com
BERKELEY - 1677 SHATTUCK AVE (BTWN CEDAR & LINCOLN STS)
TEL: 510.540.7210 HOURS: M-SA 11-6; SU 11-5
Parking: street parking

North Bay

Baby Nook ★★★★★

GREENBRAE - 250 BON AIR RD (AT MARIN GENERAL HOSPITAL)
TEL: 415.925.7474 HOURS: M W F 10:30-4:30; T TH SA 10:30-1:30
Parking: lot in front of building

❝...you can rent or buy great pumps here...just excellent customer service - always friendly...I wish the lactation consultant was there full time...the best place in Marin to get a breast pump...some of the lactation specialists even make house calls...the store also has darling baby clothes, diapers, maternity bras and other breastfeeding items that are a must for first time moms...❞

Criteria

Rentals available .... ✓ $$ .... Prices
Staff knowledge .... ❺   ❺ .... Customer service

Center for Creative Parenting

NOVATO - 446A IGNACIO BLVD (IGNACIO BLVD EXIT OFF 101)
TEL: 415.883.4442 HOURS: M-SA 10-5:30
Parking: lot in front of store

Heller's for Children ★★★★

SAN RAFAEL - 514 4TH ST (AT GRAND AVE)
TEL: 415.456.5533 HOURS: M-SA 9:30-6; SU 11-5
Parking: lot in front of store

❝...wide selection of medela products...convenient location and helpful staff...pricey, but lots of breast pump options available...the staff seemed knowledgeable...❞

Criteria

Rentals available .... ✗ $$$ .... Prices
Staff knowledge .... ❹   ❹ .... Customer service

Outgrown

SAN RAFAEL - 1417 4TH ST (BTWN D & E)
TEL: 415.457.2219 HOURS: M-SA 10-4
Parking: lot behind store

Target

www.target.com

ROHNERT PARK - 475 ROHNERT PARK EXPY W (AT LABATH AVE)
TEL: 707.586.2901 HOURS: M-SA 8-10; SU 8-9
Parking: big lot in front of store

Healthy Horizons Breastfeeding Ctr

DALY CITY - 1900 SULLIVAN AVE (AT EASTMOOR AVE)
TEL: 650.992.4000 HOURS: M W F 4-7; SA 12-3

"...they are very knowledgeable, helpful and willing to take the time to meet your needs...Sheila and her partner are great - I can't say enough good things about them...their weekly support group meetings are wonderful and definitely worth going to... **"**

Criteria

Rentals available......................✓ $$$ .... Prices
Staff knowledge ....❺   ❹ ....Customer service

Lullaby Lane

★ ★ ★ ★

www.lullabylane.com
SAN BRUNO - 556 SAN MATEO AVE (AT SYLVAN AVE)
TEL: 650.588.7644   HOURS: M TU TH F 10-6; W 10-8; SA 9:30-5:30; SU 12-5
Parking: lot behind store

"...excellent selection of breast pumps and accessories...I rented their medela pump for both my children - the staff was very courteous and knowledgeable and worked with me on drop offs...the only problem is that it sometimes gets so busy that it's hard to get help...worth the drive from anywhere in the Bay Area... **"**

Criteria

Rentals available......................✓ $$.................................. Prices
Staff knowledge ....❺   ❺ ....Customer service

Maternal Connections

MOUNTAIN VIEW - 2400 HOSPITAL DR # 1B (AT GRANT RD)
TEL: 650.988.8287 HOURS: M-SA 10-4
Parking: street parking

Tiny Tots Togs

www.tinytots.com
CAMPBELL - 138 RAILWAY AVE (AT E CAMPBELL AVE)
TEL: 408.866.2925 HOURS: M-SA 9-5
Parking: lot in front of store
Service Area: Alameda, Contra Costa, San Francisco, San Mateo, Santa Clara & Santa Cruz Counties

"...they carry a nice supply of breastfeeding essentials...I rented a hospital grade pump - wonderful service and great equipment... **"**

Criteria

Rentals available......................✓ $$.......................... Prices
Staff knowledge ....❺   ❺ ....Customer service

Online

Baby Center
☆☆☆☆
www.babycenter.com

"...products and delivery are quite satisfactory, and prices are good...also a good information source on any number or parenting topics...awesome customer service... **"**

Criteria

Rentals available...................... ✗ $$$ .... Prices

❺ .... Customer service

Birth Experience
www.birthexperience.com

Breastfeeding.com
www.breastfeeding.com

KNOX Breastfeeding Accessories
www.knoxbreastfeeding.com

To say that you will rely heavily on your pediatrician during your baby's first year is to engage in gross understatement. And as your baby grows, you'll continue to see your pediatrician until high school graduation day.

That being so, you may feel some pressure to find the **perfect doctor** as soon as possible. It's perfectly okay to take your time, maybe **check out several physicians** before choosing the right one.

This section can help. However, do keep in mind that rating physicians is a complex undertaking, and it's important to note that none of the ratings provided here are intended to reflect on these doctors' medical abilities. Our implicit assumption is that all the physicians listed are board certified and licensed to practice their specialty. Instead we focused on the more consumer oriented criteria including **parking**, the practice's **overall appearance**, waiting room magazine selection, and **administrative competency**.

San Francisco

Alban, Jan MD

SAN FRANCISCO - 3838 CALIFORNIA ST #815 (AT ARGUELLO BLVD)
TEL: 415.221.6476 HOURS: M T TH F 9-6; W 9-12
Parking: garage in building
PEDIATRICIANS: Jan Alban, MD

Huie & Tang

SAN FRANCISCO - 3905 SACRAMENTO ST #100 (AT CHERRY ST)
TEL: 415.379.6700 Parking: lot by building
PEDIATRICIANS: Sonja Huie, MD; Diana Tang, MD

"...*great practice if you can get in...the doctors all have kids themselves and are especially good about responding to new parents anxieties...* **"**

Criteria

Administrative efficiency .... ❹   ❹ ....Office decor

Kaiser Permanente

www.kp.org

SAN FRANCISCO - 2425 GEARY BLVD (AT DIVISADERO ST)
TEL: 415.833.2200 HOURS: CALL FOR DETAILS
Parking: garage underneath building
PEDIATRICIANS: call for names

Kaufman, Stephen MD

SAN FRANCISCO - 3905 SACRAMENTO ST #205 (AT ARGUELLO BLVD)
TEL: 415.752.3664 HOURS: M-F 9-5
Parking: street parking
PEDIATRICIANS: Stephen Kaufman, MD

"...*Dr Kaufman has an excellent sense of humor and is good about explaining to his patients what he's going to be doing...I would recommend him if you don't want a super busy practice...his assistant Kimberly is very personable too...* **"**

Criteria

Administrative efficiency .... ❹   ❹ ....Office decor

Mitchell Sollod Practice

SAN FRANCISCO - 595 BUCKINGHAM WY #355 (AT WINSTON DR)
TEL: 415.566.2727 HOURS: M-F 9-5
Parking: garage underneath building
PEDIATRICIANS: Martin Fung, MD; Judy Daddio, MD; Marvin Kolotkin, MD; Mitchell Sollod, MD; Nanci Tucker, MD; Colleen Halloran, MD

"...*Dr Halloran is wonderful - she puts even the most uptight new mom at ease with her calm and centered demeanor...Dr Tucker is very accessible and nice...the office staff is courteous*

and the wait is generally short...my daughter still thinks Dr Fung's name is Dr Fun, which I find appropriate and amusing... **"**

Criteria

Administrative efficiency .... ❹   ❸ .... Office decor

Noe Valley Pediatrics ★★★★

SAN FRANCISCO - 3700 24TH ST (AT DOLORES ST)
TEL: 415.641.1019 HOURS: M-F 9-5
Parking: lot next to building
PEDIATRICIANS: Nayana Anne, MD; Gianna Frazee, MD; James Schwanke, MD

"...*A friendly environment with a very San Francisco feel...Dr Anne is very laid back, but highly professional...Dr Frazee always has a big smile to brighten your day...a great pediatric group if you can get in...* **"**

Criteria

Administrative efficiency .... ❹   ❸ .... Office decor

Pacific Family Practice

SAN FRANCISCO - 2300 CALIFORNIA ST, #103 (AT WEBSTER ST)
TEL: 415.921.5762 HOURS: M-F 9-5
Parking: garage off California St

Pacific Pediatrics ★★★★

SAN FRANCISCO - 45 CASTRO ST, STE 232 (AT DUBOCE AVE)
TEL: 415.565.6810 HOURS: M-F 9-5
Parking: garage next to building
PEDIATRICIANS: Daniel Kelly, MD; Molly Prindiville, MD; Barry Rostek, DO; William Solomon, MD

"...*Dr Rostek always manages to reassure me, no matter what the issue...Dr Solomon is a great doc, but so busy that you need to make appointments well in advance...I have nothing but good things to say about every experience we've had with Drs Kelly and Prindiville...they never make us feel rushed, even though the practice is incredibly busy...* **"**

Criteria

Administrative efficiency .... ❹   ❸ .... Office decor

Patton & Piel Pediatric Practice - CPMC ★★★★★

SAN FRANCISCO - 3641 CALIFORNIA ST (BTWN SPRUCE & MAPLE STS)
TEL: 415.668.0888 HOURS: M-F 9-5
Parking: lot in front of building
PEDIATRICIANS: Eileen Aicardi, MD; Lisa Dana, MD; Martin Ernster, MD; William Gonda, MD; Robert Patton, MD; Mary Piel, MD; Laura Schultz, MD; Paul Silvestre, MD

"...we've seen 3 different doctors there and really liked them all...Dr Aicardi is a first rate diagnostician and presents her findings and treatment plans with warmth and compassion...Dr Patton is a brilliant and kind doctor who truly loves his job...Dr Gonda would call himself to set up appointments in order to expediate things...the office staff is very friendly and always remember my daughters name..."

Criteria

Administrative efficiency ....Office decor

San Francisco General Hospital - Childrens Health Ctr ★★★★

SAN FRANCISCO - 1001 POTRERO AVE 6M5 (AT 22ND ST)
TEL: 415.206.8376 HOURS: DAILY 7-10:45 PM
Parking: garage at 23 Potrero
PEDIATRICIANS: Elena Fuentes-Afflick, MD; Grace Kwok, MD; Steve Shochet, MD; Chris Stewart, MD; Shannon Thyne, MD; Cam Tu Tran, MD

"...Dr Afflick is a very experienced doctor...Dr Thyne is smart, hip and fun...Dr Tran is an amazing pediatrician...the only drawback is the SFGH is really busy, and kind of a run-down looking place..."

Criteria

Administrative efficiency ....Office decor

Town & Country Pediatrics ★★★★

SAN FRANCISCO - 3838 CALIFORNIA ST #111 (AT ARGUALLO BLVD)
TEL: 415.666.1860 HOURS: M-F 9-5
Parking: garage at 460 Cherry St
PEDIATRICIANS: Brock Bernsten, MD; Martha Kosinski, MD; Stephen Rosenbaum, MD; Robert Saffa, MD; Carolyn Wright, MD

"...Dr Wright is business like with parents and wonderful with babies - she explains everything you want to know clearly...Dr Kosinski puts the kids at ease and takes the time to talk to the parents...Dr Bernsten is very easy going, calm and has a terrific bedside manner...office staff can be a bit rushed at times but the waiting time is always minimal..."

Criteria

Administrative efficiency ....Office decor

UCSF Pediatric Clinic ★★★★★

SAN FRANCISCO - 400 PARNASSUS AVE, 2ND FL (AT UCSF MED CTR)
TEL: 415.353.2000 HOURS: M-F 9-4:30
Parking: garage off Parnassus
PEDIATRICIANS: David Becker, MD; Carol Miller, MD; Marina Tan, MD; Martha Taylor, MD; Bob Pantell, MD; Alan Uba, MD

"...It doesn't get any better than Dr Miller - first class...Dr Becker is the best pediatrician ever - caring, gentle, responsive

and very attentive...Dr Uba knows his stuff and is relaxed about the rules of parenting - he has kids of his own so I really trust him...the wait times can be kind of rough... **"**

Criteria

Administrative efficiency .... ❹   ❹ .... Office decor

UCSF/Mt Zion Medical Ctr ★★★★★

SAN FRANCISCO - 2330 POST ST #320 (AT DIVISADERO ST)
TEL: 415.885.7478   HOURS: M-F 9-5
Parking: garage on Sutter St at Divisadero
PEDIATRICIANS: Jane Anderson, MD; William DeGoff, MD; Eileen Gallagher, MD; Elisa Song, MD; Kara Wright, MD

"...*Dr Song is wonderful, very enthusiastic and extremely available...Dr DeGoff allows plenty of time during visits for questions and provides literature for parents to take home and read...Dr Anderson is especially good for brand new parents, she has a very relaxed attitude with the kids and they love her...Dr Wright is attentive and caring, has a good, warm sense of humor...* **"**

Criteria

Administrative efficiency .... ❹   ❹ .... Office decor

Winchell Quock, MD - Private Practice ★★★★

SAN FRANCISCO - 402 8TH AVE #202 (AT GEARY BLVD)
TEL: 415.751.1411 HOURS: M-F 10-6; SA 9-2
Parking: street parking
PEDIATRICIANS: Berty Liau, MD; Winchell Quock, MD

"...*Dr Quock has a great manner with children and is honest, open and nonjudgmental about parent's decisions...the office is funky, not super modern looking or slick, but everyone there is very, very nice...* **"**

Criteria

Administrative efficiency .... ❹   ❸ .... Office decor

East Bay

Alameda Pediatrics

★ ★ ★ ★

www.alamedapediatrics.com
ALAMEDA - 1332 PARK ST, STE 202 (AT ENCINAL AVE)
TEL: 510.523.3417 HOURS: M-F 9:30-12:30 1:30-5:30
Parking: street parking
PEDIATRICIANS: Robert Butts MD; Penny B. Harris, MD; Norman
Lewak, MD; B. Anne Parker, MD; Karin Schiffman, MD

" *...great clinic - efficient and professional...Dr Butts is good with children and worried parents...Dr Parker is an amazing resource for developmental questions...all of the docs we've seen here are first rate - punctual, attentive and knowledgeable...* **"**

Criteria

Administrative efficiency .... ❹   ❸ .... Office decor

Bancroft Pediatrics

SAN LEANDRO - 1300 BANCROFT AVE #204 (AT ESTUDILLO AVE)
TEL: 510.483.2600 HOURS: M-F 9-12 2-5
Parking: lot behind building
PEDIATRICIANS: Maria Beamer, MD; Laura Denenberg, MD; George
Ezekiel, MD; Laura Grunbaum, MD; Clifford Harris, MD; Stephen
Santucci, MD

Bay Valley Medical Group

www.bayvalleymedicalgroup.com
CASTRO VALLEY - 20130 LAKE CHABOT RD, STE 302 (AT CASTRO
VALLEY BLVD)
TEL: 510.581.2559 HOURS: M W TH F 8:30-5:30; T 8:30-12:30
Parking: lot at building
DANVILLE - 319 DIABLO RD (AT HARTZ AVE)
TEL: 925.314.0260 HOURS: M-TH 8-7; F 8-5; SA 9-4; SU 10-3
HAYWARD - 27212 CALAROGA AVE (AT W TENNYSON RD)
TEL: 510.785.5000 HOURS: M 8-7; T 8:30-7; W 8:30-5:30; TH 8:30-7; F
8:30-5:30; SA 9-1
PLEASANTON - 4725 FIRST ST (AT BERNAL AVE)
TEL: 925.462.7060 HOURS: M-TH 7:30-7; F 8:30-5:30
PEDIATRICIANS: Carolyn Hudson, MD; John Nackley, MD; Lilia
Oceguera, MD; Frederick Osborne, MD; Misha Roishteyn, MD

" *...Dr Nackley is a pro with an incredibly soothing demeanor...* **"**

Criteria

Administrative efficiency .... ❸   ❹ .... Office decor

Bayside Medical Group

www.baysidemed.com

ALAMEDA - 2500 CENTRAL AVE (AT PARK ST)
TEL: 510.523.8162 HOURS: M-F 9-5:30
Parking: street parking

OAKLAND - 3100 TELEGRAPH AVE (AT SUMMIT MEDICAL CTR)
TEL: 510.452.5231 HOURS: M-TH 9-7; F 9-5
Parking: lot behind building

PINOLE - 2160 APPIAN WY, STE 100 (AT MANN DR)
TEL: 510.724.8300 HOURS: M-F 9-5:30
Parking: lot next to building

PLEASANTON - 5720 STONERIDGE MALL RD, STE 240 (AT
STONERIDGE DR)
TEL: 925.463.1234 HOURS: M-F 8:30-5:30; SA 9-12
Parking: lot in front of building

WALNUT CREEK - 590 YGNACIO VALLEY RD, STE 160 (AT HILLSIDE
AVE)
TEL: 925.933.4383 HOURS: M-F 9-5:30
Parking: lot next to building

PEDIATRICIANS: Lisa Asta, MD; Sara Buckelew, MD; James Eichel, MD; Beverly Anne Estes, MD; Donald Fones, MD; Carol Gill, MD; Stephen Hart, MD; Tina Hong, MD; Toril Jelter, MD; Anna Rebecca Kerr, MD; Michael Linn, MD; J.D. Maynard, MD; Stephanie Moses, MD; Thi Sui Le Nguyen, MD; Janet Perlman, MD; Cynthia Quan, MD; Asha Ramchandran, MD; Budd Shenkin, MD; Marianne Tosick, MD; Jody Ullom, MD; Ting Wai Wang, MD; Howard Wax, MD; Charles Woodard, MD

❝...Dr Maynard really makes an effort to get to know our family...Dr Hong is full of energy and always willing to answer questions that firt-time parents have...Dr Perlman is easy to talk to and makes me and my child feel comfortable and relaxed...all the pediatricians strike me as very competent... ❞

Criteria

Administrative efficiency ....Office decor

Berkeley Pediatrics ★ ★ ★ ★

www.bpmg.salu.net

BERKELEY - 1650 WALNUT ST (AT CEDAR ST)
TEL: 510.848.2566 HOURS: M-F 9-5
Parking: street parking

PEDIATRICIANS: Ragna Boynton, MD; James Cuthbertson, MD; Elaine Davenport, MD; Annemary Franks, MD; Howard Gruber, MD; Aarti Kulshrestha, MD; Olivia Lang, MD

❝...great care and very responsive all around...they have two waiting rooms - one for sick kids...Dr Franks is an exceptional pediatirician who pays careful attention to the whole child, physically, emotionally and developmentally...Dr Lang really takes her time to answer my questions in a clear and understandable way - even the silly ones... ❞

Criteria

Administrative efficiency .... **4**   **4** ....Office decor

East Bay Pediatrics   ★ ★ ★ ★

www.eastbaypediatrics.medem.com
BERKELEY - 2999 REGENT ST #325 (AT ASHBY AVE)
TEL: 925.254.9203 HOURS: M-F 9-5
Parking: street parking
ORINDA - 96 DAVIS RD #2
TEL: 925.438.1100 HOURS: M-F 9-5
Parking: street parking
PEDIATRICIANS: Myles Abbott, MD; Dorit Bardin, MD; Sara Cahn, MD;
Marcia Charles-Mo, MD; Tracy Evans-Ramsey, MD; Mark Hodgson, MD;
Mary Jones, MD; Richard Oken, MD; William Rhea, MD

"*...Dr Cahn's gentle and patient demeanor helped her connect with my daughter from the start...Dr Evans-Ramsey talks to the child as well as the parent...our kids love Dr Jones and they actually look forward to going to the doctor...everyone from the office staff to the nurses to the pediatricians are friendly, helpful, understanding and concerned...* **"**

Criteria

Administrative efficiency .... **4**   **3** ....Office decor

John Muir Medical Ctr Pediatrics   ★ ★ ★ ★ ★

WALNUT CREEK - 2121 YGNACIO VLY RD #E106 (WALNUT AVE)
TEL: 925.935.2333 HOURS: M-F 9-5
Parking: lot in front of office
PEDIATRICIANS: Thomas Bell, MD; Arthur Law, MD; Tessie Okamura,
MD; Nancy Schwarzman, MD

"*...this group is top notch with smart doctors who obviously love babies and kids...Dr Law is easy to talk to and wonderful with kids...* **"**

Criteria

Administrative efficiency .... **5**   **5** ....Office decor

Kaiser Permanente

www.kp.org
HAYWARD - 27400 HESPERIAN BLVD (AT ARF AVE)
TEL: 510.784.4000 HOURS: CALL FOR DETAILS
OAKLAND - 280 W MACARTHUR BLVD (AT BROADWAY)
TEL: 510.752.1200 HOURS: CALL FOR DETAILS
Parking: lot next to building
PLEASANTON - 7601 STONERIDGE DR (AT FOOTHILL RD)
TEL: 925.847.5050 HOURS: CALL FOR DETAILS
Parking: lot in front of building

RICHMOND - 901 NEVIN AVE (AT 9TH ST)
TEL: 510.307.1543 HOURS: CALL FOR DETAILS
WALNUT CREEK - 320 LENNON LN (AT YGNACIO VALLEY RD)
TEL: 925.906.2525 HOURS: CALL FOR DETAILS
PEDIATRICIANS: call for names

Kiwi Pediatrics

BERKELEY - 1178 SAN PABLO AVE (AT HARRISON ST)
TEL: 510.524.9400 HOURS: M-F 10-12 2-5; SA 9-3
Parking: street parking
PEDIATRICIANS: David Kittams, MD; Elizabeth Salsburg, MD; Robin
Winokur, MD; Wilson Wong, MD

"...Dr Salsburg never appears to get annoyed at my worried
mommie-ness...Dr Kittams came highly recommended by my
midwife because her kids are there...**"**

Criteria
Administrative efficiency .... **5**   **4** .... Office decor

Palo Alto Medical Foundation

www.pamf.org
FREMONT - 3200 KEARNEY ST (AT PASEO PADRE PKWY)
TEL: 510.490.1222 HOURS: M-F 7-7; SA 8:30-12
Parking: lot in front of clinic
PEDIATRICIANS: Marietta Frey, MD; Holly Ginsberg, MD; Lilia
Hernandez, MD; Li-Min Hu, MD; Henry Sanchez, MD; Tina Scobel, MD;
Lanshin Yang, MD

Pediatric Medical Group

BERKELEY - 2320 WOOLSEY ST, STE 301 (AT TELEGRAPH AVE)
TEL: 510.849.1744 HOURS: M-F 9-5 BY APPT
Parking: small lot located behind building
PEDIATRICIANS: Ralph Berberich, MD; Jane Hunter MD; Steve
Kowalski, MD; Petra Landman, MD; Liz Moffitt, MD

"...Dr Landman exudes great confidence - she's not an alarmist
and very reassuring...comfortable, friendly office...**"**

Criteria
Administrative efficiency .... **4**   **4** .... Office decor

Pleasanton Pediatric Office

www.pleasantonpediatrics.yourmd.com
PLEASANTON - 5565 WEST LAS POSITAS BLVD, SUITE 240 (AT
SANTA RITA RD)
TEL: 925.460.8444 HOURS: M-F 9-5; SA 9-12
Parking: street parking
PEDIATRICIANS: Mary Anastasiou, MD; Stephen Anastasiou, MD;
Lionel Herrera, MD; Sam Pejham, MD

"*...the office is conveniently located right next to Valley Care Hospital...Dr Pejham is always willing to answer questions and is extremely gentle with young babies...***"**

Criteria

Administrative efficiency .... **4**   **2** .... Office decor

Primary Pediatric Medical Group ★★★★

ALAMEDA - 2258 SANTA CLARA AVE (AT OAK ST)
TEL: 510.523.3123 HOURS: M-F 9-5
Parking: lot behind building

OAKLAND - 411 30TH ST #212 (BTWN TELEGRAPH AVE & BROADWAY)
TEL: 510.433.1045 HOURS: M-F 9-5
Parking: garage on 30th St
PEDIATRICIANS: Patricia Chiang, MD; Jim Florey, MD; Neil Hoglund, MD; Bruce Horwitz, MD; Ricci Larese, MD; Roy Lin, MD; Thu Ha Pham, MD; Kenneth Plicker, MD; Laura Saldivar, MD; Kathleen Smith, MD; Michael Usem, MD

"*...Dr Usem is personable and has a knack for explaining things to new parents...Dr Horwitz is experienced, knowledgeable, realistic and warm...Dr Saldivar helped us more in 20 minutes than any other doctor had helped us in 3 years...in my experience the staff always goes above and beyond...***"**

Criteria

Administrative efficiency .... **4**   **4** .... Office decor

Rainbow Pediatrics Lafayette

www.baydocs.com/offices/rainbow/index.htm

LAFAYETTE - 3210 OLD TUNNEL RD STE A (AT PLEASANT HILL RD)
TEL: 925.287.9220 HOURS: M-F 9-5; SA 9-12; HOURS VARY, CALL FOR DETAILS
Parking: street and lot parking
PEDIATRICIANS: Maria Steelman, MD; Sharlene Pereria, MD; Sujay Banerjee, MD

Rainbow Pediatrics Pinole ☆☆☆☆☆

www.baydocs.com/offices/rainbow/index.htm

PINOLE - 1063 SAN PABLO AVE # B (AT ROGERS WAY)
TEL: 510.724.6269 HOURS: M-F 8-5; EXTENDED HOURS ON TU
Parking: lot parking
PEDIATRICIANS: Wolffe Nadoolman, MD; Helain Pleet, MD; Michael Zwerdling, MD

"*...Dr Nadoolman is an extraordinary pediatrician because of the amount of time he spends with his patients...***"**

Criteria

Administrative efficiency .... **4**   **2** .... Office decor

Summit Pediatrics Medical Group

ORINDA - 4 COUNTRY CLUB PLAZA (AT ORINDA WY)
TEL: 925.254.9500 HOURS: M-F 9-5
Parking: lot in front of building
PEDIATRICIANS: Philip Chamberlain, MD; Seymour Harris, MD; Lloyd
Takao, MD

Walnut Creek Pediatrics

WALNUT CREEK - 1822 SAN MIGUEL DR (AT SIERRA MIGUEL
PROFESSIONAL CENTER)
TEL: 925.934.9339 HOURS: M-F 8-12 1:30-5 SA EMERGENCY BASIS
ONLY
Parking: lot parking
PEDIATRICIANS: Cristina Chua-Lim, MD; Montgomery Kong, MD; Toby
Lustig, MD

"...Dr Kong is superb in every way - I drive way out of my way to
bring my children to him... **"**

Criteria

Administrative efficiency .... ❸   ❸ .... Office decor

North Bay

Kaiser Permanente

www.kp.org

NOVATO - 97 SAN MARIN DR (AT SAN RAMON WY)
TEL: 415.899.7414 HOURS: CALL FOR DETAILS
SAN RAFAEL - 99 MONTECILLO RD (AT NOVA ALBION WY)
TEL: 415.444.4460 HOURS: CALL FOR DETAILS
Parking: lot in front of building
PEDIATRICIANS: call for names

Marin Pediatric Associates ★★★★

GREENBRAE - 1100 S ELISEO DR, STE 106 (AT BON AIR RD)
TEL: 415.461.8828 HOURS: M-F 9:30-5
Parking: lot in front of building
PEDIATRICIANS: Beth Berghausen, MD; Jane Meill, MD; Scott Werner, MD; Kara Ornstein, MD

"...Dr Meill is fairly laid back and I really appreciate how easy going she is...Dr Berghausen clearly loves being a pediatrician...... **"**

Criteria

Administrative efficiency .... Office decor

Mill Valley Pediatric Associates ★★★★★

www.mvkids.salu.net

MILL VALLEY - 1206 STRAWBERRY VLG (OFF TIBURON BLVD)
TEL: 415.388.3364 HOURS: M-F 9-5; SA BY APPT
Parking: lot in front of office
PEDIATRICIANS: Melissa Congdon, MD; Kathryn Brown, MD; Richard Dow, MD; Michael Harris, MD

"...Dr Dow is smart, caring and makes my son laugh every time...Dr Brown is a delight - she takes her time, listens to your concerns, and makes sure she's thorough and attentive every time...I was a patient here as a kid and it still has the same feel it had thirty years ago - I feel my son is in the best hands... **"**

Criteria

Administrative efficiency ....  .... Office decor

Pediatric Alternatives ★★★★★

MILL VALLEY - 33 MILLWOOD ST (AT MILLER AVE)
TEL: 415.380.8448 HOURS: M-F 9-5
Parking: street parking
PEDIATRICIANS: Stacia Lansman, MD; Lindy Woodard, MD

"...Dr Woodard called me back personally to answer my questions about insurance...Drs Lansman and Woodard are knowledgeable about health alternatives and support a spirit-based lifestyle - priceless...... **"**

Sexton Joffe Urbach Pediatrics ★★★★

GREENBRAE - 1000 S ELISEO DR # 1A (OFF BON AIR RD)
TEL: 415.461.5436 HOURS: M-F 9-5
Parking: lot in front of building
PEDIATRICIANS: Martin Joffe, MD; Kathryn Sexton, MD; Katrina Urbach, MD

❝...Dr Joffe has well-informed, no-nonsense advice for new parents...Dr Sexton is a wonderful pediatrician and I am grateful that we were able to get into her practice... ❞

Criteria

Administrative efficiency .... **4**   **4** .... Office decor

Tiburon Pediatrics ★★★★

BELVEDERE TIBURON - 21 MAIN ST (AT MAIN ST & TIBURON BLVD)
TEL: 415.435.3154 HOURS: M-F 9-5
Parking: street parking
PEDIATRICIANS: Catherine Crosby, MD; Susan Dab, MD; Alan Johnson, MD; Gary Gin, MD; Margaret Miller, MD; Michelle Pepitone, MD

❝...Dr Johnson is warm, caring, extremely responsive and knowledgeable...the group is especially good with preemies and dealing with the referral, special authorizations, etc. that are often needed... ❞

Criteria

Administrative efficiency .... **5**   **3** .... Office decor

Troy & Yamaguchi ☆☆☆☆☆

SAN RAFAEL - 920 NORTHGATE DR #9 (AT LAS GALLINAS AVE)
TEL: 415.479.9797 HOURS: M-F 9-12 2-5
Parking: lot at 920 Northgate
PEDIATRICIANS: Ann Troy, MD; Michael Yamaguchi, MD

❝...Excellent, caring pediatricians...during the appointments they spend quality time and don't rush you...they also have back-up coverage during the evenings and weekends... ❞

Criteria

Administrative efficiency .... **5**   **5** .... Office decor

Peninsula

ABC Pediatrics

SAN MATEO - 50 S SAN MATEO DR #260 (BTWN TILTON & E 3RD AVES)
TEL: 650.579.6500 HOURS: M-TH 8-12 1:30-6; F 8-12 1:30-5; SA 9-12
Parking: lot adjacent to Mills Hospital
PEDIATRICIANS: Jeanne Beymer, MD; Alger Chapman, MD; Howard Chau, MD; Rosen Kerstin, MD; Nina Rezai, MD; Patricia Soong, MD

Bay Area Pediatrics ★★★★

www.bayareapediatrics.com
DALY CITY - 1500 SOUTHGATE #104 (AT SULLIVAN AVE)
TEL: 650.992.4200 HOURS: M-F 7:30-5
Parking: street parking
PEDIATRICIANS: Devi Ananda, MD; Emanuel Berston, MD; Jan Gilless, MD; Rachel Malina, MD; Robert Zaglin, MD

DALY CITY - 1800 SULLIVAN AVE #202 (AT EASTMOOR AVE)
TEL: 650.756.4200 HOURS: M-F 8-5
PEDIATRICIANS: Alice Breder, MD; Debra Barra-Stevens, MD; Amita Jain, MD; Eric Perez, MD; Marie Ribeiro, MD; Marie-Jeanne Takis, MD

SAN MATEO - 29 BAYWOOD AVE #1 (AT EL CAMINO)
TEL: 650.343.4200 HOURS: M-TH 8-9 PM; F 8-5; SA 9-12
Parking: lot in front of building
PEDIATRICIANS: James Ferrara, MD; Ken Rosenbaum, MD; Diane Suwabe, MD; Christina Tan, MD; James Wall, MD; Vincent Mason, MD

Criteria

Administrative efficiency .... ❹ ❹ ....Office decor

Camino Medical Group

www.caminomedical.com
SANTA CLARA - 2734 EL CAMINO REAL (AT KIELY BLVD)
TEL: 408.524.5952 HOURS: M-F 9-5
Parking: lot in front of building
PEDIATRICIANS: James Kim, MD; Mary Jane Pionk, MD; Vasuki Thangamuthu, MD; Kenneth Vereschagin, MD

Care First Pediatrics

LOS GATOS - 812 POLLARD RD # 1 (AT W PARR AVE)
TEL: 408.374.1212 HOURS: M-F 9-12 1-5; SA 9-12
Parking: street parking
PEDIATRICIANS: Christine Buchanan, MD; Margaret DeVilliers, MD; James Mellema, MD; Meenal Pabari, MD

❝...Dr DeVilliers is soft spoken and somewhat reserved, but a fountain of knowledge...the staff is always friendly and helpful... ❞

Criteria

Administrative efficiency .... ❹ ❹ .... Office decor

Good Samaritan Pediatrics ★★★★★

www.sjgsmedgrp.com

SAN JOSE - 2585 SAMARITAN DR (AT LOS GATOS BLVD)
TEL: 408.357.1030 HOURS: M-F 9-5
Parking: free valet
PEDIATRICIANS: Michael Eisenfeld, MD; Patricia Ferrari, MD; Marybeth Hughes, MD; James Hull, MD; Tahira Malik, MD; David Trager, MD; Jamie Wallach, MD

"...Dr. Wallach is the greatest pediatrician - she always takes the extra time to help and be there for patients...the office staff is helpful and knows many of the kids by name... **"**

Criteria

Administrative efficiency .... ❹ ❸ .... Office decor

Kaiser Permanente

www.kp.org

REDWOOD CITY - 1150 VETERANS BLVD (AT MAPLE ST)
TEL: 650.299.2015 HOURS: CALL FOR DETAILS
SOUTH SAN FRANCISCO - 1200 EL CAMINO REAL (AT ARROYO DR)
TEL: 650.742.2050 HOURS: CALL FOR DETAILS
PEDIATRICIANS: call for names

Kid Kare Associates ★★★★★

www.kidkareassociates.yourmd.com

REDWOOD CITY - 595 PRICE AVE, SUITE E (OFF VETERANS BLVD)
TEL: 650.369.4147 HOURS: M-F 9-5; SA 9-12 (SICK VISITS ONLY)
Parking: lot behind building
PEDIATRICIANS: Eileen Chan, MD; Laurie Rubenstein, MD; Niki Saxena, MD

"...Dr Chan is wonderful with our baby - she takes the time to talk to us about her development, feeding, etc. even though she is obviously very busy...all the docs I've seen there are top notch... **"**

Criteria

Administrative efficiency .... ❹ ❹ .... Office decor

Palo Alto Medical Foundation - Pediatrics ★★★★★

www.pamf.org

PALO ALTO - 795 EL CAMINO REAL (AT EMBARCADERO RD)
TEL: 650.853.2992 HOURS: M-F 8-9; SA-SU 8:30-5
Parking: garage located beneath building
PEDIATRICIANS: Mary Ann Carmack, MD; Ross DeHovitz, MD; Harry Dennis, MD; Charlotte Drew, MD; Lora Eichner, MD; Richard Greene, MD; Kimberly Jones, MD; Frederick Lloyd, MD; Kelly Look, MD; Jasmine

Makar, MD; Bettina McAdoo, MD; Robin Drucker, MD; Kellen Glinder, MD; Sally Harris, MD

"...Dr. Greene has a wonderful, comforting way about him...Dr Dennis has all of the qualities I was looking for in a pediatrician...Dr Look has a warm personality and great sense of humor..."

Criteria

Administrative efficiency .... **4**   **4** .... Office decor

Peninsula Pediatric Medical Group   ★★★★

BURLINGAME - 1720 EL CAMINO REAL 205TEL: 650.259.5050 HOURS: M-F 8:30-12 1:30-5; SA 9-12

Parking: street parking

PEDIATRICIANS: Robert Jacobs, MD; Albert Kasuga, MD; Anna Pollack, MD; Jeffrey Tan, MD; Tara Tanaka, MD; Lauri Yang Marsh, MD

"...Dr Marsh is friendly and always trying to make our baby feel at ease...Dr Tan is caring, supportive and open to new ideas...Dr Kasuga routinely schedules new infant's first appointment as a house call...all the physicians I have come into contact with are extremely personable and have excellent bedside manner..."

Criteria

Administrative efficiency .... **4**   **4** .... Office decor

A set of car keys buys nine to eleven minutes of baby happiness. The shoulders of your shirts will be perpetually stained with drool. And you will never, ever be on time for anything ever again. There. That's all you need to know about parenting.

Okay, there are some other things you may want to learn. And thankfully, the Bay Area has several organizations and businesses that focus on education and general parenting support. These places are typically staffed with specialists who provide Lamaze training and other birthing classes, post partum support and early childhood developmental information. They are also a great place to meet other parents. The quality of classes varies considerably, as do the prices. Also, some places are known to be better at organizing and presenting the information which often creates waiting lists that can be quite long.

San Francisco

Children's Council ☆☆☆☆
www.childrenscouncil.org
SAN FRANCISCO - 445 CHURCH ST (BTWN 16TH & 17TH STS)
TEL: 415.276.2900 HOURS: M-TH 9-4; F 9-12
Parking: street parking

"...great resource for parenting information in San Francisco...their choosing childcare class is very good and it's free...additionally they offer free childcare referrals... **"**

Criteria
Staff knowledge .... ❺ $$... Prices
Class selection........................ ❹   ❹ ....Info presentation

DayOne ★★★★
www.dayonecenter.com
SAN FRANCISCO - 3490 CALIFORNIA ST, STE 203 (AT LOCUST ST)
TEL: 415.440.3291 HOURS: M-F 9:30-6; SA 11-6; SU 11-5
Parking: garage on Locust St

"...the perfect place for a new mother to start getting out of the house with her baby...great selection of pre and post-natal parenting classes...smart classes with smart instructors...very convenient because you can take classes and shop for products all in one place...a little pricey but a great way to connect with other moms...amazing resource...I would not have made it through my pregnancy and beginning days without it...it made me a saner new mom... **"**

Criteria
Staff knowledge .... ❺ $$$..................................... Prices
Class selection........................ ❺   ❺ ....Info presentation

Great Expectations ★★★
SAN FRANCISCO - 400 PARNASSUS AVE (AT UC MEDICAL CTR)
TEL: 415.353.2667 HOURS: M-W & F 9-5; TH 9-8
Parking: garage on Parnassus Ave

"...some classes were great at providing the basics since this was our first baby...occasionally a bit too long...classes are large and can be a gun way to meet other expectant parents...very knowledgeable instructors...good to see videos of real births... they even provided information about accupressure... **"**

Criteria
Staff knowledge .... ❹ $$... Prices
Class selection........................ ❹   ❸ ....Info presentation

Kaiser Pre-natal Health and
Women's Health Education

SAN FRANCISCO - 2200 OFARRELL ST (AT DIVISADERO ST)
TEL: 415.833.4120 HOURS: CALL FOR SCHEDULE
Parking: lot next to store

"...*very informative, basic, pre-natal health classes...good breastfeeding classes...I was pleasantly surprised at how good these classes were...my husband took the fatherhood class and actually enjoyed it...* **"**

Criteria
Staff knowledge .... ❹ $ .... Prices
Class selection......................... ❹   ❹ ....Info presentation

Natural Resources Childbirth

www.naturalresourcesonline.com
SAN FRANCISCO - 1307 CASTRO ST (AT 24TH ST)
TEL: 415.550.2611 HOURS: M-F 10:30-6; SA 11-5; SU 12-4
Parking: street parking

"...*the best around for a holistic look at pregnancy and child rearing...Natural Resources is a gem - one of the places every pregnant woman needs to know about...great birthing classes, though heavily slanted toward natural birth methods...I appreciate that they are so available and try to offer so much...their classes fill up really quickly...parking can be tough...* **"**

Criteria
Staff knowledge .... ❹ $$$ .... Prices
Class selection......................... ❹   ❹ ....Info presentation

Newborn Connections

www.cpmc.org/newbornconnections
SAN FRANCISCO - 3698 CALIFORNIA ST, 1ST FL (AT MAPLE ST)
TEL: 415.600.2229 HOURS: M T TH F 9-5; W 9-6; SA 10-2
Parking: garage on Locust St

"...*operated by California Pacific Medical Center, they offer a great variety of classes not only for moms, but for dads and siblings too...the instructors really were very knowledgeable and the material was taught at a pace that kept your attention...super affordable, and it thus attracts all kinds of different people from diverse backgrounds making the classes very interesting...for a first-time mother/parent they offered just the right classes...* **"**

Criteria
Staff knowledge .... ❹ $$ .... Prices
Class selection......................... ❺   ❹ ....Info presentation

Parents Place ★★★★

www.jfcs.org

SAN FRANCISCO - 1710 SCOTT ST (AT SUTTER ST)
TEL: 415.359.2454 HOURS: M-TH 8:30-8; F 8:30-5
Parking: street parking

"...they deserve the fabulous reputation they have...super resource for all kinds of parenting needs...a good selection of parenting experts that teach a range of informative classes...great new mom/baby support groups...they provide child care while parents attend classes...whether it's their job boards or the emails that tell you which classes are up and coming, I always appreciate their professionalism and care... **"**

Criteria

Staff knowledge .... ❺ $$$ .... Prices
Class selection......................... ❹   ❹ ....Info presentation

Sage Femme Midwifery Svc

SAN FRANCISCO - 877 BRYANT ST, # 210 (AT 7TH ST)
TEL: 415.552.6600 HOURS: M-F 10-6
Parking: lot parking

Zann Erick - Private Practice ★★★★★

SAN FRANCISCO - PRIVATE RESIDENCE
TEL: 415.333.3394 HOURS: BY APPOINTMENT ONLY

"...we took her class for the birth of our 2nd child, and my birthing experience with the 2nd was night and day from the first...due to her instruction, I felt extremely prepared and relaxed about the birthing process as did my husband...the classes were fun and we stayed in touch with classmates for years...this class revolutionized the way I though about childbirth... **"**

Criteria

Staff knowledge .... ❺ $$ .... Prices
Class selection......................... ❺   ❺ ....Info presentation

East Bay

Alta Bates Parent Education Program

★★★★

www.altabates.com

BERKELEY - 2450 ASHBY AVE (AT FLORENCE ST)
TEL: 510.204.1334   HOURS: SCHEDULE IS ONLINE
Parking: lot on site

❝...sign up for classes early because they fill up fast...they cover everything from birthing and becoming a dad, to breastfeeding and preparing sibling classes...classes are totally reasonably priced given the quality of the instructors...essential for first-time parents... ❞

Criteria

Staff knowledge .... ❹ $$$ .... Prices
Class selection .... ❹   ❹ .... Info presentation

Bananas

★★★★★

www.bananasinc.org

OAKLAND - 5232 CLAREMONT AVE (AT 51ST ST)
TEL: 510.658.0381   HOURS: M-TH 10-4 (TU 7PM-9PM); F 10-1
Parking: street parking

❝...our community is very lucky to have the services that Bananas offers - childcare referrals, excellent classes and workshops, consultations - and the expertise of people who know their stuff...THE place to go for all your parenting questions...they even provide parent support in other languages such as Spanish, Cambodian and Vietnamese... ❞

Criteria

Staff knowledge .... ❺ $$ .... Prices
Class selection .... ❹   ❹ .... Info presentation

Birth & Bonding Family Ctr

★★★

www.birthbonding.org

ALBANY - 1126 SOLANO AVE (AT SAN PABLO AVE)
TEL: 510.527.2121   HOURS: M-SA 10-5
Parking: street parking

❝...small, intimate classes...the owner is very knowledgeable...a great resource for the parent who wants to know all the alternatives that hospitals may not tell you about ❞

Criteria

Staff knowledge .... ❹ $$$ .... Prices
Class selection .... ❸   ❸ .... Info presentation

Birthways

www.birthways.org

OAKLAND - 478 SANTA CLARA ST (AT GRAND AVE)
TEL: 510.864.8480 HOURS: F 12-2; 1ST SA OF EACH MONTH 10-2
Parking: street parking

Hayward Adult School - Parenting Ctr

www.haywardadult.com

HAYWARD - 2652 VERGIL CT (AT GROVE WY)
TEL: 510.293.8599 HOURS: CHECK ONLINE FOR SCHEDULE
Parking: lot in front of building

John Muir Mt Diablo Health System - Womens Health Ctr

www.jmmdhs.com

WALNUT CREEK - 1656 N CALIFORNIA BLVD (AT CIVIC DR)
TEL: 925.941.7900 HOURS: M-TH 9-7; F 9-5
Parking: street parking

"...hands down the best choice for East Bay parents...a lot of great pre-natal/newborn classes...birthing class, CPR/first aid, caring for a newborn and so on...all of the instructors were helpful and knowledgeable... **"**

Criteria

Staff knowledge **4**
Class selection......................... **5**

$$ .... Prices
5 ....Info presentation

Nurture Ctr

www.nurturecenter.com

LAFAYETTE - 3399 MT DIABLO BLVD (AT BROWN AVE)
TEL: 925.283.1346   HOURS: M-W & F-SA 10-5; TH 10-8
Parking: lot in front & back of store

Support Services For Mothers

www.supportgroupformothers.com

BERKELEY - P.O. BOX 7151
TEL: 510.524.0821 HOURS: CHECK ONLINE FOR SCHEDULE

"...a total lifesaver, especially if you don't have family in the area....Sherry Reinhardt has been facilitating these groups for many years and is a great resource for all things baby related...an Sherry Reinhardt is awesome...excellent forum to discuss all the changes that come with motherhood...the groups are formed from the beginning with the idea that they will provide support and friendship as your child grows...we talk about everything - from how to get your baby to sleep, to the physical and emotional changes to relationships with loved ones...... **"**

Criteria

Staff knowledge .... ❹ $$$ .... Prices
Class selection........................ ❹   ❹ ....Info presentation

Waddle & Swaddle

www.waddleandswaddle.com

BERKELEY - 1677 SHATTUCK AVE (BTWN CEDAR & LINCOLN STS)
TEL: 510.540.7210 HOURS: M-SA 11-6; SU 11-5
Parking: street parking

"...*super warm and supportive and really provided a nice atmosphere for meeting other new moms and getting lots of your new-mom questions answered...excellent 6 week new mom groups...* **"**

Criteria

Staff knowledge .... ❹ $$ .... Prices
Class selection........................ ❹   ❹ ....Info presentation

North Bay

California Parenting Institute

SANTA ROSA - 3650 STANDISH AVE (AT TODD RD)
TEL: 707.585.6108

Center for Creative Parenting ★★★★

www.creativeparenting.com

NOVATO - 446A IGNACIO BLVD (AT ALAMEDA DEL PRADO)
TEL: 415.883.4442 HOURS: M-SA 10-5:30
Parking: lot parking

"...*a great place to go when your baby is small and you have a ton of questions...classes are facilitated by a nurse so they are very informative...classes range from preconception through toddlerhood...CPR, nursing, feeding classes...they also have support groups, play groups, a small retail store and a good quarterly newsletter...* **"**

Criteria

Staff knowledge .... ❺ $$... Prices
Class selection......................... ❹   ❹ ....Info presentation

Marin Child Care Council

www.mc3.org

SAN RAFAEL - 555 NORTHGATE DR (AT LOS RANCHITOS RD)
TEL: 415.472.1092 HOURS: CALL FOR SCHEDULE

Parents Place ☆☆☆☆☆

www.jfcs.org

SAN RAFAEL - 600 5TH AVE (AT IRWIN ST)
TEL: 415.491.7959 HOURS: M-F 8:30-5
Parking: lot behind building

"...*they deserve the fabulous reputation they have...super resource for all kinds of parenting needs...a good selection of parenting experts that teach a range of informative classes...great new mom/baby support groups...they provide child care while parents attend classes...whether it's their job boards or the emails that tell you which classes are up and coming, I always appreciate their professionalism and care...* **"**

Criteria

Staff knowledge .... ❺ $ .... Prices
Class selection......................... ❺   ❹ ....Info presentation

Peninsula

Blossom Birth Services
www.blossombirth.com
PALO ALTO - 1000 ELWELL CT (AT SAN ANTONIO RD)
TEL: 650.964.7380 HOURS: CHECK SCHEDULE ONLINE
Parking: lot in front of building

Mills Health Ctr

www.millspeninsula.org
SAN MATEO - 100 S SAN MATEO DR (AT BALDWIN AVE)
TEL: 650.696.5400 HOURS: M-F 8:30-4:30
Parking: lot and street parking

❝...excellent support groups that cover a range of different topics...helpful pre-natal classes - not the run-of-the-mill info, but presented in a fun and engaging way...experienced teachers...parking near the hospital doors is tough, but there is plenty of space in the lower stretches of the parking lot...❞

Criteria
Staff knowledge .... ❹ $$.. Prices
Class selection......................... ❹   ❹ ....Info presentation

Except for maybe making it through the final moments before the epidural sets in, trusting your newborn to the care of a stranger may be the hardest thing you have to go through as a new parent. However, a **good nanny** can be a great help. And whether you need full-time help because you are going back to work, or simply need someone to fill in for a few hours a week, there are many resources here in the Bay Area.

The businesses listed on the following pages range from places that provide **bulletin boards** with nanny ads and sitters to more developed **recruiting services**. Some resources screen applicants, while others simply provide a convenient mechanism for parents to find nannies. The **presentation of information** varies from searchable, electronic databases to large, paper-based bulletin boards. Accordingly, **prices** vary from free to several hundred dollars per search or class session.

San Francisco

Core Group

www.thecoregroup.org

SAN FRANCISCO - 2616 JACKSON ST (AT PIERCE ST)
TEL: 415.567.0568 HOURS: CALL FOR DETAILS
Parking: street parking
Service Area: San Francisco, Alameda, Contra Costa, San Mateo and Marin counties.

❝*...they came through in a pinch when we were desperate for a babysitter...they do all kinds of stuff including child care and party organization...quite responsive and knowledgeable...*❞

Criteria

Info selection .... ❹ $$$ .... Prices
Info presentation .... ❹   ❺ .... Customer service
Staff knowledge .... ❺

In-house Staffing at Aunt Ann's   ★★★★

www.in-housestaffing.com

SAN FRANCISCO - 2722 GOUGH STREET (AT UNION ST)
TEL: 415.749.3650 HOURS: M-F 8:30-5
Parking: street parking
Service Area: Bay Area

❝*...very helpful and fast...they understand what you are looking for and deliver...as with all agencies they are quite expensive, but at least you don't have to pay upfront...if you need help in a pinch this is a great place to turn...*❞

Criteria

Info selection .... ❹ $$$ .... Prices
Info presentation .... ❹   ❹ .... Customer service
Staff knowledge .... ❺

Parents Place   ★★★★

www.jfcs.org

SAN FRANCISCO - 1710 SCOTT ST (AT SUTTER ST)
TEL: 415.359.2454 HOURS: M-TH 8:30-8; F 8:30-5
Parking: street parking
Service Area: San Francisco

❝*...A very easy way to find listings of people looking for child care positions, as well as people to share nannies with...a great first stop...the nanny board is helpful and free, but it can also be overwhelming and time consuming...they do a good job keeping board clean and orderly...especially useful if you are looking for specific language nannies or household help...*❞

Criteria

Info selection .... ❹ $ .... Prices
Info presentation .... ❹   ❸ .... Customer service
Staff knowledge .... ❹

Town & Country Resources ★★★★

www.tandcr.com

SAN FRANCISCO - 1388 SUTTER ST, STE 904 (AT FRANKLIN ST)
TEL: 415.567.0956 HOURS: M-F 8:30-5
Parking: street parking
Service Area: Alameda, Contra Costa, San Francisco, San Mateo, Santa
Clara and Marin Counties

❝...high quality service that produces top-notch candidates...but
you definitely pay for it...I went to several agencies and they
were by far the best...although they were very quick, I felt very
secure that the candidates were trustworthy and high
quality...they made the entire nanny search process stress
free... ❞

Criteria

Info selection .... ❺ $$$$ .... Prices
Info presentation .... ❺   ❹ .... Customer service
Staff knowledge .... ❹

University of San Francisco
Career Ctr ☆☆☆☆

SAN FRANCISCO - 2130 FULTON ST (AT COLE ST)
TEL: 415.422.6216 HOURS: M TH F 9:30-5; TU & W 9:30-7
Parking: street parking
Service Area: San Francisco Area

❝...a great place to find part-time, inexpensive sitters...the
babysitter list is how we found someone to cover our evenings
when we can't get home in time to pick up our daughter - we
love our babysitter, and couldn't be happier...you'll probably have
to screen many prospective sitters before you find the right
match... ❞

Criteria

Info selection .... ❺ $ .... Prices
Info presentation .... ❺   ❹ .... Customer service
Staff knowledge .... ❹

East Bay

A Nanny Connection

www.nannyconnection.com

DANVILLE - PO BOX 1038TEL: 925.743.0587 HOURS: M-F 9-5
Service Area: East Bay

"...*Robin really makes it her job to find you a great nanny...they can help you find pretty much any type of nanny help you are looking for...they screen all of the candidates for you...they only get paid if you find someone that works for you...* **"**

Criteria

Info selection .... ❺	$ .... Prices	
Info presentation .... ❺	❺ .... Customer service	
Staff knowledge .... ❺		

Bananas

★ ★ ★ ★

www.bananasinc.org

OAKLAND - 5232 CLAREMONT AVE (AT 51ST ST)
TEL: 510.658.0381 HOURS: M-TH 10-4 (TU 7PM-9PM); F 10-1
Parking: street parking
Service Area: Oakland, Berkeley, Piedmont, Alameda, Emeryville, Albany

"...*a good place to start the child care search...a great place to ask for advice - they know the East Bay really well...they really helped me narrow down what I was looking for...the biggest shortcoming is that their system is all paper-based which is very time consuming especially when you have the little one with you...* **"**

Criteria

Info selection .... ❸	$ .... Prices	
Info presentation .... ❸	❹ .... Customer service	
Staff knowledge .... ❹		

Bay Area 2nd Mom

www.2ndmom.com

EMERYVILLE - 6400 HOLLIS ST, STE 8 (AT 65TH ST)
TEL: 888.926.3666 HOURS: M-F 9-5
Parking: street parking and parking at back of building
Service Area: Alameda, Contra Costa, San Francisco, San Mateo and Marin Counties

"...*they can help you with pretty much any nanny situation...especially great for temporary or emergency nannies...once you're signed up you can call first thing in the morning and have someone there by around noon...all the nannies they've sent seemed good and well-qualified...* **"**

Criteria

Info selection .... ❹

Info presentation .... ❹

Staff knowledge .... ❹

$$$$ .... Prices

❹ .... Customer service

Contra Costa Child Care Council

www.cocokids.org

CONCORD - 2280 DIAMOND BLVD, STE 500 (AT CONCORD AVE)
TEL: 925.676.5437 HOURS: M-W 8-4; TH 8-8; F 8-12

North Bay

Rent-A-Parent Personnel Svc

★★★★

www.rentaparent.net

BELVEDERE TIBURON - 1640 TIBURON BLVD (BTWN BEACH AND MAIN)

TEL: 415.435.2642 HOURS: M-F 9-5

Parking: parking lot in front of building

Service Area: Marin County

"...a great fallback resource...a bit pricey, but that is the reality for last minute, screened referrals...you do need to do your own phone interview before you just take anyone off the list...all the referrals are CPR and first aid certified ... **"**

Criteria

Info selection .... ❹

Info presentation .... ❹

Staff knowledge .... ❺

$$$ .... Prices

❺ .... Customer service

Peninsula

Bay Area 2nd Mom

www.2ndmom.com

CUPERTINO - 10682 FLORA VISTA AVE (AT GREENLEAF DR)
TEL: 408.863.0553 HOURS: MONDAY-FRIDAY 9:00AM-5:00PM
Parking: street parking and parking at back of building
Service Area: Alameda, Contra Costa, San Francisco, San Mateo and
Marin Counties

"...they can help you with pretty much any nanny
situation...especially great for temporary or emergency
nannies...once you're signed up you can call first thing in the
morning and have someone there by around noon...all the
nannies they've sent seemed good and well-qualified...**"**

Criteria

Info selection .... ❹
Info presentation .... ❹
Staff knowledge .... ❹

$$$$................................... Prices
❹ .... Customer service

Town & Country Resources

★ ★ ★ ★

www.tandcr.com

PALO ALTO - 425 SHERMAN AVE, STE 130 (AT ASH ST)
TEL: 650.326.8570 HOURS: M-F 8:30-5
Parking: street parking
Service Area: Alameda, Contra Costa, San Francisco, San Mateo, Santa
Clara and Marin Counties

"...high quality service that produces top-notch candidates...but
you definitely pay for it...I went to several agencies and they
were by far the best...although they were very quick, I felt very
secure that the candidates were trustworthy and high
quality...they made the entire nanny search process stress
free...**"**

Criteria

Info selection .... ❹
Info presentation .... ❹
Staff knowledge .... ❹

$$$$................................... Prices
❹ .... Customer service

Online

Bay Area Sitters

☆ ☆ ☆ ☆ ☆

www.bayareasitters.com
Service Area: Bay Area

"...well organized...produces results... **"**

Criteria

Info selection **5**
Info presentation **5**

.... Prices

Craigslist

★ ★ ★ ★

www.craigslist.org
Service Area: Bay Area

"...awesome resource...we've gotten so many responses from highly qualified child care providers...ads are updated real time and we were able to find our caregiver by using this for one day...you have to do all the background work yourself, but we have found several good nannies this way...the best part is that it's free... **"**

Criteria

Info selection **4**
Info presentation **4**

$ .... Prices

Nanny Bank

www.nannybank.com
432 NORTH CANAL ST, STE 12

If you were to line up the number of diapers you'll change during your baby's first year, you'd have one awfully long line of diapers (and the EPA authorities on your doorstep). The point is that diapers are going to be an omnipresent part of your baby rearing equation.

And with that comes the age-old question: washable or disposable? If you decide to go the washable cloth diaper route, you'll probably be signing up with one of the services listed in this section. Although there isn't a tremendous amount of choice in the Bay Area for diaper services, you'll want to discuss their pricing policy and drop off schedules.

Bay Area

Abc Diaper Svc Inc

★★★★

BERKELEY - 1800 2ND ST (AT VIRGINIA ST)
TEL: 510.549.1133   HOURS: M-F 8-5
Service Area: Marin, Alameda, Contra Costa & Solano Counties

"...terrific service...they'll help you figure out what you need and deliver with a smile...always willing to answer questions and change my order... **"**

Criteria

Punctuality.............................. ❺ $$.. Prices
Customer service .... ❹

Tiny Tots

★★★★

www.tinytots.com

CAMPBELL - 138 RAILWAY AVE (AT E CENTRAL AVE)
TEL: 408.866.2900 HOURS: M-F 9-3
Service Area: Alameda, Contra Costa, San Francisco, San Mateo, Santa Clara & Santa Cruz Counties

"...they make the cloth diaper decision as painless as disposable...reasonably priced...always on time and very reliable...also sell diapering accessories such as wipes, disposable, diaper covers, nursing accessories, etc.... **"**

Criteria

Punctuality.............................. ❺ $$.. Prices
Customer service .... ❹

Tidee Didee

★★★★

www.tideedidee.com

SACRAMENTO - 153 OTTO CIR
TEL: 916.427.6161 HOURS: M-F 8:30-4:30
Service Area: Marin & Sonoma Counties

"...on-time deliveries and friendly service...extremely convenient and easy to use...can get costly, but that's part of making the choice to go with cloth diapers... **"**

Criteria

Punctuality.............................. ❺ $$.. Prices
Customer service .... ❹

Yeah, sure. The extra weight is necessary for the health of the baby and all, but you want to look like yourself again. So whether you're exercising to **prepare for birth**, or working to shed some weight **after the birth** of your little one, the Bay Area, as you might suspect, has lots of exercise programs to offer.

The programs available range from traditional classes in **gyms** to yoga in **studios** to **outdoor workouts**. There are even specialty training programs. **Prices** vary greatly depending on the type of program you are interested in as do class sizes. You'll also want to ask whether you can bring your baby with you. In all cases, we recommend calling ahead to get **class schedules**. Exercise programs are good for your general well-being and can also be a great way to meet other like-minded parents and their babies.

San Francisco

24 Hour Fitness ☆☆☆

www.24hourfitness.com

SAN FRANCISCO - 1850 OCEAN AVE (AT MIRAMAR AVE)
TEL: 415.334.1400 HOURS: DAILY 5AM-2AM
Parking: share parking lot with Rite Aid

"...one of the few gyms in the city that provides baby-sitting services on the premises...toddlers love the gym...no reservation policy for infants...good selection of classes... **"**

Programs

		Criteria
Pre-natal	✗	$$ .... Prices
Classes with infants	✗	❺ .... Staff knowledge
Child care available	✓	❹ .... Decor
		❸ .... Customer service

Baby Boot Camp ★★★★★

www.babybootcamp.net

SAN FRANCISCO
TEL: 415.290.2764 HOURS: CHECK ONLINE FOR SCHEDULE

"...what a great concept - work out and bring your baby along...an awesome way to get in shape, get out doors and enjoy time with new moms and your baby...like a play group/moms' group with a fitness twist...excellent class for when your infant is still happy to be sleeping and hanging out in a stroller...if you want to get back in shape and have fun doing it then you've got to check this out...classes throughout the Bay Area **"**

Programs

		Criteria
Pre-natal	✗	$$ .... Prices
Classes with infants	✓	❺ .... Staff knowledge
Child care available	✗	❺ .... Decor
		❺ .... Customer service

Castro Yoga ☆☆☆☆

www.castroyoga.com

SAN FRANCISCO - 4450 18TH ST (BTWN EUREKA & DOUGLASS STS)
TEL: 415.552.9644 HOURS: SCHEDULE IS ONLINE
Parking: street parking

"...pre-natal classes are relaxing, challenging and extremely well-guided...private lessons are great in addition to classes... **"**

Programs

		Criteria
Pre-natal	✓	$$$ .... Prices
Classes with infants	✗	❺ .... Staff knowledge
Child care available	✗	❺ .... Decor
		❺ .... Customer service

Dailey Method ★★★★★

www.thedaileymethod.com
SAN FRANCISCO - 3249 SCOTT ST (AT LOMBARD ST)
TEL: 415.345.9992 HOURS: SCHEDULE ONLINE
Parking: garage on Pierce St btwn Chestnut & Lombards Sts

❝...a low impact, yet very challenging workout that keeps you strong and lean...nothing else could have prepared my body as well or kept me in such great shape during/after pregnancy...the owner recently had a baby and she is a great example of what this method can do for you...they pay special attention to pregnant clients and customize exercises for each individual...**❞**

Programs		Criteria	
Pre-natal	✓	$$$$	Prices
Classes with infants	✗	❺	Staff knowledge
Child care available	✓	❹	Decor
		❺	Customer service

Integral Yoga Institute ☆☆☆☆

www.integralyogasf.org
SAN FRANCISCO - 770 DOLORES ST (BTWN 21ST & LIBERTY STS)
TEL: 415.252.5725 HOURS: SCHEDULE IS ONLINE

❝...from Hatha to Raja yoga, they do a great job at it all...excellent post-natal mom and baby yoga class...very philosophical and meditative approach...**❞**

Programs		Criteria	
Pre-natal	✓	$$	Prices
Classes with infants	✓	❺	Staff knowledge
Child care available	✗	❹	Decor
		❹	Customer service

It's Yoga

www.itsyoga.net
SAN FRANCISCO - 848 FOLSOM ST (BTWN 4TH & 5TH ST)
TEL: 415.543.1970 HOURS: SCHEDULE IS ONLINE

Iyengar Yoga Institute of San Francisco

www.iyisf.org
SAN FRANCISCO - 2404 27TH AVE (BTWN 26TH & 27TH AVES)
TEL: 415.753.0909 HOURS: CHECK ONLINE FOR SCHEDULE OR CALL

Mindful Body ★★★★

www.themindfulbody.com
SAN FRANCISCO - 2876 CALIFORNIA ST (BTWN DIVISADERO & BRODERICK STS)
TEL: 415.931.2639 HOURS: CHECK ONLINE FOR SCHEDULE
Parking: street parking

"...they provided the physical, emotional and spiritual well-being I needed...the instructor in the mom & baby class was incredibly sensitive and helpful...the center is clean and bright and the staff are helpful and knowledgeable...they have pre and post-natal massages as well...parking can be quite challenging..."

Programs   **Criteria**

Pre-natal .... ✓ $$ .... Prices
Classes with infants .... ✓   ❹ .... Staff knowledge
Child care available .... ✗   ❹ .... Decor
                                                ❹ .... Customer service

Open Door Yoga   ★★★★

www.opendooryoga.com
SAN FRANCISCO - 1500 CASTRO ST (AT 25TH ST)
TEL: 415.824.5657 HOURS: SCHEDULE ONLINE
Parking: street parking

"...the pre and post-natal classes are fabulous...great way to meet lots of moms and babies too...I had great a terrific time taking pre-natal yoga classes here and am looking forward to baby-and-me classes..."

Programs   **Criteria**

Pre-natal .... ✓ $$ .... Prices
Classes with infants .... ✓   ❺ .... Staff knowledge
Child care available .... ✗   ❹ .... Decor
                                                ❹ .... Customer service

Outfit Fitness

www.outfitfitness.com
SAN FRANCISCO - 1505 NORTHPOINT ST (AT LAGUNA ST)
TEL: 415.441.4631 HOURS: SCHEDULE ONLINE
Parking: lot by Marina Green

San Francisco Bay Club

www.sfbayclub.com
SAN FRANCISCO - 150 GREENWICH ST (AT SANSOME ST)
TEL: 415.433.2200 HOURS: CALL FOR SCHEDULE
Parking: garage in building

Strong Heart Strong Body   ★★★★

www.strongheartstrongbody.com
SAN FRANCISCO - 3556 SACRAMENTO ST (BTWN LOCUST & LAUREL STS)
TEL: 415.353.5616 HOURS: M-F 6-8; SA 10-6; SU 11-5
Parking: garage at Locust & California

"...excellent pre and post-natal classes...one-on-one and semi-private workouts...children are always welcome and can play with the different sized balls, mini-trampolines, and big foam blocks...a beautiful place to workout...kind of expensive..."

Programs

Pre-natal .... ✓
Classes with infants .... ✓
Child care available .... ✓

Criteria

$$$$ .... Prices
5 .... Staff knowledge
4 .... Decor
4 .... Customer service

Therapeia

www.etherapeia.com

SAN FRANCISCO - 1801 BUSH ST (AT OCTAVIA ST)
TEL: 415.885.4450 HOURS: CHECK ONLINE FOR SCHEDULE
Parking: street parking

YMCA - Presidio Community ★ ★ ★ ★

www.ymcasf.org

SAN FRANCISCO - LINCOLN BLVD (AT FUNSTON)
TEL: 415.447.9622 HOURS: M-F 5:45-9:45; SA 7:30-6:30; SU 8:30-5:30
Parking: lot in front of building

❝...an awesome facility that includes machines, free weights, group exercise and other classes...they also have a swimming pool and racquetball courts...a great way to shape up and meet other moms...classes for moms with new babies...child care for older kids...good pre and post-natal aerobics classes... **❞**

Programs

Pre-natal .... ✓
Classes with infants .... ✓
Child care available .... ✓

Criteria

$$ .... Prices
4 .... Staff knowledge
3 .... Decor
4 .... Customer service

YMCA - Stonestown ☆ ☆ ☆

www.ymcasf.org/stonestown

SAN FRANCISCO - 333 EUCALYPTUS DR (AT 21ST AVE)
TEL: 415.242.7100 HOURS: M-F 5-10; SA 7-8; SU 7-6
Parking: lot in front of building

❝...great facility with tons to do...no group classes specifically geared towards new or expecting mothers , although you can take some gentle yoga classes, or modify other classes to suit your needs...baby-sitting services are provided at an extra cost - reservations required... **❞**

Programs

Pre-natal .... ✗
Classes with infants .... ✗
Child care available .... ✓

Criteria

$$$ .... Prices
3 .... Staff knowledge
3 .... Decor
4 .... Customer service

Yoga Tree

★ ★ ★ ★

www.yogatreesf.com

SAN FRANCISCO - 1234 VALENCIA ST (BTWN 23RD & 24TH STS)
TEL: 415.647.9707 HOURS: SCHEDULE IS ONLINE
Parking: street parking

SAN FRANCISCO - 519 HAYES ST (AT OCTAVIA ST)
TEL: 415.626.9707 HOURS: SCHEDULE IS ONLINE
Parking: street parking

SAN FRANCISCO - 780 STANYAN ST (AT WALLER ST)
TEL: 415.387.4707 HOURS: SCHEDULE IS ONLINE
Parking: street parking

"...*their instructors are a pregnant woman's best resource for mind and body well-being...every possible kind of yoga is taught here...nice comfortable studios...* **"**

Programs		Criteria
Pre-natal	✓	
Classes with infants	✗	$$ .... Prices
Child care available	✗	❹ .... Staff knowledge
		❺ .... Decor
		❺ .... Customer service

East Bay

4th Street Yoga

www.4thstreetyoga.com

BERKELEY - 1809 4TH ST (AT UNIVERSITY AVE)
TEL: 510.845.9642 HOURS: CHECK ONLINE FOR SCHEDULE
Parking: street parking

"...very well taught classes in a beautiful setting...fantastic post-natal yoga classes that include babies...the pre-natal classes helped prepare my body for labor...the post-natal classes helped put my body back into shape while having my baby next to me during the classes...4th Street parking can be tricky, but spots are usually available for morning classes..."

Programs		Criteria
Pre-natal	✓	$$$ .... Prices
Classes with infants	✓	❺ .... Staff knowledge
Child care available	✗	❹ .... Decor
		❹ .... Customer service

7th Heaven Body Awareness Ctr

www.7thheavenyoga.com

BERKELEY - 2820 7TH ST (AT GRAYSON ST)
TEL: 510.665.4300 HOURS: CHECK ONLINE FOR SCHEDULE
Parking: lot on 7th St

"...excellent pre-natal yoga instructors...their special pre and post-natal class was a life saver both before and after my pregnancy...check out their other non-yoga classes too, they're great for mixing things up a little..."

Programs		Criteria
Pre-natal	✓	$$$ .... Prices
Classes with infants	✓	❹ .... Staff knowledge
Child care available	✗	❺ .... Decor
		❹ .... Customer service

Mind-Body Connection

www.mindbodyfitness.net

OAKLAND - 5255 COLLEGE AVE (AT BROADWAY TER)
TEL: 510.420.0444 HOURS: CHECK SCHEDULE ONLINE
Parking: street parking

New Mother's Workout

BERKELEY - 1432 DERBY ST (AT SACRAMENTO ST)
TEL: 510.644.2066 HOURS: CALL FOR SCHEDULE
Parking: street parking

"...Karen Casino is very knowledgeable about the postpartum body and her exercises are geared to getting those problem areas

back in alignment and shape...she has a great sense of humor and a gentle teaching style...classes are very small, so you get individual attention often...the workout does plateau after a while, though, so you really need to be vocal about asking for more advanced exercises... **"**

Programs		Criteria	
Pre-natal	✓	$$$ .... Prices	
Classes with infants	✓	❺ .... Staff knowledge	
Child care available	✓	❹ .... Decor	
		❹ .... Customer service	

Oakwood Athletic Club
www.oakwoodathleticclub.com

LAFAYETTE - 4000 MT DIABLO BLVD (AT ACALANES RD)
TEL: 925.283.4000 HOURS: M-F 5-11; SA 6-9; SU 7-9

Piedmont Yoga Studio   ★★★★
www.piedmontyoga.com

OAKLAND - 3966 PIEDMONT AVE (AT MACARTHUR BLVD)
TEL: 510.652.3336 HOURS: CHECK ONLINE FOR SCHEDULE

"*...good pre-natal yoga class, but not as engaging as it could be...the teachers are caring, compassionate, and really know yoga...classes can get overly crowded...* **"**

Programs		Criteria	
Pre-natal	✓	$$ .... Prices	
Classes with infants	✓	❹ .... Staff knowledge	
Child care available	✗	❹ .... Decor	
		❹ .... Customer service	

Stroller Jam Exercise   ☆☆☆☆☆
PLEASANTON - 301 MAIN ST (AT BERNAL AVE)
TEL: 650.302.1776 HOURS: CALL FOR DETAILS
Parking: lot in front of building

"*...one of the many classes offered run by Nancy Larson...a very effective and creative class - you do aerobics with your stroller...a great way to connect with other new moms who want to get their bodies back in shape...* **"**

Programs		Criteria	
Pre-natal	✓	$$ .... Prices	
Classes with infants	✓	❹ .... Staff knowledge	
Child care available	✗	❸ .... Decor	
		❺ .... Customer service	

YMCA - Albany

www.baymca.org
ALBANY - 921 KAINS AVE (AT SOLANO AVE)
TEL: 510.525.1130 HOURS: SCHEDULE ONLINE
Parking: street parking

YMCA - Downtown Berkeley

www.baymca.org
BERKELEY - 2009 10TH ST (AT UNIVERSITY AVE)
TEL: 510.848.9622 HOURS: M-F 5-10; SA-SU 7-7:30

"...lots of classes to choose from...the pre-natal yoga and water aerobics classes were amazing...the babygym and kindergym staff are so nice - I feel very comfortable leaving my child there while I work out..."

Programs

Pre-natal	✓
Classes with infants	✗
Child care available	✓

Criteria

$$	Prices
❹	Staff knowledge
❸	Decor
❹	Customer service

Yogalayam

www.yogalayam.org
BERKELEY - 1717 ALCATRAZ AVE (BTWN ELLIS & KING ST)
TEL: 510.655.3664 HOURS: CHECK ONLINE FOR SCHEDULE
Parking: street parking

"...they are miracle workers...their pre-natal class was the single most helpful activity throughout my pregnancy...I thoroughly enjoyed their pre-natal class and the mommy-and-baby yoga class too..."

Programs

Pre-natal	✓
Classes with infants	✓
Child care available	✓

Criteria

$	Prices
❺	Staff knowledge
❸	Decor
❹	Customer service

North Bay

Baby Boot Camp

★★★★★

www.babybootcamp.net

MILL VALLEY - 825 AUTUMN LN
TEL: 415.290.2764 HOURS: SCHEDULE ONLINE

"...what a great concept - work out and bring your baby along...an awesome way to get in shape, get out doors and enjoy time with new moms and your baby...like a play group/moms' group with a fitness twist...excellent class for when your infant is still happy to be sleeping and hanging out in a stroller...if you want to get back in shape and have fun doing it then you've got to check this out...classes throughout the Bay Area **"**

Programs

			Criteria
Pre-natal	✗	$$$	Prices
Classes with infants	✓	❺	Staff knowledge
Child care available	✗	❹	Decor
		❺	Customer service

Dailey Method

☆☆☆☆

www.thedaileymethod.com

CORTE MADERA - 11 1ST ST (AT TAMALPAIS & MAGNOLIA DRS)
TEL: 415.927.1133 HOURS: CALL FOR SCHEDULE
Parking: lot across on Tamalpais

"...a low impact, yet very challenging workout that keeps you strong and lean...nothing else could have prepared my body as well or kept me in such great shape during/after pregnancy...the owner recently had a baby and she is a great example of what this method can do for you...they pay special attention to pregnant clients and customize exercises for each individual... **"**

Programs

			Criteria
Pre-natal	✓	$$$$	Prices
Classes with infants	✗	❺	Staff knowledge
Child care available	✓	❹	Decor
		❺	Customer service

Elan Fitness Ctr

☆☆☆☆☆

www.elanfitness.com

SAN ANSELMO - 230 GREENFIELD AVE (AT SEQUOIA DR)
TEL: 415.485.1945 HOURS: M-TH 5:30-9:30; F 5:30-8; SA 7-6; SU 7-5
Parking: lot in front of building

"...large facilities that also include spa services...they offer great offers good aerobic classes for pre and post-natal moms...you can bring your tot with you, use him as a free weight, and when he gets bigger you can drop him off at the childcare center inside the gym... **"**

Programs

Pre-natal................................. ✓
Classes with infants .... ✓
Child care available................. ✓

Criteria

$$ .... Prices
❺ .... Staff knowledge
❺ .... Decor
❹ .... Customer service

Mill Valley Community Ctr ★★★★

www.millvalleycenter.org

MILL VALLEY - 180 CAMINO ALTO (AT E BLITHEDALE AVE)
TEL: 415.383.1370 HOURS: CALL FOR DETAILS
Parking: lot in front of building

❝...the good-hearted instructors are enthusiastic and love to share their infinite knowledge of physical fitness...a good workout for pre and post-natal women...this is where I met most of the women that formed the moms' group I'm part of...they have reasonably priced child care for parents who want to use the gym...the facility is beautiful and clean...the Taj Mahal of community centers... ❞

Programs

Pre-natal................................. ✓
Classes with infants .... ✓
Child care available................. ✓

Criteria

$$ .... Prices
❹ .... Staff knowledge
❹ .... Decor
❹ .... Customer service

Yoga Center Of Marin

www.yogacenterofmarin.com

CORTE MADERA - 142 REDWOOD AVE (AT TAMALPAIS DR)
TEL: 415.927.1850 HOURS: CHECK SCHEDULE ONLINE
Parking: lot in front of building

Yoga Garden

www.yogagardenstudio.com

SAN ANSELMO - 412 RED HILL AVE, STE 12 (AT SIR FRANCIS DRAKE BLVD)
TEL: 415.485.5800 HOURS: SCHEDULE ONLINE

Yoga Studio ★★★★

www.yogastudiomillvalley.com

MILL VALLEY - 650 E BLITHEDALE AVE (AT LOMITA DR)
TEL: 415.380.8800 HOURS: CHECK SCHEDULE ONLINE

❝...the pre-natal yoga and mom and baby yoga instructor is wonderful...you'll get a good workout, have time to relax and learn lots about how to cope with the many changes your body endures during pregnancy and the postpartum period...nice way to get to know a variety of women and different stages in pregnancy...they're studios are beautiful, people are wonderful and the most knowledgeable instructors I've ever had... ❞

Programs

Pre-natal................................. ✓
Classes with infants .... ✗
Child care available................. ✗

Criteria

$$$ .... Prices
❺ .... Staff knowledge
❹ .... Decor
❹ .... Customer service

Peninsula

Baby Boot Camp

www.babybootcamp.net
BURLINGAME
TEL: 415.290.2764 HOURS: CHECK ONLINE FOR SCHEDULE

"...what a great concept - work out and bring your baby along...an awesome way to get in shape, get out doors and enjoy time with new moms and your baby...like a play group/moms' group with a fitness twist...excellent class for when your infant is still happy to be sleeping and hanging out in a stroller...if you want to get back in shape and have fun doing it then you've got to check this out...classes throughout the Bay Area "

Programs			Criteria
Pre-natal	✗	$$	Prices
Classes with infants	✓	❺	Staff knowledge
Child care available	✗	❺	Decor
		❺	Customer service

Mills Health Ctr - Aquatic Program

www.millspeninsula.org
SAN MATEO - 100 S SAN MATEO DR (BTWN TILTON & E 3RD AVES)
TEL: 650.696.5600 HOURS: M-F 6:30-8:30; SA 8-3
Parking: lot at hospital

"...they offer several great pre-natal aquatic classes...instructors are knowledgeable about stretching and aerobic exercise while pregnant...prices are reasonable... "

Programs			Criteria
Pre-natal	✓	$$	Prices
Classes with infants	✗	❹	Staff knowledge
Child care available	✗	❹	Decor
		❹	Customer service

Pacific Athletic Club

www.pacclub.com
REDWOOD SHORES - 200 REDWOOD SHORES PKWYTEL:
650.593.9100 HOURS: M-F 5-11; SA-SU 7-9
Parking: lot in front of building

San Carlos Recreation Ctr

www.ci.san-carlos.ca.us
SAN CARLOS - 1017 CEDAR ST (AT BRITTAN AVE)
TEL: 650.802.4385 HOURS: CHECK ONLINE FOR SCHEDULE
Parking: lot at 1001 Chestnut

On the universal scale of challenging events, dressing a monkey ranks number one. Cutting the hair of a squirming child is a close second. Many consider the **first haircut** to be a rite of passage for the parents and child. However, cutting children's hair can be tricky and you want to make sure you find someone who can handle it and make it a special event all at the same time.

Many of the kid-oriented places have toys, videos and other **distractions** to make the experience enjoyable as well as memorable. Furthermore, **speed** is a characteristic highly valued by parents of less-than-interested kids.

San Francisco

Kids Cuts

SAN FRANCISCO - 85 29TH ST (AT SAN JOSE AVE)
TEL: 415.643.8582 HOURS: M-F 9:30-6:30; SA 8:30-5
Parking: street parking

"...a blast from the past - the perfect place for good old fashioned kids' cuts...plenty of activities to keep the little one occupied - fire truck seat, toys, balloons and lollipops...Esmerelda is great, and kept my son's hands busy with a toy while she quickly cut his hair...the best thing about them is they're across the street from Mitchell's ice cream - for an after haircut treat... **"**

Criteria

Speed .... **4** $$ .... Prices
Decor **4**

Peppermint Cuts

SAN FRANCISCO - 1772 LOMBARD ST (AT LAGUNA ST)
TEL: 415.292.6177 HOURS: BY APPOINTMENT ONLY
Parking: street parking

Snippety Crickets

SAN FRANCISCO - 3562 SACRAMENTO ST (BTWN LAUREL & LOCUST STS)
TEL: 415.441.9363 HOURS: M-F 10-6; SA 9-5; SU 10-5
Parking: street parking

"...they were very adept at cutting hair under very difficult circumstances – my fighting toddler...wonderful Thomas train set up for kids to play with afterwards...fun atmosphere...a bit pricey, but worth the effortless haircut experience - excellent distraction toys, and a lollipop to boot... **"**

Criteria

Speed .... **4** $$$ .... Prices
Decor **4**

Supercuts

www.supercuts.com

SAN FRANCISCO - 2947 GEARY BLVD (AT BLAKE ST)
TEL: 415.752.0656 HOURS: M-F 9-8; SA 8-7; SU 10-5
Parking: street parking

"...staff tries hard to make kids feel special...they still get my daughter's hair cut even though she is upset - amazing...they usually have toys to play with during the haircut and a balloon after...lines can get long but you can call for appointments... **"**

Criteria

Speed .... ❹ $ $ .... Prices
Decor .... ❸

East Bay

Cool Tops

★ ★ ★ ★

LAFAYETTE - 3367 MT DIABLO BLVD (AT HAMPTON RD)
TEL: 925.284.5360 HOURS: T-TH 9:30-6; SA-SU 9-5
Parking: street parking

❝...a really fun lively place with cheerful staff...great animal barber chairs and videos at each station...great place to go, especially for first haircut...the cuts are decent and do the job...the owner and employees do not mind if kids run around in the place...❞

Criteria

Speed .... ❺ $$$ .... Prices
Decor .... ❺

Dublin Beauty College

DUBLIN - 7305 VILLAGE PKWY (AT AMADOR VALLEY BLVD)
TEL: 925.829.7644 HOURS: TU-SA 8-3
Parking: street parking

Genray Hair Salon

OAKLAND - 6093 CLAREMONT AVE (AT COLLEGE AVE)
TEL: 510.655.2262 HOURS: BY APPOINTMENT ONLY
Parking: street parking

Great Clips for Hair - Rockridge Ctr

OAKLAND - 5118 BROADWAY (AT COLLEGE AVE)
TEL: 510.594.1689 HOURS: M-F 9-9; SA 9-6; SU 11-6
Parking: mall has a lot

Pony Tails For Children

★ ★ ★ ★

LAFAYETTE - 3413 MT DIABLO BLVD (AT BROWN AVE)
TEL: 925.283.7432 HOURS: M 9:30-5; TU-F 9-5; SA 9-2:30
Parking: lot in front of store

❝...nice little salon for kids...their shop is inside a consignment shop so there is a great waiting room for parents to shop while they wait for their kids....kids can choose to sit on a merry-go-round horse or a regular stylist chair...❞

Criteria

Speed .... ❹ $$$ .... Prices
Decor .... ❹

Rich's Barber Shop

RICHMOND - 12645 SAN PABLO AVE (AT SOLANO AVE)
TEL: 510.237.1107 HOURS: CALL FOR APPOINTMENT
Parking: street parking only

Shear Adventures ★ ★ ★ ★

DANVILLE - 320 HARTZ AVE (AT DIABLO RD)
TEL: 925.820.3697 HOURS: TU-F 9-6; SA 9-4
Parking: street parking

❝...you can tell this place has it down with little ones...great place for a first haircut and it's worth the money to pay for someone who knows what to expect when cutting a young child's hair...fun and cheerful environment...can be busy, often running behind schedule... ❞

Criteria

Speed .... ❺ $$$ .... Prices
Decor .... ❺

Snippety Crickets ★ ★ ★

BERKELEY - 1753 SOLANO AVE (AT COLUSA AVE)
TEL: 510.527.3987 HOURS: M-F 10-6; SA 9-6; SU 10-5
Parking: street parking

❝...the haircutters are quick, friendly and generally do what you want them to do...fun atmosphere...a little pricey for a kids cuts... ❞

Criteria

Speed .... ❹ $$$ .... Prices
Decor .... ❹

Snips ★ ★ ★

OAKLAND - 5335 COLLEGE AVE # 4 (AT CLIFTON ST)
TEL: 510.547.7277 HOURS: T-SA 10-5
Parking: street parking

❝...my daughter loves to go here for the toys they provide while her hair gets cut...stylist quality varies a bit but overall stylists are good with young children and work very quickly... ❞

Criteria

Speed .... ❹ $$$ .... Prices
Decor .... ❹

Supercuts

www.supercuts.com
OAKLAND - 6046 COLLEGE AVE (AT CHABOT RD)
TEL: 510.653.4702 HOURS: M-F 8-9; SA 8-7; SU 8-6
Parking: street parking

North Bay

Children's Hair Club

SAN RAFAEL - 1726 LINCOLN AVE (AT HAMILTON CT)
TEL: 415.453.9111 HOURS: BY APPOINTMENT ONLY ON SA-W

Cuts Etc

ROHNERT PARK - 125 SOUTHWEST BLVD # BTEL: 707.795.2887
HOURS: M-F 10-7; SA 9-5; SU 10-3
Parking: lot in front of store

Lions & Tigers & Hair

PETALUMA - 42 KENTUCKY ST (AT B ST)
TEL: 707.773.3711 HOURS: T-F 10-5; SA 10-3
Parking: street parking

Locks & Lollipops ☆ ☆ ☆ ☆

SAN RAFAEL - 1563 4TH ST (BTWN E & F STS)
TEL: 415.457.5211 HOURS: M 2-5; TU-F 10-5; SA 10-4
Parking: street parking

"...wonderful, professional and child-friendly...totally kid-friendly, designed only for children...kids can watch videos and completely forget about getting their hair trimmed...lots of books and toys... **"**

Criteria

Speed .... ❺ $$... Prices
Decor .... ❺

Panda Room ★ ★ ★ ★

CORTE MADERA - 127 CORTE MADERA TOWN CTR (AT TAMALPAIS DR)
TEL: 415.924.2288 HOURS: M-SA 10-5:30; SU 10-3
Parking: mall has a lot

FAIRFAX - 1573 SIR FRANCIS DRAKE BLVD
TEL: 415.459.1288 HOURS: TU F SA 10-5; TH 12-7
Parking: street parking

NOVATO - 132 VINTAGE WY # F3 (AT ROWLAND BLVD)
TEL: 415.892.2889 HOURS: M-SA 10-5:30; SU 10-3
Parking: mall has a lot

"...funky, downhome decor that kids and parents love...the staff is so patient with difficult, unwilling kids...wonderful place for a first haircut...they give my son a basket of toys which just about keeps him occupied for the duration of the haircut...often crowded, appointments are recommended... **"**

Criteria

Speed .... ➍

Decor .... ➍

$ $ $ .... Prices

Peninsula

Balloon Cuts

SAN JOSE - 4684 MERIDIAN AVE (AT FOXWORTHY AVE)
TEL: 408.266.5466 HOURS: M-F 10-6:30; SA 9-5:30
Parking: lot in front of store

Just Kids Cuts

★ ★ ★

BURLINGAME - 1200 HOWARD AVE (AT N DELAWARE ST)
TEL: 650.548.1490 HOURS: T-F 9:30-6; SA 9-5; SU10-3
Parking: street parking

"...fun, friendly and quick...they had tv's everywhere and a waiting/play room... **"**

Criteria

Speed .... ❹
Decor .... ❹

$$$ .... Prices

You can't accost complete strangers with a wallet full of baby photos if you don't get some good ones taken!

If you're interested in having a professional take pictures of you and your baby, there are several photographers to choose from. Most will make **appointments** and come to your home or other place of your choice. Finding a photographer who understands what you are looking for and who can **coax some cooperation** out of your baby is important. Also, do realize that hiring professional photographers can often be rather **costly**, but they are helping you document some of the best days of your life.

San Francisco

Gail Mallimson Photography

www.archetypicalproductions.com/photo

SAN FRANCISCO - 2130 23RD ST (BTWN DE HARO & RHODE ISLAND STS)

TEL: 415.648.5019 HOURS: BY APPOINTMENT

Parking: street parking

Service Area: Bay Area-wide

❝...Gail's creativity captured our family together in a very playful way...her pictures are soulful and playful at the same time...she's a true professional and provides professional service...the fact that she's a mother is an incredible asset - she is able to create delightful and truthful pictures...❞

Criteria

Speed .... ❺ $$$$ .... Prices
Customer service .... ❺

Kathi O'Leary Photography

SAN FRANCISCO - 1033 HAYES ST (AT STEINER ST)

TEL: 415.552.0905 HOURS: W-SA 9-4

Parking: street parking

Leslie Corrado Photography

www.lesliecorrado.com

SAN FRANCISCO - 2 HENRY ADAMS ST #M2 (AT DIVISION ST)

TEL: 415.431.3917 HOURS: BY APPOINTMENT ONLY

Parking: street parking

Service Area: Bay Area & in-studio

Criteria

Speed .... ❹ $$$ .... Prices
Customer service .... ❺

Picture People

www.picturepeople.com

SAN FRANCISCO - 3251 20TH AVE (AT STONESTOWN GALLERIA)

TEL: 415.566.7803 HOURS: M-SA 10-9; SU 11-6

Parking: mall has a lot

Service Area: in-studio only

❝...they always seem to have coupons for a free something or other...the wait can be quite long and they do seem to run behind schedule a fair bit...they have tons of props and poses for you to strike...compared to some photos I had taken for which I paid a ton, they are very good...portraits were ready the same day...❞

Criteria

Speed .... ❹

Customer service .... ❸

$$ .... Prices

Tami DeSellier Photography ★★★★

www.tamiland.com

SAN FRANCISCO - TEL: 415.668.5930 HOURS: BY APPOINTMENT ONLY

Service Area: in-studio only

"...*Tami was fabulous...she captured the spirit of our family and son...selecting the prints out of the huge number of wonderful proofs was the toughest part...Tami is expensive, but she's definitely worth it - she's a pro with kids...* **"**

Criteria

Speed .... ❹

Customer service .... ❹

$$$$ .... Prices

East Bay

Abc Harrell Photography
www.abcharrell.com
OAKLAND - 2507 BROADWAY (AT 27TH ST)
TEL: 510.655.2099 HOURS: BY APPOINTMENT ONLY
Parking: street parking

Angela Lang Photography
www.angelalang.com
EMERYVILLE
TEL: 510.420.0541 HOURS: BY APPOINTMENT ONLY

Christina Shook Photography

www.cshook.com
ORINDA - 19 CHARLES HILL CIR (OFF ST STEPHENS DR)
TEL: 415.713.9717 HOURS: BY APPOINTMENT ONLY
Parking: street parking
Service Area: Bay Area & in-studio

"...a warm and smiling artist...Christina is an all 'round top professional with years of experience in photographing both families and celebrities...the black and whites were crisp and dramatic...the color shots were so vibrant...she came to our home and shot some beautiful pictures...great studio gardens... **"**

Criteria
Speed .... **5** $$.. Prices
Customer service **5**

Eliot Khuner Photography
www.ekphoto.com
BERKELEY - 1029 CEDAR (AT 10TH ST)
TEL: 510.524.3569 HOURS: BY APPOINTMENT ONLY
Parking: street parking

James Brian Studios
www.jamesbrian.com
WALNUT CREEK - 1727 BONANZA ST (AT CALIFORNIA BLVD)
TEL: 925.934.4455 HOURS: T-F 10-4 AND BY APPOINTMENT
Parking: lot parking

Jamie Westdal Photography
www.jamiewestdal.com
ORINDA - 2 THEATRE SQ # 112 (AT MORAGA WY)
TEL: 925.254.9689 HOURS: BY APPOINTMENT ONLY
Parking: garage at Theatre Sq

JCPenney Portrait Studio

www.jcpenney.com

PLEASANTON - 1500 STONERIDGE MALL RD (AT STONERIDGE DR)
TEL: 925.463.9780 HOURS: M-SA 10-9; SU 11-7
Parking: mall has a lot

RICHMOND - 1000 HILLTOP MALL RD (OFF BLUME DR)
TEL: 510.222.4411 HOURS: M-SA 10-9; SU 11-7
Parking: mall has a lot

Picture People

www.picturepeople.com

ALAMEDA - 2237 S SHORE CTR (AT OTIS & PARK)
TEL: 510.814.8856 HOURS: M-F 10-9; SA 10-6; SU 11-6
Parking: mall has a lot

RICHMOND - 2141 HILLTOP MALL RD (OFF BLUME DR)
TEL: 510.223.2932 HOURS: M-SA 10-9; SU 11-7
Parking: mall has a lot

Sandra Eatons Photography

LAFAYETTE - 13 FIESTA LN (AT MT DIABLO BLVD)
TEL: 925.284.1929 HOURS: BY APPOINTMENT ONLY
Parking: lot or street parking

Sears Portrait Studio   ☆ ☆ ☆ ☆

www.searsportrait.com

CONCORD - 1001 WILLOW PASS RD (AT CONTRA COSTA BLVD)
TEL: 925.246.1969 HOURS: M-F 9:30-8; SA 9:30-8; SU 10-5
Parking: mall has a lot
Service Area: in-studio only

HAYWARD - 660 W WINTON AVE (OFF 880)
TEL: 510.784.5369 HOURS: M-F 10-8; SA 9-8; SU 10-6
Parking: mall has a lot

OAKLAND - 1955 BROADWAY (AT 22ND ST)
TEL: 510.267.2069 HOURS: M-F 10-6; SA 10-6; SU 11-5
Parking: parking lot

PLEASANTON - 1700 STONERIDGE MALL RD (OFF STONERIDGE DR)
TEL: 925.469.5469 HOURS: M-SA 10-8; SU 11-6
Parking: mall has a lot

RICHMOND - 2300 HILLTOP MALL RD (OFF BLUME DR)
TEL: 510.262.4169 HOURS: M-F 9:30-8; SA 9-8; SU 10-7
Parking: mall has a lot
Service Area: in-studio only

❝...best to make an appointment, or go on the less hectic
weekdays...use coupons and it's best to buy the smile saver
plan...I love that they take pictures with a digital camera so you
can choose the ones you want right away...**❞**

Criteria

Speed .... ❸ $ $ .... Prices
Customer service .... ❸

Sharon Muraco Photography

OAKLAND
TEL: 510.531.7881   HOURS: BY APPOINTMENT ONLY

Stratford Candids

www.stratfordcandids.com

BERKELEY - 3149 LEWISTON AVE (AT ALCATRAZ AVE)
TEL: 510.595.7300   HOURS: BY APPOINTMENT ONLY
Parking: street parking

North Bay

Benoit Photography
www.photobenoit.com
ROHNERT PARK - 5430 COMMERCE BLVD # I (AT CASCADE CT)
TEL: 707.584.0361 HOURS: BY APPOINTMENT
Parking: street parking

Carolyn O'Neill Fine Art Photography
★★★★★
www.carolynoneill.com
SAN RAFAEL - 10 SMITH RANCH RD (AT LUCAS VALLEY RD)
TEL: 415.491.4249 HOURS: BY APPOINTMENT ONLY
Service Area: Bay Area

❝...the Bay Area's best kept secret...her work is fabulous ..high-end photography and service for a great value...very professional...very intuitive in that she know what parents are looking for in photos...she has quite a knack with kids... ❞

Criteria
Speed .... ❹ $$$ .... Prices
Customer service .... ❺

Hyla Molander Photography
SAN RAFAEL - 4340 REDWOOD HWY (AT TAMALPAIS DR)
TEL: 415.491.4573 HOURS: BY APPOINTMENT ONLY
Parking: street parking

Lisa Knutson Photography
www.lisakphoto.com
LARKSPUR - PO BOX 936
TEL: 415.256.9597 HOURS: BY APPOINTMENT ONLY

Nancy Manning Photography
LARKSPUR
TEL: 415.924.2932 HOURS: BY APPOINTMENT ONLY

Picture People
★★★★
www.picturepeople.com
SAN RAFAEL - 5600 NORTHGATE MALL (AT LAS GALLINAS AVE)
TEL: 415.479.4430 HOURS: M-SA 10-9; SU 11-6
Parking: mall has a lot
Service Area: in-studio only

❝...they always seem to have coupons for a free something or other...the wait can be quite long and they do seem to run behind schedule a fair bit...they have tons of props and poses for you to strike...compared to some photos I had taken for which I *paid a ton, they are very good...portraits were ready the same day...* **"**

Criteria

Speed .... ❹ $$ .... Prices
Customer service .... ❹

San Anselmo One Hour Photo

SAN ANSELMO - 560 SAN ANSELMO AVE (AT MAGNOLIA AVE)
TEL: 415.459.7538 HOURS: M-F 10-6; SA 10-5

Sears Portrait Studio   ★ ★ ★

www.searsportrait.com

SAN RAFAEL - 9000 NORTHGATE MALL (AT FREITAS PKWY)
TEL: 415.507.2368 HOURS: M-F 10-8; SA 9:30-8; SU 11-5
Parking: mall has a lot
Service Area: in-studio only

Criteria

Speed .... ❸ $$ .... Prices
Customer service .... ❸

Theresa Vargo Photography   ☆ ☆ ☆ ☆

www.theresavargophotography.com

MILL VALLEY - 469 MILLER AVE #A (AT REED ST)
TEL: 415.388.9210 HOURS: BY APPOINTMENT ONLY

"...nice and friendly, good with kids and very flexible...wonderful photographer and her pictures were gorgeous...* **"**

Criteria

Speed .... ❺ $$$ .... Prices
Customer service .... ❺

Peninsula

Classic Kids

☆☆☆☆

www.classickids.net

SAN MATEO - 1501 S B ST (AT 15TH AVE)

TEL: 650.522.9705 HOURS: M-F 9-5

Parking: lot or street parking

"...they had my daughter dancing and laughing the whole time...they calmly engaged each one of my children and inspired world class photographs...wonderful experience...excellent results...**"**

Criteria

Speed .... ❹ $$$ .... Prices

Customer service .... ❺

JCPenney Portrait Studio

www.jcpenney.com

SAN JOSE - 2230 TULLY RD (AT EAST RIDGE SHOPPING CENTER)

TEL: 408.238.0300 HOURS: M-SA 10-7; SU 11-6

Parking: mall has a lot

Olan Mills Portrait Studio

www.olanmills.com

SAN JOSE - 777 STORY RD (AT ROBERTS AVE)

TEL: 408.279.3128 HOURS: M-SA 10-7; SU 1-5

Parking: lot in front of building

Picture People

★ ★ ★

www.picturepeople.com

SAN MATEO - 3400 S EL CAMINO REAL # 300

TEL: 650.377.0124 HOURS: M-SA 9-9; SU 10-7

Parking: mall has lot

Service Area: in-studio only

"...they always seem to have coupons for a free something or other...the wait can be quite long and they do seem to run behind schedule a fair bit...they have tons of props and poses for you to strike...compared to some photos I had taken for which I paid a ton, they are very good...portraits were ready the same day... **"**

Criteria

Speed .... ❸ $$ .... Prices

Customer service .... ❸

Sears Portrait Studio

☆ ☆ ☆ ☆

www.searsportrait.com

SAN BRUNO - 1178 EL CAMINO REAL (AT SNEATH LN)
TEL: 650.553.8869 HOURS: M-F 9:30-8; SA 9-8; SU 10-7
Parking: lot in front of building

SAN MATEO - 40 HILLSDALE MALL RD (AT 31ST AVE)
TEL: 650.295.2069 HOURS: M-SA 9:30-8; SU 10-6
Parking: mall has a lot
Service Area: in-studio

Criteria

Speed .... ❸ $$ .... Prices
Customer service .... ❸

Wine And Jam Photography

www.wineandjam.com

MOUNTAIN VIEW
TEL: 415.970.8995 HOURS: BY APPOINTMENT ONLY

This you will realize much sooner than you may expect: more than anything else, activities get you through your sleep-deprived day.

The Bay Area has tons to offer parents and their kids. The appropriateness of activities varies for infants and toddlers but there is no shortage of things to do with kids of all ages. Play groups, music classes, museums, outings and indoor activities abound. Class availability may be an issue for some programs and prices vary from free to annual memberships/subscriptions.

San Francisco

AcroSports

www.acrosports.org

SAN FRANCISCO - 639 FREDERICK ST (AT WILLARD ST)
TEL: 415.665.2276 HOURS: CHECK ONLINE FOR SCHEDULE
Parking: street parking

"...my son loves to run and tumble, climb the walls, and swing from the trapeze...instructors range from super fun and enthusiastic to quieter and reserved...it seems like there's something here for everyone...the classes fill up fast so you need to sign up early...parents watch from the bleachers as the little ones aim to impress... **"**

Criteria

Staff.....................................❸ $$$$..................................... Prices

American Gymnastics

www.americangymnasticsclub.com

SAN FRANCISCO - 2520 JUDAH ST (BTWN 30TH & 31ST AVES)
TEL: 415.731.1400 HOURS: SCHEDULE IS ONLINE
Parking: street parking

Baker Beach

SAN FRANCISCO - BOWLEY ST (AT LINCOLN BLVD & 25TH AVE)
Parking: multiple lots & street parking

Basic Brown Bear Factory

www.basicbrownbear.com

SAN FRANCISCO - 444 DE HARO ST (AT MARIPOSA ST)
TEL: 415.626.0781 HOURS: DAILY 10-5

"...although pricey, there's nothing like making your own stuffed bear...my kids loved picking out the shell, stuffing, dressing and naming their bear...even a leisurely trip will have you in and out the door in about an hour... **"**

Criteria

Staff.....................................❹ $$$ .... Prices

California Academy of Sciences

www.calacademy.org/aquarium

SAN FRANCISCO - 1 MARITIME PLZ (AT 9TH AVE IN GG PARK)
TEL: 415.750.7145 HOURS: WINTER: DAILY 10-5; SUMMER:
DAILY 9-6
Parking: street parking

"...the aquarium, natural history museum and planetarium are the best place in the city on a rainy day...where else can you go and see dinosaurs, alligators, fish, and the stars all in an *afternoon...the roundabout aquarium is a treasure...they have a neat, special play area for toddlers with books, games, and instruments in the African section...can get pretty crowded...the first Wednesday of each month is free...* **99**

Criteria

Staff.. ❹ $$$ .... Prices

Exploratorium   ★ ★ ★ ★

www.exploratorium.edu

SAN FRANCISCO - 3601 LYON STREET (AT MARINA BLVD)
TEL: 415.561.0394 HOURS: TU-SU 10-5; W 10-9
Parking: lot in front of museum

66*...as soon as your child can run around this is a good place to go...lots of stuff to touch, smell, use, and play with...tons of mirrors, bubbles and a play area for toddlers...lots of cool, interactive exhibits...a great place to let your kids tear about - they definitely won't get bored...small, but packed with activities...the first Wednesday of each month is free...* **99**

Criteria

Staff.. ❹ $$$ .... Prices

Golden Gate Mother's Group   ★ ★ ★ ★

www.ggmg.org

SAN FRANCISCO
TEL: 415.789.7219

66*...a good way to connect especially with your first baby...a convenient way to join a playgroup and meet other moms...the monthly meetings usually have some interesting and helpful topics...the group's monthly newsletter is chock-full of information and resources...* **99**

Criteria

Staff.. ❹ $$ .... Prices

Golden Gate Park - Merry Go Round   ★ ★ ★ ★ ★

SAN FRANCISCO - SHARON MEADOWS (AT KEZAR & MLK JR DRVS)
Parking: small lot near playground

66*...a beautiful, classic merry-go-round in a park setting...kids love the funky old organ and colorful animals...a fabulous ride for the money...the only negative is that the ticket line can take a while since it is also the line for the snack bar...weekdays are very uncrowded and you can combine it with some of the other great activities and sights in the park...* **99**

Criteria

Staff.. ❹ $ .... Prices

Gymboree Play Programs ★★★

www.gymboree.com

SAN FRANCISCO - 1525 SLOAT BLVD (AT 34TH AVE)
TEL: 415.242.5637 HOURS: CHECK SCHEDULE ONLINE
Parking: mall has a lot

SAN FRANCISCO - 2675 GEARY BLVD (AT MASONIC AVE)
TEL: 415.776.2111 HOURS: CHECK SCHEDULE ONLINE
Parking: lot in front of mall

"...the equipment is terrific for toddlers and the music is fun...make sure you preview the class you want to join to see if you like the instructor since there is variability in their styles - some are more engaging than others...safe environment for both walkers and crawlers...wait until your kids are very mobile and need a lot of physical activity before joining...can get kind of expensive... **"**

Criteria

Staff....................................... ❹ $$$ .... Prices

Herbst Pool ★★★★

SAN FRANCISCO - 207 SKYLINE BLVD (AT ARMORY RD)
TEL: 415.665.4100 HOURS: CALL FOR SCHEDULE
Parking: street parking

"...wonderful warm water...parents join kids in the pool for their class...the best thing is that classes are an hour as opposed to half-hour most other places... **"**

Criteria

Staff....................................... ❹ $$ .... Prices

Kindermusik with Deedee

www.kindermusikwithdeedee.com

SAN FRANCISCO - 4620 CALIFORNIA ST (AT 8TH AVE)
TEL: 415.561.9754 HOURS: SCHEDULE IS ONLINE
Parking: street parking

Metreon - Where the Wild Things Are ★★★★

www.metreon.com

SAN FRANCISCO - 101 FOURTH ST (AT MISSION ST)
TEL: 415.369.6000 HOURS: M 10-5; F-SA 10-7; SU 10-6
Parking: garage on Mission at 4th St

"...parents and kids alike will love this fantasy land exhibit taken straight from the pages of everyone's favorite book...good to go there when the weather is bad because your little one can run and jump and scream to his heart's content...it seems a bit pricey for many families and big groups... **"**

Criteria

Staff....................................... ❸ $$$ .... Prices

Milberry Recreation & Fitness Center Pool

★★★★

www.cas.ucsf.edu/mps

SAN FRANCISCO - 500 PARNASSUS AVE (AT UCSF MEDICAL CTR)
TEL: 415.476.1115 HOURS: FAMILY SWIM ON SA & SU 2:30-4:30
Parking: garage at UC campus

"...the infant swim classes can be terrific, depending on the instructor...at 7 dollars per class they are great value...check out family swim time on weekends - a great way to spend the afternoon meeting other kids...**"**

Criteria

Staff......................................❸ $$..Prices

Moscone Recreation Ctr

★★★★

SAN FRANCISCO - 1800 CHESTNUT ST (AT FILLMORE ST)
TEL: 415.292.2006 HOURS: CALL FOR SCHEDULE
Parking: street parking

"...an amazing space for playgroups...the kids gym programs on Thursdays and Fridays are great...lots of toys and things to do - paint, draw, play-doh...if you buy the discount book the prices aren't bad...**"**

Criteria

Staff......................................❸ $ ....Prices

Music Together: Golden Gate Music Together

SAN FRANCISCO - FT MASON CTR
TEL: 415.454.7194 HOURS: CALL FOR DETAILS

Music Together: Music Together of San Francisco

★★★★

www.musictogethersf.com

SAN FRANCISCO - 500 DE HARO (AT MARIPOSA ST)
TEL: 415.596.0299 HOURS: CALL FOR SCHEDULE
Parking: street parking

"...Paul is very animated and great with kids...full of energy and able to engage the children actively...the pace is quick and fun...our daughter started when she was one - now she's two and she still sings the songs from the class all the time - when she's getting dressed, taking a bath, eating meals and always in the car...kids love it...**"**

Criteria

Staff......................................❹ $$$ ....Prices

Music Together: San Francisco
Music Together

www.sfmusictogether.com

SAN FRANCISCO - 776 HAIGHT ST (AT SCOTT ST)
TEL: 415.431.9793 HOURS: CHECK ONLINE FOR SCHEDULE
Parking: street parking

"...*a beautiful, bright urban studio space and a hip, creative and energetic teacher...Amy has so much energy and spirit...there are about 7-10 other parent/child pairs in the class...we go through songs, tones, chants and jam sessions - all with a backup CD, tape and workbook to repeat at home...* **"**

Criteria

Staff...................................... **5** $$.. Prices

Noe Strolls

www.noestrolls.com

SAN FRANCISCO - HOURS: CHECK SCHEDULE ONLINE

"...*the newsletter is an awesome resource for activities each day of the week across the city...lectures, activities, events - this is a really helpful resource...a clearinghouse of information on what to do with your baby or toddler...* **"**

Criteria

Staff...................................... **5** $ .... Prices

North Beach Playground & Pool

SAN FRANCISCO - 651 LOMBARD ST (BTWN POWELL & MASON STS)
TEL: 415.274.0200 HOURS: PRESCHOOL SWIM T&TH 11-11:45; W 3:15-3:45; CALL FOR SCHEDULE OF OTHER PROGRAMS
Parking: street parking

Playsongs

www.sfplaysongs.com

SAN FRANCISCO - 25 LAKE ST (AT ARGUELLO BLVD)
TEL: 415.567.7838 HOURS: CALL FOR SCHEDULE
Parking: street parking

SAN FRANCISCO - THE PRESIDIO - BLDG 49 (NEXT DOOR TO THE OFFICER'S CLUB ON THE MAIN POST)
TEL: 415.567.7838 HOURS: CHECK ONLINE FOR SCHEDULE
Parking: street parking

"...*Chris Molla, the instructor, is very special and talented with kids of all ages...the class has structure and a theme but gives children the opportunity to explore and enjoy the music...a great way to introduce music to your little one...wonderful, but pretty pricey...* **"**

Criteria

Staff...................................... **5** $$$ .... Prices

Randall Museum

www.randallmuseum.org

SAN FRANCISCO - 199 MUSEUM WY (OFF ROOSEVELT WY)

TEL: 415.554.9600 HOURS: T-SA 10-5

Parking: lot in front of museum

"...a small wonderful space for young children...there are animals to feed and observe, a working model railroad, and lots of drop-in arts and crafts projects...go in the weekday afternoons when you have the squawking eagles and hawks practically to yourselves...there is a nice little reading nook with animal books just right for the setting...nothing beats it for hands on with furry critters...you can't beat the price - free!...**"**

Criteria

Staff... ❹ $ .... Prices

Richmond Recreation Ctr

SAN FRANCISCO - 251 18TH AVE (BTWN CALIFORNIA & CLEMENT STS)

TEL: 415.666.7020 HOURS: KIDS PROGRAMS: T&F 10-12; CALL FOR OTHER SCHEDULES

Parking: small lot in front of ctr

"...excellent kids gym in the morning with a whole room full of toys plus activity area with paints and crafts...there is a baby area and plenty for older kids too...it is so clean and the toys are well-maintained...Tuesdays are great, Fridays are a zoo...**"**

Criteria

Staff... ❹ $ .... Prices

San Francisco Gymnastics

www.sanfranciscogymnastics.com

SAN FRANCISCO - 920 MASON ST (AT CRISSY FIELD)

TEL: 415.561.6260 HOURS: CHECK ONLINE FOR SCHEDULE

Parking: lot behind building

San Francisco Zoo

www.sfzoo.org

SAN FRANCISCO - 1 ZOO RD

TEL: 415.753.7080 HOURS: DAILY 10-5

Parking: street parking

"...a wonderful place - petting zoo, carousel, and steam train rides all available...the one membership that never wears out...wow, they have done a great job renovating the zoo...you can rent a private area for birthday parties too...a great deal for any train loving kids is to join the little puffer club as a junior engineer - there are special Saturday mornings when you get to go before the zoo opens and you can ride the train as much as you want....staff is generally available to answer questions...the first Wednesday of each month is free...**"**

Criteria

Staff.................................... ❹ $$.. Prices

Sherith Israel Play Groups ★★★★★

www.sherithisrael.org

SAN FRANCISCO - 2266 CALIFORNIA ST (AT WEBSTER ST)
TEL: 415.346.1720 HOURS: M 10:30-12 & 2-3:30; T&TH 10:30-12; F 10-11:30

Parking: garage on Webster St

❝...Mimi is a blessing - she exudes wonderful enthusiasm and tremendous support and guidance...the Tuesday morning music sessions are a great energy boost for moms and babes...groups take place in a huge carpeted room filled with toys geared towards birth to 2 years...a good place to meet other parents... ❞

Criteria

Staff.................................... ❺ $$.. Prices

Upper Noe Recreation Ctr

SAN FRANCISCO - 299 DAY ST (AT SANCHEZ ST)
TEL: 415.695.5011 HOURS: CALL FOR SCHEDULE

Parking: street parking

Zeum - Yerba Buena Gardens ★★★★

www.zeum.org

SAN FRANCISCO - 221 4TH ST (AT HOWARD ST)
TEL: 415.777.2800 HOURS: W-SU 11-5

Parking: garage on Mission St btwn 4th & 5th St

❝...deep in the heart of downtown, this play space has something for everyone...good place to go when you get tired of playgrounds...plenty of room to run around in an architecturally interesting setting that suits both parents and kids....a sand pit, water table, slides, and climbing gym make this a definite must-do...don't miss the carousel...close to shopping and the Metreon... ❞

Criteria

Staff.................................... ❹ $$$ .... Prices

East Bay

Beth Abraham Temple Play Group

www.tbaoakland.org

OAKLAND - 327 MACARTHUR BLVD (AT ADAMS ST)
TEL: 510.832.0936 HOURS: CALL FOR SCHEDULE
Parking: street parking

"...*nice bright space with lots of activities for kids...bubbles, toys, ball pit, parachute time, free play and songs...Dawn is a magical group leader for this fun free-form indoor gym...at the end there's juice and a story...* **"**

Criteria

Staff.. **4** $$.. Prices

Castro Valley Mothers Club   **904**

www.castrovalleymothersclub.com

CASTRO VALLEY - 20103 LAKE CHABOT RD (EDEN HOSPITAL CONF CTR) (AT CASTRO VALLEY BLVD)
TEL: 510.475.6864 HOURS: CALL FOR DETAILS
Parking: hospital lot

Children's Fairyland

www.fairyland.org

OAKLAND - 699 BELLEVUE AVE (AT GRAND AVE)
TEL: 510.452.2259 HOURS: CALL FOR DETAILS

"...*a quaint story book park originally built in the 50s - it has since been remodeled...good to do several times over...many of the rides are only suitable for older children...lots of places for climbing, exploring and discovering...get there early - parking fills up fast...* **"**

Criteria

Staff.. **4** $$.. Prices

East Bay Moms

www.eastbaymoms.com

OAKLAND - 6000 CONTRA COSTA RD (AT CHAUMONT PATH)
TEL: 510.653.7867 HOURS: CALL FOR SCHEDULE

"...*great for meeting other moms and learning about all the cool stuff to do with kids in the Bay Area...the founder, Lee Eisman, is super energetic and a fountain of creativity...an excellent group for mothers who love to hike...extremely organized...good newsletter...offers so many activities for families with children of all ages...we've been members for over a year and have really enjoyed our hikes and stroller walks...* **"**

Criteria

Staff.. **4** $$$ .... Prices

FUN Mothers Club

www.funmothersclub.org

FREMONT - PO BOX 891
TEL: 510.475.6864

"...geared towards moms in the Fremont, Union City, and Newark area...the people are very friendly...there are playgroups, baby sitting co-ops, mothers night out - just to name a few activities..."

Criteria

Staff.. ❹ $$.. Prices

Gymboree Play Programs

www.gymboree.com

CONCORD - 1975 DIAMOND BLVD, STE C-130 (AT WILLOW PASS RD)
TEL: 925.685.7773 HOURS: CHECK SCHEDULE ONLINE
Parking: mall has a lot

PLEASANTON - 5460 SUNOL BLVD # 9 (BTWN BERNAL AVE & 680)
TEL: 925.249.0006 HOURS: CHECK SCHEDULE ONLINE
Parking: lot out front

SAN RAMON - 3191 CROW CANYON PL (AT 680 & CROW CANYON RD)
TEL: 925.866.8315 HOURS: CHECK SCHEDULE ONLINE
Parking: mall has a lot

"...the equipment is terrific for toddlers and the music is fun...make sure you preview the class you want to join to see if you like the instructor since there is variability in their styles - some are more engaging than others...safe environment for both walkers and crawlers...wait until your kids are very mobile and need a lot of physical activity before joining...can get kind of expensive..."

Criteria

Staff.. ❹ $$$ .... Prices

Habitot Children's Museum

www.habitot.org

BERKELEY - 2065 KITTREDGE ST. (AT SHATTUCK AVE)
TEL: 510.647.1111 HOURS: M W 9:30-1; T F 9:30-5; TH 9:30-7; SA 10-5; SU 11-5 (NOT OPEN ON SU DURING SUMMER)

"...painting, water works, train sets - lots of stimulation before nap time...the staff is personable and involved...great for rainy day activities since it's all indoors...parking is really tough...can be expensive since they also charge adults, but when you see how much fun the kids have, it's all worth it..."

Criteria

Staff.. ❹ $$$ .... Prices

Itty Bitty Kiddie Gym

www.lakemerrittumc.com/itty_bitty_kiddie_gym.htm

OAKLAND - 1255 FIRST AVE (AT E 11TH ST)
TEL: 510.465.4793 HOURS: CHECK ONLINE FOR SCHEDULE
Parking: street parking

"...*a wonderful toddler movement program for kids nine months to three years...it's run by two experienced teachers who are stay-at-home dads...a nice range of activities for small kids from songs and art projects to play equipment and toys...the physical space is light and airy and also has an outdoor play area...***"**

Criteria

Staff....................................**❺** $$.. Prices

Jungle Fun & Adventure

www.junglefunandadventure.com

CONCORD - 1975 DIAMOND BLVD (AT WILLOW WY)
TEL: 925.687.4386 HOURS: SU-TH 10-9; F 10-10; SA 9-10
Parking: lot in front of building

"...*my children's' favorite place to go...because it is indoors, it gets crowded during the winter...there is a play area for under 3 years as well as the gigantic structure for all other kids...they also have games and a cafeteria...there is a quiet room for parents and plenty of tables to sit and relax....***"**

Criteria

Staff....................................**❹** $ .... Prices

Kennedy Park

www.hard.dst.ca.us

HAYWARD - 19501 HESPERIAN BLVD (AT BARTLETT AVE)
TEL: 510.881.6715 HOURS: SA-SU 11:30-4:30
Parking: lot near entrance

"...*a train, merry-go-round, pony ride, bounce house and a petting zoo...they also have a wonderful playground...tables can be rented to parties and large groups...***"**

Criteria

Staff....................................**❹** $ .... Prices

Kids 'N Dance

LAFAYETTE - 3369 MT. DIABLO BLVD (AT HAMPTON RD)
TEL: 925.284.7388 HOURS: CALL FOR SCHEDULE

Lamorinda Mothers Club

www.lamorindamomsclub.org

LAFAYETTE - PO BOX 1002
TEL: 925.941.4714

"...*moms dinners, playgroups, monthly and weekly activities...your level of involvement is totally up to you - you can* *sit on the sidelines and read the newsletter or get involved in leadership roles and social activities...a definite recommendation for new moms...* **"**

Criteria

Staff..................................... ❺ $ .... Prices

Lindsay Wildlife Museum

www.wildlife-museum.org

WALNUT CREEK - 1931 FIRST AVE (AT BUENA VISTA)
TEL: 925.935.1978 HOURS: CALL FOR DETAILS; SUMMER AND
WINTER HOURS VARY
Parking: lot in front of museum

"*...a wonderful live museum filled with animals that you would find all over California...an excellent way for kids to see animals like bobcats, falcons, snakes and eagles close up...there is a park next door where you can eat lunch and play either before or after your visit...don't miss the downstairs traveling exhibits...* **"**

Criteria

Staff..................................... ❺ $ .... Prices

Montclair Recreation Ctr

www.oaklandnet.com/parks/facilities

OAKLAND - 6300 MORAGA AVE (AT LA SALLE AVE)
TEL: 510.482.7812 HOURS: CALL FOR ACTIVITIES SCHEDULE
Parking: street parking

Neighborhood Parents Network

www.parentsnet.org

BERKELEY - PO BOX 8597
TEL: 510.527.6667

Oakland Zoo

www.oaklandzoo.org

OAKLAND - 9777 GOLF LINKS RD (AT KNOWLAND PARK)
TEL: 510.632.9523 HOURS: DAILY 10-4

"*...a great little zoo that you can see in a single afternoon...they have a small petting zoo with goats and sheep...there is also a small amusement park area with rides and a train, and the park is always a great place for a picnic...parking is easy...a sure kid pleaser...* **"**

Criteria

Staff..................................... ❹ $$ .... Prices

Orinda Community Center

www.ci.orinda.ca.us

ORINDA - 26 ORINDA WY (AT SANTA MARIA WY)
TEL: 925.254.2445 HOURS: SCHEDULE ONLINE
Parking: street parking

Piedmont Gardens Retirement Community Volunteer Program

OAKLAND - 110 41ST ST (AT PIEDMONT AVE)
TEL: 510.654.7172 X113 HOURS: T 9:30-10:30
Parking: street parking

"...*a super, volunteer intergenerational program...we play in the center of a large room, and residents gather around to watch - it is wonderful for everyone involved...the elderly residents light up when the kids arrive...Liz Chamish has been organizing this program for over a decade and is phenomenal...* **"**

Criteria
Staff.. ❺ $ .... Prices

Pixieland Amusement Park

www.pixieland.com
CONCORD - 2740 E OLIVERA RD (NEAR WILLOW PASS RD)
TEL: 925.689.8841 HOURS: HOURS VARY - CHECK WEB SITE

"...*nothing fancy, but the kids really love it...the train is particularly fun and there are lots of areas for picnics...a very small amusement park for toddlers...cute, inexpensive, kind of grungy...but fun, fun, fun...* **"**

Criteria
Staff.. ❸ $$.. Prices

Pleasant Hill/Walnut Creek Mothers Club

www.mom4mom.org
PLEASANT HILL - 2590 PLEASANT HILL RD (AT TAYLOR BLVD)
TEL: 925.939.6466 HOURS: CALL FOR DETAILS.

Pleasanton Mothers Club

www.pleasantonmothersclub.homestead.com
PLEASANTON - PO BOX 10141
TEL: 925.927.2444 HOURS: CALL FOR MEETING TIMES

Sulphur Creek Nature Ctr

HAYWARD - 1801 D ST (AT 7TH ST)
TEL: 510.881.6747 HOURS: TU-SU 10-5
Parking: small lot and street parking

"...*an animal rescue place and it's free to come in and see the adorable animals...wildlife, bugs, nature experience...the toddler programs are excellent and the big reason is the staff...Christine Blakely who leads the reasonably priced children's programs is extraordinary...very exciting for little people...* **"**

Criteria
Staff.. ❺ $ .... Prices

Support Services For Mothers ☆☆☆☆☆

www.supportgroupformothers.com
BERKELEY - PO BOX 7151
TEL: 510.524.0821 HOURS: CHECK ONLINE FOR SCHEDULE

Criteria

Staff.................................... ❹ $ .... Prices

Tilden Park - Steam Train ★★★★★

ORINDA - GRIZZLY PEAK BLVD (AT LOMAS CANTADAS)
TEL: 510.548.6100 HOURS: SA-SU 11-DARK
Parking: lot in front at entrance

"...this train ride is a real treat...an inexpensive way to spend the afternoon...it gets pretty windy up there so don't forget to bring sweatshirts and lip balm...the larger train is wonderful and the miniature trains are just terrific...a bay area kids classic...**"**

Criteria

Staff.................................... ❹ $$ .... Prices

Tilden Park - The Little Animal Farm ★★★★★

www.ebparks.org/parks/tna.htm
BERKELEY - 600 CANON DR (IN TILDEN PARK)
TEL: 510.525.2233 HOURS: DAILY 8:30-4
Parking: lot in front of farm

"...a perfect, toddler-sized farm...there is a cow, a pack of sheep, a bunch of goats, pigs, chickens, bunnies, geese and sometimes ducks...no petting but you can feed the animals and get lots of close up viewing...bring fresh lettuce and celery for the animals to eat...there also is a nice picnic area nearby...a great and free way to spend time outside with the kids...**"**

Criteria

Staff.................................... ❹ $ .... Prices

Wee Play ☆☆☆☆☆

www.wee-play.com
ALBANY - 1228 SOLANO AVE (AT TALBOT AVE)
TEL: 510.524.1318 HOURS: CHECK ONLINE FOR SCHEDULE
Parking: street parking

"...a safe, colorful, stimulating and enclosed playground...open play sessions are wonderful for toddlers...**"**

Criteria

Staff.................................... ❺ $$ .... Prices

North Bay

Bay Area Discovery Museum

www.badm.org
SAUSALITO - 557 FORT BAKER TEL: 415.331.2129 HOURS: TU-F 9-4;
SA-SU 10-5
Parking: lot in front of museum

"...the exhibits are wonderful and engaging with tons of fun and educational things to do...an excellent place to take toddlers - especially in bad weather...it's an indoor/outdoor place in a lovely setting...very cool place, even for a one year old...the kids love it and so will you...a great view of the golden gate bridge and there are also some walking trails from the parking lot...**"**

Criteria
Staff.. ❹ $$$ .... Prices

Center for Creative Parenting

www.creativeparenting.com
NOVATO - 446A IGNACIO BLVD (AT ALAMEDA DEL PRADO)
TEL: 415.883.4442 HOURS: M-SA 10-5:30
Parking: mall has a lot

"...the center has facilitated playgroups for 6-12 months, and unfacilitated drop-in play...there are lots of toys and structures and the play area is extremely safe...I just let my 11 month old loose to stretch her legs and run wild...**"**

Criteria
Staff.. ❺ $ .... Prices

Grateful Dads

www.gratefuldads.com
SAN ANSELMO - 61 SAIS AVETEL: 415.307.0505 HOURS: CALL FOR
SCHEDULE

"...an excellent, free group for fathers that meet once every three weeks to go on hikes with their kids...Jonathan Marks, the founder of the group, picks out new hikes all over Marin and emails the info to the group...hikes are usually on Sundays, about four to five miles long and always very scenic...**"**

Criteria
Staff.. ❺ $ .... Prices

Gymboree Play Programs

www.gymboree.com
MILL VALLEY - 406 STRAWBERRY VLG (BTWN SEMINARY DR & E
BLITHDALE)
TEL: 415.383.9771 HOURS: CHECK SCHEDULE ONLINE
Parking: lot in front of building

"...the equipment is terrific for toddlers and the music is fun...make sure you preview the class you want to join to see if you like the instructor since there is variability in their styles - some are more engaging than others...safe environment for both walkers and crawlers...wait until your kids are very mobile and need a lot of physical activity before joining...can get kind of expensive..."

Criteria

Staff...................................... ❹ $ $ $ .... Prices

Kindermusik   ★★★★
www.mykindermusik.com

MILL VALLEY - TEL: 415.383.6174 HOURS: CALL FOR SCHEDULE

"...great way to play with other children while being exposed to musical instruments and song...Lara thoroughly engages the kids and has a beautiful voice...the CDs that are included in the tuition are my daughter's favorites..."

Criteria

Staff...................................... ❹ $ $ $ .... Prices

Kindermusik of Marin
www.kindermusikofmarin.com

SAN RAFAEL - 10 BAYVIEW DR (IN ST LUKE'S PRESBYTERIAN CHURCH)

TEL: 415.721.1929 HOURS: CHECK ONLINE FOR SCHEDULE

Marine World
www.sixflags.com

VALLEJO - 2001 MARINE WORLD PKWY (OFF RT 37)
TEL: 707.644.4000 HOURS: CHECK ONLINE FOR HOURS
Parking: big lot in front of park

Mill Valley Community Ctr   ☆☆☆
www.millvalleycenter.org

MILL VALLEY - 180 CAMINO ALTO DR (AT E BLITHEDALE AVE)
TEL: 415.383.1370 HOURS: CALL FOR SCHEDULE
Parking: lot in front of building

"...they have a wide variety of classes year round for children at a very reasonable prices...all ages are welcome...the best place to go if you have babies/kids in the North Bay...they have childcare available for parents who want to use the gym..."

Criteria

Staff...................................... ❸ $ $ .... Prices

Mill Valley Public Library

www.millvalleylibrary.org

MILL VALLEY - 375 THROCKMORTON AVE (AT OLD MILL PARK)
TEL: 415.389.4292 HOURS: CALL FOR SCHEDULE
Parking: street parking

Criteria

Staff...................................... ❹ $ .... Prices

Music Together of Marin

www.music4families.com
MILL VALLEY - TEL: 415.388.2464 HOURS: CHECK SCHEDULE
ONLINE

Novato Mother's Club

www.novatomothersclub.com

NOVATO - PO BOX 1306
TEL: 415.458.3203

❝...in addition to playgroups, there are a number of special interest groups such as cooking, wine, hiking, camping, book, etc...a very supportive group...❞

Criteria

Staff...................................... 0 $ .... Prices

Ross Valley Mother's Club

ROSS
TEL: 415.721.4576

❝...terrific and informative newsletter and dedicated palygroup coordinators...a great group of moms that work to reach out and support other moms...❞

Criteria

Staff...................................... ❹ $ .... Prices

San Anselmo Library - Story Time

www.townofsananselmo.org/library

SAN ANSELMO - 110 TUNSTEAD AVE (AT SIR FRANCIS DRAKE BLVD)
TEL: 415.258.4656 HOURS: M W 10-9; T TH 10-6; F SA 10-5; CALL
FOR PRESCHOOL STORY TIME SCHEDULE

San Rafael Mothers Club

www.srmoms.org

SAN RAFAEL - PO BOX 4003
TEL: 415.451.7355

Southern Marin Mother's Club   ★★★★

www.southernmarinmoms.com

MILL VLLEY
TEL: 415.273.5366

"...a must for Marin moms...great group of women with lots to offer at a very reasonable rate...playgroups, newsletter, special events, new member get-togethers, general meetings with interesting speakers...excellent way to meet other moms and introduce you to future playmates for baby...very informative newsletters with useful articles and local recommendations...especially great for parents new to the area...**"**

Criteria

Staff....................................... ❹ $$.. Prices

Toobtown

ROHNERT PARK - 6591 COMMERCE BLVD (AT GOLF COURSE DR)
TEL: 707.588.5810 HOURS: SU-TH 10-8; F-SA 10-9
Parking: lot in front of building

Peninsula

Aitken's Peninsula Swim School ★★★★

www.peninsulaswim.com

REDWOOD CITY - 1602 STAFFORD ST (BTWN B & C STS)

TEL: 650.366.9211 HOURS: M-F 9-9; SA 8:30-2:30

Parking: street parking

"...their staff is friendly and knowledgeable and has a real knack for chilrden...very warm indoor/outdoor pool...playhouse, yard and outdoor play equipment for non-swimming siblings...gummy bears for everyone... **"**

Criteria

Staff.. ❹ $$.. Prices

Burlingame Mothers Club

www.burlingamemothers.org

BURLINGAME

TEL: 650.635.6777

Burlingame Recreation Ctr

www.burlingame.org

BURLINGAME - BURLINGAME AVE (AT ROLLINS RD)

TEL: 650.558.7300 HOURS: CALL FOR SCHEDULE

Parking: street parking

Coyote Point Museum ★★★★

www.coyoteptmuseum.org

SAN MATEO - 1651 COYOTE POINT DR (OFF 101 AT COYOTE POINT EXIT)

TEL: 650.342.7755 HOURS: TU-SA 10-5; SU 12-5

Parking: lot in front

"...very good museum for small as well as older kids...they have a toddler program every other Tuesday...if you are going to see the animals, don't go at midday because they are all asleep...a family membership here is the best deal in town - not only does it give you free admission to Coyote Point, which has a nifty tiny zoo, but it also gets you into other zoos including San Francisco and Oakland...first Wednesday of each month is free... **"**

Criteria

Staff.. ❹ $$.. Prices

Foster City Mothers Club

www.fostercitymothersclub.org

FOSTER CITY

TEL: 650.634.976

Gymboree Play Programs

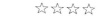

www.gymboree.com

REDWOOD CITY - 2531 EL CAMINO REAL (NEAR INTERSECTION OF 84 & 82)
TEL: 650.364.3420 HOURS: CHECK SCHEDULE ONLINE
Parking: lot in front of store

SAN BRUNO - 731 KAINS AVE (AT SAN BRUNO AVE W)
TEL: 650.875.3588 HOURS: CHECK SCHEDULE ONLINE
Parking: lot behind building

SAN JOSE - 925 BLOSSOM HILL RD # 222 (AT SANTA TERESA BLVD)
TEL: 408.629.5813 HOURS: CHECK SCHEDULE ONLINE
Parking: mall has a lot

"...the equipment is terrific for toddlers and the music is fun...make sure you preview the class you want to join to see if you like the instructor since there is variability in their styles - some are more engaging than others...safe environment for both walkers and crawlers...wait until your kids are very mobile and need a lot of physical activity before joining...can get kind of expensive... **"**

Criteria

Staff...................................... **4** $$...................................... Prices

La Petite Baleen Swim School

www.swimlpb.com

SAN BRUNO - 434 SAN MATEO AVE (AT EL CAMINO AVE)
TEL: 650.588.7665 HOURS: CALL FOR CLASS SCHEDULE.
Parking: lot in front and back

"...warm water and a fun environment to meet other parents and kids...small class sizes so your little one gets plenty of attention... **"**

Criteria

Staff...................................... **4** $$$ .... Prices

Los Gatos-Saratoga Community Ctr

www.lgsrecreation.org

LOS GATOS - 123 EAST MAIN ST (OFF RT 17)
TEL: 408.354.8700 HOURS: SCHEDULE IS ONLINE

Mothers Club of Palo Alto & Menlo Park

☆ ☆ ☆

PALO ALTO
TEL: 650.306.8182

"...excellent resource and support network...regular playgroups and outings... **"**

Criteria

Staff...................................... **3** $$$ .... Prices

Music Together

BURLINGAME - 850 BURLINGAME AVENUE (AT ANITA RD)
TEL: 650.558.7300 HOURS: CALL FOR SCHEDULE
Parking: street parking

Palo Alto Children's Library

☆ ☆ ☆ ☆ ☆

www.city.palo-alto.ca.us/library
PALO ALTO - 1276 HARRIET ST (AT HOPKINS AVE)
TEL: 650.329.2134 HOURS: SU 1-5; M & W 12-8; T,TH,F SA 10-5

"...extensive toddler and childrens programs, including story times and in the summer events such as magicians, jugglers, singers, musicians, puppets and animals...great selection of videos, DVDs and computers for kids...staff is always friendly and interested in the kids... **"**

Criteria

Staff.. ❺ $ .... Prices

Rinconada Pool

☆ ☆ ☆ ☆

PALO ALTO - 777 EMBARCADERO RD (AT NEWELL RD)
TEL: 650.329.2351 HOURS: CALL HOURS AND CLASS SCEDULE

"...pretty good for a public swimming pool...nice large children's pool that is no deeper than 3 feet throughout...lots of fun stuff for water play - jets of water, slides, stationary bikes that spray water...there's a park adjacent to the pool for cook outs and outdoor activity... **"**

Criteria

Staff.. ❸ $$ .... Prices

San Carlos Recreation Ctr

www.ci.san-carlos.ca.us
SAN CARLOS - 1017 CEDAR ST (AT BRITTAN AVE)
TEL: 650.802.4385 HOURS: CHECK ONLINE FOR SCHEDULE
Parking: lot at 1001 Chestnut

As a new parent, you will get used to certain things: drool on your shirts, old raisins on your car seats, and sand, well, everywhere. If you go to the playground, expect to bring some of it home. But that's perfectly okay when you see how much fun your child has playing on the swings and slides. So whether you want to take a walk with your child in a stroller or are looking for a fully equipped playground, there's plenty to choose from.

As you know, **parking** in the city can be challenging and there is considerable variability in the **cleanliness** and **maintenance** of the play structures. There are also lots of parks with picnic areas and water sprinklers for hot summer days.

San Francisco

Alamo Square Park

★ ★ ★

SAN FRANCISCO - STEINER ST (AT HAYES ST)
Parking: street parking

"...gorgeous setting but the park equipment is not very inviting - it really needs an update...the playground isn't that great but lots of trees that are easy to climb on and plenty of grass on...dogs run free in a separate area... **"**

Criteria

Parking .... ❷   ❷ .... Equipment/play structures
Setting/location .... ❺   ❸ .... Maintenance

Alta Plaza Park

★ ★ ★ ★

www.parks.sfgov.org/recpark/facilities.htm

SAN FRANCISCO - 3301 LYON ST (AT JACKSON & STEINER)
TEL: 415.292.2002 Parking: street parking

"...great view, but always kind of windy...beautiful setting...small enclosed play area so you can keep in eye on your children...great equipment for kids of all ages and lots of sand...swings, merry go round and slides...good place for interacting with other children... **"**

Criteria

Parking .... ❸   ❹ .... Equipment/play structures
Setting/location .... ❹   ❹ .... Maintenance

Aquatic Park

★ ★ ★ ★

www.parks.sfgov.org/recpark/facilities.htm

SAN FRANCISCO - BEACH ST (AT BOTTOM OF HYDE ST)
Parking: lot at bottom of Hyde St

"...little beach to walk around on...very close to Fort Mason and other places to stop in for a snack... **"**

Criteria

Parking .... ❷   ❷ .... Equipment/play structures
Setting/location .... ❹   ❹ .... Maintenance

Argonne Playground

☆ ☆ ☆ ☆

www.parks.sfgov.org/recpark/facilities.htm

SAN FRANCISCO - 18TH AVE (BTWN ANZA & GEARY STS)
Parking: street parking

"...a nice neighborhood playground near Geary Blvd so it's a convenient stop while doing errands...equipment is due for an overhaul...the rec center is sometimes open for additional indoor activities...lots of other moms, nannies and babies to meet... **"**

Criteria

Parking .... ❹	❹ .... Equipment/play structures
Setting/location .... ❹	❹ .... Maintenance

Balboa Park   ☆ ☆ ☆

SAN FRANCISCO - SAN JOSE AVE (AT 22ND ST)
TEL: 415.337.4701 HOURS: CALL FOR SCHEDULE
Parking: street parking

"...never crowded which is great when you're looking for a break from the more popular sandboxes...baby swings are pretty tattered...the washrooms aren't the greatest...pretty safe since the police station is right next door... **"**

Criteria

Parking .... ❹	❹ .... Equipment/play structures
Setting/location .... ❸	❸ .... Maintenance

Bernal Heights Playground   ★ ★ ★ ★

www.parks.sfgov.org/recpark/facilities.htm
SAN FRANCISCO - 500 MOULTRIE (AT CORTLAND AVE)
TEL: 415.695.5007 Parking: street parking

"...standard equipment...nice neighborhood playground... sometimes I call this Dad Park because there are so many dads with their kids here at all times...a real gathering place for the neighborhood and we are always guaranteed to see a kid we know- - no need to set up playdates...nearly always sunny... **"**

Criteria

Parking .... ❸	❹ .... Equipment/play structures
Setting/location .... ❹	❹ .... Maintenance

Buena Vista Park   ☆ ☆ ☆

www.parks.sfgov.org/recpark/facilities.htm
SAN FRANCISCO - HAIGHT ST (AT LYON ST)
Parking: street parking

"...the play structures are just okay, but you can't beat the setting...a steep trail takes you to the top of the park that has incredible views...the playground in the park is small but never crowded...urban campers occasionally use the park for napping... **"**

Criteria

Parking .... ❸	❷ .... Equipment/play structures
Setting/location .... ❹	❸ .... Maintenance

China Beach   ☆ ☆ ☆ ☆

SAN FRANCISCO - SEACLIFF AVE (AT 28TH AVE)
Parking: street parking

"...peaceful and quiet, especially on weekdays...the surroundings are overwhelmingly beautiful...great for kids who don't need equipment to play with..."

Criteria

Parking .... ❹   ❶ .... Equipment/play structures
Setting/location .... ❺   ❹ .... Maintenance

Christopher Playground

SAN FRANCISCO - 5210 DIAMOND HEIGHT BLVD (AT 27TH ST)
TEL: 415.695.5000 Parking: street parking

Civic Center Plaza Playground   ☆ ☆ ☆

SAN FRANCISCO - MCALLISTER ST (AT LEAVENWORTH ST)
Parking: street parking

"...fairly well-maintained for a city park...all adults need to be with a kid as the area does have a homeless population...right by the Main Library which is always a fun activity...parking is metered so watch for tickets...no swings, but plenty to climb on..."

Criteria

Parking .... ❷   ❹ .... Equipment/play structures
Setting/location .... ❸   ❸ .... Maintenance

Corona Heights Playground

SAN FRANCISCO - MUSEUM WY (BELOW RANDALL MUSEUM)
Parking: lot in front of Randall Museum

Cow Hollow Playground   ★★★★

SAN FRANCISCO - MILEY ST (AT BAKER ST)
TEL: 415.292.2003
Parking: street parking

"...safe and clean...fenced-in playground...small enough and not too crowded so it is easy to keep track of your child...beautiful and hidden location...diaper changing stations in the men's and women's bathrooms...wonderful wild parrots that live in the neighborhood...not the most ideal place for parking..."

Criteria

Parking .... ❸   ❹ .... Equipment/play structures
Setting/location .... ❹   ❹ .... Maintenance

Crissy Field   ★★★★

www.crissyfield.org

SAN FRANCISCO - 603 MASON ST (AT HALLECK ST)
TEL: 415.427.4779 Parking: lot at the Warming Hut

"...the most beautiful park in the city...always filled with moms and babies in strollers...a little windy along the shore...there is no play equipment at Crissy Fields but it's great to take a walk or

run...great place for kids to run aroud...the view of the Bay and Golden Gate Bridge is fantastic...lots of dogs running around to add to the atmosphere... **"**

Criteria
Parking .... ❺   ❶ .... Equipment/play structures
Setting/location .... ❺   ❺ .... Maintenance

Dolores Park ★★★
SAN FRANCISCO - DOLORES ST (AT 18TH ST)
Parking: street parking

"*...nice place to go for family picnics...a lot of open space so you have to keep watching the little ones, once they start walking...lots of dogs...playground for older children - swings are the only thing for infants/toddlers...park is not enclosed and is surrounded by busy streets...not condusive to those under five...terrific views...* **"**

Criteria
Parking .... ❷   ❸ .... Equipment/play structures
Setting/location .... ❹   ❸ .... Maintenance

Douglass Park ★★★★
SAN FRANCISCO - DOUGLASS ST (AT 26TH ST)
TEL: 415.695.5017
Parking: street parking

"*...wonderful park nestled against the hillside...clean and friendly...doesn't have a separate toddler area...the play structures are rather limited...nice grassy area for picnics and great place for birthday parties...parking is always available...* **"**

Criteria
Parking .... ❹   ❹ .... Equipment/play structures
Setting/location .... ❹   ❹ .... Maintenance

Duboce Park ★★★★★
SAN FRANCISCO - 50 SCOTT ST (AT DUBOCE AVE)
TEL: 415.666.7200
Parking: street parking

"*...excellent for smaller kids...good variety of equipment - sand box, swings, slides, climbing equipment...very safe and clean...fenced in play yard with a spongy surface...along the N-Judah route so easy to get there by muni train...for sleep deprived parents, coffee and pastries are nearby at Cooper's and Jumpin Java...bathroom could be closer...* **"**

Criteria
Parking .... ❸   ❹ .... Equipment/play structures
Setting/location .... ❹   ❹ .... Maintenance

Eureka Valley Playground
www.parks.sfgov.org/recpark/facilities.htm
SAN FRANCISCO - 100 COLLINGWOOD ST (AT 18TH ST)
TEL: 415.695.5012 Parking: street parking

Excelsior Playground
www.parks.sfgov.org/recpark/facilities.htm
SAN FRANCISCO - 579 MADRID ST (AT RUSSIA ST)
TEL: 415.337.4709
Parking: street parking

Fulton Playground
www.parks.sfgov.org/recpark/facilities.htm
SAN FRANCISCO - 27TH AVE (AT FULTON ST)
TEL: 415.666.7009
Parking: street parking

Glen Canyon Park Playground
www.parks.sfgov.org/recpark/facilities.htm
SAN FRANCISCO - BOSWORTH ST (AT ELK ST)
TEL: 415.337.4705
Parking: street parking

"...nice families, great structures...good walk/hike along the pretty trails..."

Criteria
Parking .... **4**   **4** .... Equipment/play structures
Setting/location .... **5**   **4** .... Maintenance

Golden Gate Park - Sharon Meadows Playground ★★★★★
www.parks.sfgov.org
SAN FRANCISCO - LINCOLN WY (AT 4TH AVE)
TEL: 415.831.2700
Parking: lot off South Dr

"...the biggest, most varied playground in the city...worth braving the terrible weekend parking...the variety of equipment for all ages is wonderful...great place to meet other parents...important to watch your kids since access from the main park provides for some occasional unsavory characters...can be cold and windy so wear layers...close to the Academy of Sciences..."

Criteria
Parking .... **2**   **4** .... Equipment/play structures
Setting/location .... **5**   **4** .... Maintenance

Grattan Playground

www.parks.sfgov.org/recpark/facilities.htm

SAN FRANCISCO - 165 GRATTAN ST (AT STANYAN ST)

TEL: 415.759.2815

Parking: street parking

J.P. Murphy Playground

www.parks.sfgov.org/recpark/facilities.htm

SAN FRANCISCO - 1960 9TH AVE (AT ORTEGA ST)

TEL: 415.753.7099

Parking: street parking

Jackson Playground ★★★★

www.parks.sfgov.org/recpark/facilities.htm

SAN FRANCISCO - ARKANSAS ST (AT 17TH ST)

TEL: 415.554.9527

Parking: street parking

"...a well designed playground with two areas - one for toddlers and another for older ones...the park is very clean...next to the Brown Bear Factory and gets overrun when older kids take their lunch break from touring the facility... **"**

Criteria

Parking .... ❹	❹	Equipment/play structures
Setting/location .... ❹	❹	Maintenance

Julius Kahn Park ★★★★

www.parks.sfgov.org/recpark/facilities.htm

SAN FRANCISCO - PACIFIC AVE (AT SPRUCE ST)

TEL: 415.292.2004

Parking: street parking

"...beautiful setting inside the Presidio...good all around park for kids of all ages...easy parking, great sun and shade...grassy area for babies not ready for sandboxes...play on the playground, hike the presidio, enjoy a picnic on the large grassy area or play in the indoor art/activity room... **"**

Criteria

Parking .... ❹	❹	Equipment/play structures
Setting/location .... ❺	❹	Maintenance

Larsen Park

www.parks.sfgov.org/recpark/facilities.htm

SAN FRANCISCO - 19TH AVE (AT VICENTE ST)

TEL: 415.753.7000

Parking: street parking

Laurel Hill Playground

www.parks.sfgov.org/recpark/facilities.htm

SAN FRANCISCO - EUCLID ST (AT BLAKE ST)
TEL: 415.666.7007
Parking: street parking

"...good for little babies because of the sand and equipment...not the nicest park in the city, but a good place to meet other moms...a parent-child class meets there through City College, so you need to sign up if you want to go to the neat clubhouse..."

Criteria

Parking .... ❸   ❸ .... Equipment/play structures
Setting/location .... ❹   ❹ .... Maintenance

Michelangelo Playground

www.parks.sfgov.org/recpark/facilities.htm

SAN FRANCISCO - GREENWICH ST (AT JONES ST)
Parking: street parking

"...small but well laid out...pretty gardens...wonderful, quiet, safe feeling with great grassy areas, fun equipment...no toilet facilities...very urban, but also very protected and well-maintained...surrounded by buildings..."

Criteria

Parking .... ❸   ❹ .... Equipment/play structures
Setting/location .... ❺   ❺ .... Maintenance

Midtown Terrace Playground

www.parks.sfgov.org/recpark/facilities.htm

SAN FRANCISCO - CLARENDON (AT OLYMPIA WY)
TEL: 415.753.7036
Parking: street parking

Mission Playground

SAN FRANCISCO - 19TH ST (NEAR VALENCIA ST)
Parking: street parking

"...a great toddler playground...new equipment over a fairly well-maintained sand pit...it's right next door to the only outdoor pool in the city...the actual playground is clean and feels safe, but the area right around it is dirty..."

Criteria

Parking .... ❷   ❹ .... Equipment/play structures
Setting/location .... ❸   ❸ .... Maintenance

Moscone Playground

SAN FRANCISCO - CHESTNUT ST (AT LAGUNA ST)
TEL: 415.292.2006
Parking: street parking

"...new equipment...this is a modern playground...fun for all ages...nice and clean...we love this park because it's all new and beautiful...very crowded, but it's a large playground with lots of play equipment...no shade...a San Francisco favorite...lots of extra sand toys to play with..."

Criteria

Parking .... ❸ ❺ .... Equipment/play structures
Setting/location .... ❺ ❺ .... Maintenance

Mountain Lake Park ★★★★

SAN FRANCISCO - LAKE ST (AT 12TH AVE)
TEL: 415.831.2700

"...a lovely discovery in the city...nice setting, although you can always hear background traffic...good for kids of all ages...good place for a brisk walk with your stroller...nice lake for duck feeding and grass for kids to run around..."

Criteria

Parking .... ❸ ❹ .... Equipment/play structures
Setting/location .... ❹ ❹ .... Maintenance

Noe Courts Playground ★★★★

SAN FRANCISCO - 24TH ST (BTWN ELIZABETH & 24TH STS)
Parking: street parking

"...the perfect place for babies just getting the hang of stairs and slides...quiet little neighborhood park with as many dogs as kids - but in separate areas...I wouldn't go out of my way to go to the park but it is great if you live in the neighborhood and have small children..."

Criteria

Parking .... ❸ ❹ .... Equipment/play structures
Setting/location .... ❹ ❸ .... Maintenance

North Beach Playground ☆☆☆

SAN FRANCISCO - LOMBARD ST (AT MASON ST)
TEL: 415.274.0200
Parking: street parking

"...a heavily used, slightly run down urban playground...it has a separate, gated tiny tots play area, plus a bathroom...close to the library, swimming pool, tennis courts...dated play structure that needs some loving..."

Criteria

Parking .... ❷ ❷ .... Equipment/play structures
Setting/location .... ❸ ❸ .... Maintenance

Panhandle Playground ★★★★

SAN FRANCISCO - ASHBURY ST (AT OAK ST)
Parking: street parking

"...a great neighborhood park where you will get to know most of the local kids, moms and nannies...the occasional waft of pot shouldn't keep you away from this great park...great shaded playground - good for those hot days...great swings, a fun car toy and lots of centralized sand activity so it's easy to keep an eye on your kid and have a coffee with the other moms..."

Criteria

Parking .... ❸   ❹ .... Equipment/play structures
Setting/location .... ❹   ❹ .... Maintenance

Precita Park

SAN FRANCISCO - PRECITA AVE (AT FOLSOM ST)
Parking: street parking

Richmond Playground

SAN FRANCISCO - 19TH AVE (BTWN CALIFORNIA & LAKE STS)
TEL: 415.666.7013
Parking: street parking

Rochambeau Playground

SAN FRANCISCO - 25TH AVE (AT CALIFORNIA ST)
TEL: 415.666.7012
Parking: street parking

Rocky Mountain Preschool Playground

SAN FRANCISCO - 2475 15TH ST (OFF ROOSEVELT WY)
TEL: 415.552.2929
Parking: street parking

Rossi Playground

SAN FRANCISCO - ARGUELLO BLVD (AT ANZA)
TEL: 415.666.7014
Parking: street parking

South Park   ☆☆☆

SAN FRANCISCO - SOUTH PARK AVE (BTWN 2ND & 3RD STS)
Parking: street parking

"...a nice little area for kids in SOMA...parents can get lunch from one of the many tasty eateries that line the park and relax on the grass while babies nap or crawl around nearby...not worth an extra trip, but great for an urban park......"

Criteria

Parking .... ❷   ❹ .... Equipment/play structures
Setting/location .... ❹   ❸ .... Maintenance

Strybing Arboretum

www.strybing.org
SAN FRANCISCO - GOLDEN GATE PARK (9TH AVE AT LINCOLN WY)
TEL: 415. 661.1316
Parking: street parking

"...a beautiful place for a long stroller walk...no play equipment, but lots of natural stuff to check out...my kid loves the pond with ducks...many nooks and crannies for little ones to explore and most things are at their eye level...frequented by mommy groups...a lovely retreat..."

Criteria

Parking .... ❸   ❸ .... Equipment/play structures
Setting/location .... ❺   ❺ .... Maintenance

Upper Noe Recreation Ctr

SAN FRANCISCO - DAY ST (BTWN SANCHEZ & CHURCH STS)
TEL: 415.695.5011
Parking: street parking

"...It has a great indoor play area...The outdoor play area has a lot of swings which is great but the main structure is starting to show signs of needing maintenance...There are tons of things to climb on and play with...sometimes there is live music on Saturday mornings, which makes for many happy kids and parent..."

Criteria

Parking .... ❸   ❹ .... Equipment/play structures
Setting/location .... ❹   ❹ .... Maintenance

Washington Square Playground

www.parks.sfgov.org/recpark/facilities.htm
SAN FRANCISCO - COLUMBUS ST (AT FILBERT ST)
Parking: street parking

West Portal Playground

SAN FRANCISCO - 131 LENNOX WY (AT ULLOA ST)
TEL: 415.753.7038
Parking: street parking

"...situated above the West Portal station so you can look down at the trains coming and going...unfortunately it is really windy and freezing in the winter and it tends to get flooded and muddy when it rains..."

Criteria

Parking .... ❸   ❹ .... Equipment/play structures
Setting/location .... ❹   ❹ .... Maintenance

East Bay

Aquatic Park ★★★★

www.ci.berkeley.ca.us/parks/
BERKELEY - BOLIVAR WY (AT FOOT OF BANCROFT WY)
TEL: 510.981.5150
Parking: street park

❝...huge, clean and so much fun...sectioned areas for different ages...the wood chips on the ground work better than sand on a post rainy day...the highlight for my toddler is watching the trains go by...strong winds can make it chilly...❞

Criteria

Parking .... ❸	❺	.... Equipment/play structures
Setting/location .... ❺	❹	.... Maintenance

Castro Valley Community Ctr Park

CASTRO VALLEY - 18988 LAKE CHABOT RD (AT QUAIL AVE)
TEL: 510.881.6700
Parking: lot at park entrance

Central Park

www.ci.san-ramon.ca.us/parks/parks.htm
SAN RAMON - 12501 ALCOSTA BLVD (AT BOLLINGER CANYON RD)
TEL: 925.973.3200
Parking: lot on Alcosta

Central Park - Lake Elizabeth

www.ci.fremont.ca.us
FREMONT - 40000 PASEO PADRE PARKWAY (AT MISSION VIEW DR)
TEL: 510.791.4340
Parking: lot at park entrance

Civic Park

www.ci.walnut-creek.ca.us/parks/parksmain.htm
WALNUT CREEK - 1375 CIVIC DR (AT N BROADWAY)
TEL: 925.943.5854
Parking: lot at park entrance

Crab Cove ★★★★

www.ebparks.org
ALAMEDA - 1252 MCKAY AVE (OFF CENTRAL AVE)
TEL: 510.521.6887 HOURS: W-SU 10-4:30
Parking: lot at visitor ctr

❝...the park extends down to the beach and another park...nice for riding bikes and strolling...the exhibits at the visitor center are always fun for curious toddlers...lots of nature hikes and a *good kite flying locale...great at low tide because you can dig and find all kinds of stuff in the sand...* **"**

Criteria

Parking .... ❹   ❸ .... Equipment/play structures
Setting/location .... ❹   ❹ .... Maintenance

FROG Park Rockridge ★★★★

www.frogpark.org
OAKLAND - HUDSON ST (AT CLAREMONT ST)
TEL: 510.420.1375
Parking: street parking

"...*a brand new innovative, imaginative playground built by neighborhood parents...two age appropriate playground areas plus a lovely, fresh water stream running through the park...perfect for summer splashing...* **"**

Criteria

Parking .... ❹   ❺ .... Equipment/play structures
Setting/location .... ❹   ❺ .... Maintenance

Heather Farm Park

www.ci.walnut-creek.ca.us/parks/parksmain.htm
WALNUT CREEK - 301 N SAN CARLOS DR (AT YGNACIO VALLEY RD)
TEL: 925.943.5854
Parking: lot at park entrance

Kennedy Park

www.ci.hayward.ca.us
HAYWARD - 19501 HESPERIAN BLVD (AT BARTLETT AVE)
TEL: 510.881.6715
Parking: lot at park entrance

Krusi Park

www.ci.alameda.ca.us
ALAMEDA - 900 MOUND ST (AT OTIS DR)
TEL: 510.748.4565
Parking: street parking

Lake Temescal

www.oaklandnet.com
OAKLAND - 6502 BROADWAY TER (OFF HWY 13)
TEL: 510.652.1155
Parking: lot at park entrance

Larkey Park

www.ci.walnut-creek.ca.us/parks/parksmain.htm

WALNUT CREEK - 1ST AVE (AT BUENA VISTA)

TEL: 925.943.5854

Parking: street parking

Livorna Park

ALAMO - LIVORNA ST (AT MIRANDA ST)

Parking: street parking

Mape Memorial Park

www.ci.dublin.ca.us

DUBLIN - SAN SABANA CT (AT CALLE VERDE RD)

Montclair Recreation Ctr - Playground

★★★★

www.oaklandnet.com

OAKLAND - 6300 MORAGA AVE

TEL: 510.482.7812

"...the park has a really nice setting - in addition to the play structures, there are ducks and grass...lots of different areas and a pretty pond...a stage coach and old west jail plus the usual slides and swings...a wonderful neighborhood playground and it has a great fenced in area for little kids... **"**

Criteria

Parking	❸	❹	Equipment/play structures
Setting/location	❹	❸	Maintenance

Moraga Commons Park

★★★★

www.ci.moraga.ca.us

MORAGA - MORAGA RD (AT ST MARYS RD)

TEL: 925.376.2520

Parking: lot at park entrance

"...on a sunny day this park is swarming with moms and kids...there are separate play areas for big and little kids...a water sprayer when it gets really hot helps cool everyone off and provides lots of fun for kids and adults... **"**

Criteria

Parking	❹	❹	Equipment/play structures
Setting/location	❺	❹	Maintenance

Osage Station Park

☆☆☆☆☆

www.ci.danville.ca.us

DANVILLE - 816 BROOKSIDE DR (AT PARAISO DR)

Parking: lot at park entrance

"...a very nice small park with a large play structure for kids of all ages to enjoy...love the water play... **"**

Criteria

Parking .... **5**   **5** .... Equipment/play structures
Setting/location .... **5**   **5** .... Maintenance

Shannon Park

www.ci.dublin.ca.us
DUBLIN - 11600 SHANNON AVE (OFF SAN RAMON RD)
TEL: 925.556.4500
Parking: lot at park entrance

Tilden Park ★ ★ ★ ★ ★

www.ebparks.org
BERKELEY - 600 CANON DR (AT WILD CAT CANYON RD)
TEL: 510.562.7275
Parking: several lots throughout park

" *...a fantastic outing...we can easily entertain an 8 year old, 4 year old and 1 year old all at the same time...little farm, steam trains, carousel, Lake Anza for swimming, Inspiration Point for walks, and much more...kind of a haul, but so worth it...it can be cool so bring layers, even if it's warm where you're coming from...* **"**

Criteria

Parking .... **4**   **4** .... Equipment/play structures
Setting/location .... **5**   **4** .... Maintenance

Totland - Virginia-McGee ★ ★ ★ ★

www.ci.berkeley.ca.us
BERKELEY - VIRGINIA ST (AT MCGEE AVE)
TEL: 510.644.6566
Parking: street parking

" *...lots of toys left by other parents/kids to play with...enclosed fence makes watching the kids easier...a great place to relax, play with kids, have a picnic and get ready for nap time...lots of stuff to do, but the whole place needs an overhaul...* **"**

Criteria

Parking .... **4**   **4** .... Equipment/play structures
Setting/location .... **4**   **3** .... Maintenance

Willard Park

www.ci.berkeley.ca.us
BERKELEY - 2727 HILLEGASS BLVD (AT DERBY ST)
TEL: 510.849.8405
Parking: street parking

North Bay

Alicia Park

www.rpcity.org
ROHNERT PARK - 300 ARLEN DR (AT ADRIAN DR)
TEL: 707.588.2200
Parking: street parking

Belvedere Tiburon Park ★★★★

BELVEDERE TIBURON - 1505 TIBURON BLVD (AT SAN RAFAEL AVE)
TEL: 415.435.4355

"...*very nice...safe and gated - kids can run around and play without worry...great for toddlers, but not much for babies...* **"**

Criteria

Parking .... ❹	❸ .... Equipment/play structures
Setting/location .... ❺	❹ .... Maintenance

Blackie's Pasture

BELVEDERE TIBURON - BLACKIE'S PASTURE RD (AT TIBURON BLVD)
Parking: lot at trailhead

Boyd Memorial Park

SAN RAFAEL - B ST (AT MISSION AVE)

Boyle Park ★★★★

www.cityofmillvalley.org
MILL VALLEY - E BLITHEDALE AVE (AT EAST DR)
TEL: 415.383.1370
Parking: street parking

"...*great for picnicing...dogs are allowed and they have BBQs also fun during Little League Baseball season...beautiful natural setting...the kind of park where you'll meet moms, not just nannies...THE source for the best Mill Valley gossip...* **"**

Criteria

Parking .... ❹	❹ .... Equipment/play structures
Setting/location .... ❹	❹ .... Maintenance

Hauke Park

www.cityofmillvalley.org/parks-facilities-main.html

MILL VALLEY - HAMILTON DR

Howarth Community Park

www.ci.santa-rosa.ca.us

SANTA ROSA - 630 SUMMERFIELD RD (AT SONOMA AVE)

TEL: 707.543.3737

Parking: lot in the park

Marinwood Park

www.marinwood.org

SAN RAFAEL - MILLER CREEK RD

TEL: 415.479.9305

Memorial Park ★★★★★

www.townofsananselmo.org/parks

SAN ANSELMO - 1000 SIR FRANCIS DRAKE BLVD (AT SAN
FRANCISCO BLVD)

TEL: 415.258.4645

Parking: lot at park entrance

❝...I love that they have a separate playground for toddlers and
another for bigger kids and both have cool play structures -
castles, trains, steering wheels, great sand play area...gets
crowded on weekends and very hot during the summer...it's
pretty big and easy to lose track of your kids... ❞

Criteria

Parking .... ❺   ❺ .... Equipment/play structures
Setting/location .... ❺   ❺ .... Maintenance

Old Mill Park ★★★★

www.cityofmillvalley.org/parks-facilities-main.html

MILL VALLEY - THROCKMORTON AVE (AT CASCADE DR)

❝...lovely park in the middle of a redwood grove right beside a
stream...go there on a warm day to get away from the heat...be
careful as there is pretty easy access to the road and
traffic...swings for babies and older kids...extensive
climbing/sliding equipment... ❞

Criteria

Parking .... ❸   ❹ .... Equipment/play structures
Setting/location .... ❹   ❹ .... Maintenance

Peacock Park

SAN RAFAEL - PEACOCK DR (AT SAN PEDRO RD)

TEL: 415.485.3377

Parking: lot at park entrance

Piper Park

www.ci.larkspur.ca.us

LARKSPUR - 250 DOHERTY DR
TEL: 415.927.6746
Parking: lot at park entrance

Santa Margarita Park

SAN RAFAEL - 1055 LAS OVEJAS (OFF OF DEL GANADO RD)

Sorich Ranch Park

www.townofsananselmo.org/parks

SAN ANSELMO - SAN FRANCISCO BLVD (AT BOTTOM OF SAN FRANCISCO BLVD)
TEL: 415.258.4645
Parking: lot at park entrance

Town Park

★ ★ ★ ★

www.ci.corte-madera.ca.us

CORTE MADERA - 498 TAMALPAIS DR (AT EASTMAN AVE)
TEL: 415.927.5072
Parking: lot at park entrance

"...wonderful, newly renovated park...busy with kids playing all day...a great place to meet other moms...biggest problem is distance to the potties...lots of different play structures and sitting areas for adults...can get hot during the summer and there is very little shade...**"**

Criteria

Parking .... ❹   ❺ .... Equipment/play structures
Setting/location .... ❺   ❹ .... Maintenance

Walnut Park

www.petalumachamber.com

PETALUMA - PETALUMA BLVD (AT D ST)
TEL: 707.762.2785
Parking: street parking

Peninsula

Burgess Park

☆ ☆ ☆ ☆

www.ci.menlo-park.ca.us

MENLO PARK - 701 LAUREL ST (AT RAVENSWOOD AVE)

TEL: 650.858.3470

Parking: lot on Laurel St

"...*shaded park adjacent to the city swimming pool and park and rec center...baseball diamonds, tennis courts and sand volleyball nets... bathrooms are located at the swimming pool...* **"**

Criteria

Parking .... ❺   ❹ .... Equipment/play structures

Setting/location .... ❹   ❹ .... Maintenance

Central Park

★ ★ ★ ★

www.ci.sanmateo.ca.us

SAN MATEO - 50 E 5TH AVE (AT EL CAMINO)

TEL: 650.522.7530

"...*a wonderful place that can keep any kid occupied for hour after hour...very large so you'll need to be one-on-one if your kid is a runner...a Japanese Tea Garden and baseball fields...this park is clean and well-maintained...one big jungle gym, a couple of swings, a sandy section and lots of grass to sit on...they also have a train that goes around in a circle...* **"**

Criteria

Parking .... ❹   ❹ .... Equipment/play structures

Setting/location .... ❹   ❹ .... Maintenance

Holbrook-Palmer Park

☆ ☆ ☆ ☆ ☆

www.ci.atherton.ca.us/holbrookpalmer.html

ATHERTON - 150 WATKINS AVE (AT MIDDLEFIELD RD)

TEL: 650.752.0534

Parking: lot at park entrance

"...*more mommies than nannies...well shaded, with neat separate sections for toddlers and infants...bring a change of clothes for the ride home because there's a section that allows wet sand play...also great for families with a large age gap - large fields for the older ones to romp...* **"**

Criteria

Parking .... ❺   ❹ .... Equipment/play structures

Setting/location .... ❺   ❺ .... Maintenance

River Glen Park

www.sjparks.org

SAN JOSE - BIRD AVE (AT PINE AVE)

Parking: street parking

San Bruno Mountain Park

www.ci.brisbane.ca.us

BRISBANE - 555 GUADALUPE CANYON PKWY
TEL: 650.992.6770
Parking: lot at park entrance

Washington Park

www.burlingame.org

BURLINGAME - 850 BURLINGAME AVE (AT EAST LN)
TEL: 650.558.7300
Parking: street parking

Okay Mom and Dad, your 5 to 6 pm Happy Hour is about to change. Drastically. Go into any restaurant around this time and you will see two things: senior citizens enjoying their 10 percent discounts and new parents trying to master the complicated dance of feeding a baby while feeding themselves.

That said, there are some restaurants that clearly cater to parents and some that would rather not have kids screaming and running around the place. Parking and stroller access vary considerably as do the quality and cleanliness of bathroom changing stations. And it's great to find a restaurant that understands eating with babies requires efficient service when it comes to bringing the food and the check.

San Francisco

Alice's Restaurant

SAN FRANCISCO - 1599 SANCHEZ ST (AT 29TH ST)
TEL: 415.282.8999 HOURS: M-TH 11-9:15; F-SA 11-10; SU 12-9:15
Parking: street parking

"...*food is wonderful and other patrons don't seem to mind a baby in tow...very friendly and accommodating staff...* **"**

Features

Children's menu .... ✗
Changing station .... ✗
High chairs available .... ✓

Criteria

$$ .... Prices
❹ .... Speed of service
❸ .... Stroller access

Amici's East Coast Pizzeria

www.amicis.com

SAN FRANCISCO - 2033 UNION ST (AT BUCHANAN ST)
TEL: 415.885.4500 HOURS: M-TH 11-10; F 11-11; SA 11:30-11; SU 11:30-10
Parking: street parking/validated garage next door

"...*good food for adults as well as kids...they understand parents and will get you out before your kids melt down...overall mellow, family-friendly atmosphere...* **"**

Features

Children's menu .... ✗
Changing station .... ✓
High chairs available .... ✓

Criteria

$$ .... Prices
❹ .... Speed of service
❹ .... Stroller access

Angelina's Cafe

SAN FRANCISCO - 6000 CALIFORNIA ST (AT 22ND AVE)
TEL: 415.221.7801 HOURS: DAILY 6:30-5
Parking: street parking

Bambino's Ristorante

www.bambinosristorante.com

SAN FRANCISCO - 945 COLE ST (AT PARNASSUS AVE)
TEL: 415.731.1343 HOURS: M-TH 11:30-10:30; F 11:30-11; SA 9-11; SU 9-10:30
Parking: street parking

Barney's Gourmet Hamburger

www.barneyshamburgers.com

SAN FRANCISCO - 3344 STEINER ST (AT LOMBARD ST)
TEL: 415.563.0307 HOURS: SU-TH 11-9; F-SA 11-10
Parking: street parking

SAN FRANCISCO - 4138 24TH ST (AT CASTRO ST)
TEL: 415.282.7770 HOURS: SU-TH 11-9:30; F-SA 11-10
Parking: street parking

❝...by far the best burgers, fries and salads around...always lots of families here...it's noisy enough that a wailing baby won't be noticed...booths have mirrors along the top that keeps older kids entertained...cheap yet generous portions...kids crayons and coloring books available...❞

Features		Criteria	
			Criteria
Children's menu .... ✓		$$... Prices	
Changing station .... ✓		❹ .... Speed of service	
High chairs available .... ✓		❹ .... Stroller access	

Bay Watch

SAN FRANCISCO - 2150 LOMBARD ST (AT FILLMORE ST)
TEL: 415.775.9673 HOURS: DAILY 7-2:30
Parking: garage on Lombard

❝...amazing consistent food and great service...fast and friendly is a good combination when you have a little one...❞

Features		Criteria	
Children's menu .... ✗		$$... Prices	
Changing station .... ✗		❹ .... Speed of service	
High chairs available .... ✓		❹ .... Stroller access	

Best Of Thai Noodle

SAN FRANCISCO - 1418 HAIGHT ST (AT MASONIC AVE)
TEL: 415.552.3534 HOURS: DAILY 11-1:30AM
Parking: street parking

Bistro Aix

www.bistroaix.com
SAN FRANCISCO - 3340 STEINER ST (AT LOMBARD ST)
TEL: 415.202.0100 HOURS: M-TH 6-10; F-SA 6-11; SU 5:30-9
Parking: street parking

❝...best for well-behaved kids...quiet and nice restaurant...service is fairly quick and food is tasty...patio seating with heat lamps...staff is accommodating...❞

Features		Criteria	
Children's menu .... ✗		$$... Prices	
Changing station .... ✗		❸ .... Speed of service	
High chairs available .... ✓		❸ .... Stroller access	

Burgermeister

SAN FRANCISCO - 86 CARL ST (AT COLE ST)
TEL: 415.566.1274 HOURS: M-SA 11-10; SU 11-9
Parking: street parking

" ...yum, great hamburgers...fast service...the jukebox and the N-Judah train going by are great entertainment for young kids...outdoor seating when it's warm outside is a plus... "

Features

Children's menu .... ✗

Changing station .... ✗

High chairs available .... ✓

Criteria

$$$ .... Prices

❹ .... Speed of service

❹ .... Stroller access

Canvas Cafe ★★★★

www.thecanvasgallery.com

SAN FRANCISCO - 1200 9TH AVE (AT LINCOLN WY)

TEL: 415.504.0060 HOURS: SU-W 8-11; TH-SA 8-12AM

Parking: street parking

" ...great place to meet other moms...food is okay and it's never too noisy so baby can nap and mom can chat with friends...fun place for a snack or lunch after a stroll in Golden Gate Park...live music on the weekends...service is cafeteria-style...there's a big space to run around when Junior gets antsy... "

Features

Children's menu .... ✗

Changing station .... ✓

High chairs available .... ✓

Criteria

$$ .... Prices

❹ .... Speed of service

❹ .... Stroller access

Cha Cha Cha ★★★

SAN FRANCISCO - 1801 HAIGHT ST (AT SHRADER ST)

TEL: 415.386.5758 HOURS: SU-TH 11:30-4 5-11; F-SA 11:30-4 5-11:30

Parking: street parking

" ...always crowded in the evenings...ear-splitting noise at night...lots of good sangria and food though...wait can be very long...if you're in the mood for tapas best to go in the afternoons before dinner when it's less crowded...not a lot of room for strollers....colorful atmosphere.... "

Features

Children's menu .... ✗

Changing station .... ✗

High chairs available .... ✗

Criteria

$$ .... Prices

❸ .... Speed of service

❷ .... Stroller access

Charanga Restaurant

SAN FRANCISCO - 2351 MISSION ST (AT 20TH ST)

TEL: 415.282.1813 HOURS: T-W 11:30-2:30 5:30-10; TH-SA 11:30-2:30 5:30-11

Parking: street parking

Cheesecake Factory ★★★

www.thecheesecakefactory.com

SAN FRANCISCO - 170 OFARRELL ST (AT POWELL ST)

TEL: 415.391.4444 HOURS: M-TH 11-11; F-SA 11-12:30AM; SU 10-11

Parking: street parking

"...yummy cheesecake and great menu variety...large portions...very busy, so expect a wait at anytime of the day...no one notices a breastfeeding mom, especially in the booths...complimentary snack plate for toddlers...moderate to high priced food...noisy..."

Features

Criteria

Children's menu	✗	$$$	Prices
Changing station	✓	❸	Speed of service
High chairs available	✓	❸	Stroller access

Chevys Fresh Mex Restaurant ★★★★★

www.chevys.com

SAN FRANCISCO - 2 EMBARCADERO CTR (AT DRUMM ST)
TEL: 415.391.2323 HOURS: SU-TH 11-10:30; F-SA 11-11:30
Parking: garage in Embarcadero complex

SAN FRANCISCO - 201 3RD ST (AT HOWARD ST)
TEL: 415.543.8060 HOURS: SU-TH 11-10:30; F-SA 11-11:30
Parking: street parking

SAN FRANCISCO - 3251 20TH AVE (AT STONESTOWN GALLERIA)
TEL: 415.665.8705 HOURS: SU-TH 11-10:30; F-SA 11-11:30
Parking: mall has a lot

SAN FRANCISCO - 590 VAN NESS AVE (AT GOLDEN GATE AVE)
TEL: 415.621.8200 HOURS: SU-TH 11-10:30; F-SA 11-11:30
Parking: street parking

"...a fun, reasonably priced place to eat...always a safe bet for a quick, tasty meal...lots of distractions for little ones such as the tortilla maker and balloons...totally kid-friendly - from the balloon at entry, to the crayons and kids' menu...usually pretty loud and busy so nobody minds if your little makes noise...the staff totally understand little children and are always quick and accommodating...changing stations aren't the greatest..."

Features

Criteria

Children's menu	✓	$$	Prices
Changing station	✓	❹	Speed of service
High chairs available	✓	❹	Stroller access

Chow ★★★★

SAN FRANCISCO - 215 CHURCH ST (AT MARKET ST)
TEL: 415.552.2469 HOURS: SU-TH 11-11; F-SA 10-12AM
Parking: street parking

"...they love babies and there is plenty of room for strollers...it gets busy so go early...excellent prices...eclectic food choices ranging from Asian dishes to pizza, pasta, fish specials and salads..."

Features

Criteria

Children's menu	✗	$$	Prices
Changing station	✗	❹	Speed of service
High chairs available	✓	❸	Stroller access

Clement Street Bar & Grill

SAN FRANCISCO - 708 CLEMENT ST (AT 8TH AVE)
TEL: 415.386.2200 HOURS: T-F 11:45-3 4:30-9:30; SA 4:30-9:30; SU 10-3 4:30-9
Parking: lot on 8th Ave

Crepes on Cole

SAN FRANCISCO - 100 CARL ST (AT COLE ST)
TEL: 415.664.1800 HOURS: M-F 7:30-11; SA-SU 7:30-MIDNIGHT
Parking: street parking

"*...yummy crepes, salads, soups and sandwiches...lots of space for strollers...quick service...casual atmosphere...located in the heart of kid-friendly Cole Valley...offers outside seating which is nice when the little one wants to screech and the sun is shining...bathrooms leave a lot to be desired...***"**

Features		Criteria
Children's menu	✗	$$ .... Prices
Changing station	✓	❹ .... Speed of service
High chairs available	✓	❸ .... Stroller access

Dragon Well Restaurant

★ ★ ★ ★

SAN FRANCISCO - 2142 CHESTNUT ST (AT SCOTT ST)
TEL: 415.474.6888 HOURS: TU-SU 11:30-10
Parking: street parking

"*...exceptional food, great staff and a warm child-friendly environment...if your stroller doesn't fit you can leave it outside with the others...the owners have young children themselves, so they understand...***"**

Features		Criteria
Children's menu	✗	$$ .... Prices
Changing station	✗	❹ .... Speed of service
High chairs available	✗	❸ .... Stroller access

Eagle Pizzeria

SAN FRANCISCO - 1712 TARAVAL ST (AT 28TH AVE)
TEL: 415.566.3113 HOURS: T-TH 2-10; F 10-10; SA 11-10; SU 4-10
Parking: street parking

Einstein's Cafe

SAN FRANCISCO - 1336 9TH AVE (AT JUDAH ST)
TEL: 415.665.4840 HOURS: M-F 11-9; SA-SU 10-9
Parking: lot on 9th Ave

"*...great for a fast, healthy meal...baby friendly staff...good food at affordable prices...lack of changing table is a negative, but you usually get out of there so quickly that it's not a problem...they have an outside patio that makes it even easier with children...***"**

Features

Children's menu .... ✗
Changing station .... ✗
High chairs available .... ✓

Criteria

$ .... Prices
❹ .... Speed of service
❸ .... Stroller access

Eliza Restaurant

SAN FRANCISCO - 1457 18TH ST (AT CONNECTICUT AVE)
TEL: 415.648.9999 HOURS: DAILY 11-3 5-10
Parking: street parking

SAN FRANCISCO - 2877 CALIFORNIA ST (AT BRODERICK ST)
TEL: 415.621.4819 HOURS: M-F 11-3 & 5-10; SA-SU 11-10
Parking: street parking

❝...large open restaurant, very relaxed and kid-friendly...bright and lively environment...great and affordable Hunan & Mandarin food...fast service...kids are always present...they provide kid-friendly plates, cups, etc...try getting there before six - once seven rolls around the wait can be long...❞

Features

Children's menu .... ✗
Changing station .... ✗
High chairs available .... ✓

Criteria

$$$$ .... Prices
❹ .... Speed of service
❹ .... Stroller access

Ella's Restaurant

SAN FRANCISCO - 500 PRESIDIO AVE (AT CALIFORNIA ST)
TEL: 415.441.5669 HOURS: M-F 7-11 & 11:30-4; SA-SU 8:30-2
Parking: street parking

❝...spoil yourself with fresh-squeezed orange juice and snazzy food as a special treat after any long night with the baby...quarters are very tight at Ellas so do not plan on bringing a stroller in...there is usually a wait on the weekends which is a bit tough with an active child...it can get so busy that they tend to rush you in and out which can be stressful if you're with kids...❞

Features

Children's menu .... ✗
Changing station .... ✗
High chairs available .... ✓

Criteria

$$$ .... Prices
❸ .... Speed of service
❸ .... Stroller access

Firewood Cafe

SAN FRANCISCO - 4248 18TH ST (AT DIAMOND ST)
TEL: 415.252.0999 HOURS: M-TH 11-10:30; F-SA 11-11; SU 11-10
Parking: street parking

Gaspare Pizza House & Restaurant

SAN FRANCISCO - 5546 GEARY BLVD (AT 20TH AVE)
TEL: 415.387.5025 HOURS: M-SA 4:30-12AM; SU 4-11
Parking: street parking

❝...a casual family restaurant...big booths which are perfect for a breastfeeding mother...comfortable place with jukeboxes, great

New Jersey style pizzas with plenty of garlic and spaghetti w/meatballs...naked spaghetti with sauce on the side for the picky child...staff will happily suggest a scoop of ice cream to put a smile on the antsy child's face... **"**

Features

Children's menu .... ✗
Changing station .... ✗
High chairs available .... ✓

Criteria

$$ .... Prices
4 .... Speed of service
4 .... Stroller access

Giorgio's Pizzeria ★★★★

SAN FRANCISCO - 151 CLEMENT ST (AT 2ND AVE)
TEL: 415.668.1266 HOURS: M-TH 11:30-10:30; F-SU 11:30-11
Parking: street parking

"*...wonderful neighborhood icon pizzeria...this place is a classic for local families...the pizza is great and there are kids everywhere - a perfect place for new parents...lots of room for strollers and high chairs...parking isn't easy...* **"**

Features

Children's menu .... ✗
Changing station .... ✗
High chairs available .... ✓

Criteria

$$ .... Prices
4 .... Speed of service
3 .... Stroller access

Houston's ★★★★

www.houstons.com

SAN FRANCISCO - 1800 MONTGOMERY ST (AT EMBARCADERO ST)
TEL: 415.392.9280 HOURS: M-TH 11-2:30 & 5-10; F-SA 11:30-11; SU 11:30-10
Parking: street parking

"*...they are ready for noise and any special meal requests...fast and efficient...quality of food is consistent...they have toys, kids menus and the staff seems to love children.. booths big enough for a car seat...best rib eye steak in town...wait can be long...* **"**

Features

Children's menu .... ✗
Changing station .... ✓
High chairs available .... ✓

Criteria

$$$ .... Prices
4 .... Speed of service
4 .... Stroller access

Il Fornaio ☆☆☆☆

www.ilfornaio.com

SAN FRANCISCO - 1265 BATTERY ST (AT LEVIS PLAZA)
TEL: 415.986.0100 HOURS: M-TH 11:30-10; F 11:30-11; SA 9-11, SU 9-10
Parking: valet parking

"*...scrumptious Italian food...not your typical child-friendly place...room next to tables for strollers...outdoor seating...a great restaurant to go with your baby, and still feels like a date...* **"**

Features		Criteria
Children's menu .... ✗	$$$$ .... Prices	
Changing station .... ✓	❸ .... Speed of service	
High chairs available .... ✓	❸ .... Stroller access	

Johnny Rockets

www.johnnyrockets.com

SAN FRANCISCO - 1946 FILLMORE ST (AT MASON ST)
TEL: 415.776.9878 HOURS: SU-TH 8-9; F-SA 8-12AM
Parking: street parking

SAN FRANCISCO - 2201 CHESTNUT ST (AT SCOTT ST)
TEL: 415.931.6258 HOURS: M-TH 11-11; F-SA 11-2AM
Parking: street parking

SAN FRANCISCO - 81 JEFFERSON ST (AT MASON ST)
TEL: 415.693.9120 HOURS: SU-TH 8-9; F-SA 8-12AM
Parking: street parking

"...fun, diner style surroundings...lots for kids to look at...great for balloons, burgers, fries and shakes...it can be a long wait at peak times and there isn't a lot of room to move around...the little table top jukeboxes keep everyone happy...there isn't a ton of room for strollers and other baby gear..."

Features		Criteria
Children's menu .... ✗	$$ .... Prices	
Changing station .... ✗	❸ .... Speed of service	
High chairs available .... ✓	❸ .... Stroller access	

Kams

SAN FRANCISCO - 3624 BALBOA ST (AT 37TH AVE)
TEL: 415.752.6355 HOURS: M-SU 11-9
Parking: street parking

Kaneyama Sushi

SAN FRANCISCO - 1380 9TH AVE (AT JUDAH ST)
TEL: 415.731.2829 HOURS: T-SU 11-2:30 5-10
Parking: street parking

La Corneta Taqueria

SAN FRANCISCO - 2834 DIAMOND ST (AT BOSWORTH ST)
TEL: 415.469.8757 HOURS: M-SA 10-10; SU 11-9
Parking: street parking

Left At Albuquerque

www.leftatalb.com

SAN FRANCISCO - 2140 UNION ST (AT FILLMORE ST)
TEL: 415.749.6700 HOURS: SU-TH 11-10; F-SA 11-11PM
Parking: street parking

"...Mexican fare...casual and noisy...a good place to go even with a new baby...not as child-friendly as they could be...no

changing station, but there is a long counter in the bathroom that works just as well...chips are a good distraction for a toddler... **"**

Features

Children's menu .... ✓
Changing station .... ✓
High chairs available .... ✓

Criteria

$$ .... Prices
4 .... Speed of service
4 .... Stroller access

Mandarin Restaurant

SAN FRANCISCO - 900 N POINT ST (AT LARKIN ST)
TEL: 415.673.8812 HOURS: DAILY 11:30-9:30
Parking: garage at Ghiradelli Sq

Maxfield's House of Caffeine

SAN FRANCISCO - 398 DOLORES ST (AT 17TH ST)
TEL: 415.255.6859 HOURS: DAILY 7-9
Parking: street parking

Mel's Drive-In ★★★★

www.melsdrive-in.com

SAN FRANCISCO - 1050 VAN NESS AVE (AT GEARY ST)
TEL: 415.292.6357 HOURS: SU-W 6-1AM; TH 6-2AM; F-SA 6-4AM
Parking: street parking

SAN FRANCISCO - 2165 LOMBARD ST (AT STEINER ST)
TEL: 415.921.3039 HOURS: M-TH 6-1AM; F-SA 24 HOURS
Parking: lot in front of building

SAN FRANCISCO - 3355 GEARY BLVD (AT BEAUMONT AVE)
TEL: 415.387.2244 HOURS: SU-TH 6-1AM; F-SA 6-3AM
Parking: lot in front of building

SAN FRANCISCO - 801 MISSION ST (AT 4TH ST)
TEL: 415.227.4477 HOURS: SU-TH 6-MIDNIGHT; F-SA 6-4AM
Parking: garage on Mission St

"_...easy place to take kids and very friendly...bright decor, music, pictures and most important - a tasty chocolate malt, cheeseburger and fries...the kids meal that is served in a cardboard car is always a hit...prices are decent...lots of crayons and enough booster chairs to go around...large menu means something for everyone..._ **"**

Features

Children's menu .... ✓
Changing station .... ✓
High chairs available .... ✓

Criteria

$$ .... Prices
4 .... Speed of service
4 .... Stroller access

Miz Brown's Restaurant ★★★★

SAN FRANCISCO - 3401 CALIFORNIA ST (AT LAUREL ST)
TEL: 415.752.2039 HOURS: M-F 7-9; SA-SU 7-8
Parking: lot and street parking

> **"**...broad range of comfort foods, including breakfast and soda fountain...it is fast, greasy, and yummy...all the neighborhood kids are there...the staff love babies...can get pretty tight for a stroller... **"**

Features		Criteria
Children's menu .... ✓	$$$ .... Prices
Changing station .... ✗	❹ .... Speed of service
High chairs available .... ✓	❸ .... Stroller access

Park Chow's Restaurant ★★★★

SAN FRANCISCO - 1240 9TH AVE (AT IRVING ST)
TEL: 415.665.9912 HOURS: M-TH 11-10; F&SA 10-11; SU 10-10
Parking: street parking

> **"**...the food rocks...mellow atmosphere - perfect for a night out with an infant...prices are reasonable...can get loud, especially on weekends...plenty of chairs for kids...friendly, helpful, fast, and welcoming to children... **"**

Features		Criteria
Children's menu .... ✗	$$$ .... Prices
Changing station .... ✗	❹ .... Speed of service
High chairs available .... ✓	❸ .... Stroller access

Pasta Pomodoro ★★★★

www.pastapomodoro.com

SAN FRANCISCO - 1865 POST ST (AT FILLMORE ST)
TEL: 415.674.1826 HOURS: DAILY 11-11
Parking: garage on Post St

SAN FRANCISCO - 1875 UNION ST (AT LAGUNA ST)
TEL: 415.771.7900 HOURS: M-TH 11-10:30; F-SA 11-11; SU 12-10
Parking: lot on Union St

SAN FRANCISCO - 2304 MARKET ST (AT 16TH ST)
TEL: 415.558.8123 HOURS: M-TH 11-11:30; F-SA 11-12AM; SU 12-11:30
Parking: street parking

SAN FRANCISCO - 3611 CALIFORNIA ST (AT SPRUCE ST)
TEL: 415.831.0900 HOURS: M-TH 11-10; F-SA 11-11; SU 12-10
Parking: street parking

SAN FRANCISCO - 4000 24TH ST (AT NOE ST)
TEL: 415.920.9904 HOURS: M-F 11-11; SA-SU 9:30-11
Parking: street parking

SAN FRANCISCO - 655 UNION ST (AT COLUMBUS AVE)
TEL: 415.399.0300 HOURS: M-TH 11-11; F-SA 11-12; SU 12-11
Parking: street parking

SAN FRANCISCO - 816 IRVING ST (AT 9TH AVE)
TEL: 415.566.0900 HOURS: M-SA 11-11; SU 12-10
Parking: street parking

> **"**...a great standard for those with active kids - quick service, a straight-forward kid-friendly menu, and enough noise and bustle

that you don't stand out with a noisy infant or toddler...the wait staff automatically brings out the kids meals first, without being asked...prices are good, food is familiar and the atmosphere is comfy...they are used to having lots of moms and strollers in the restaurant... **"**

Features

Children's menu .... ✓
Changing station .... ✓
High chairs available .... ✓

Criteria

$$ .... Prices
❹ .... Speed of service
❹ .... Stroller access

Pluto's

SAN FRANCISCO - 3258 SCOTT ST (AT CHESTNUT ST)
TEL: 415.775.8867 HOURS: SU-TH 11:30-10; F-SA 11:30-11
Parking: street parking

SAN FRANCISCO - 627 IRVING ST (AT 8TH ST)
TEL: 415.753.8867
Parking: street parking

"*...informal...tends to be a bit loud, but the food is fresh and fast...great salads and you choose the toppings...sliced meats and yummy mashed potatoes with gravy...friendly staff...order and pay at the counter...tight squeeze for strollers...great for to go orders...* **"**

Features

Children's menu .... ✗
Changing station .... ✗
High chairs available .... ✓

Criteria

$$ .... Prices
❺ .... Speed of service
❸ .... Stroller access

Rainforest Cafe

SAN FRANCISCO - 165 JEFFERSON ST (AT TAYLOR ST)
TEL: 415.440.5355

Ristorante Parma

SAN FRANCISCO - 3314 STEINER ST (AT LOMBARD ST)
TEL: 415.567.0500 HOURS: M-SA 5-10:30
Parking: street parking

Sai Jai Thai Restaurant

SAN FRANCISCO - 771 OFARRELL ST (AT LARKIN ST)
TEL: 415.673.5774 HOURS: DAILY 11-11
Parking: street parking

Savor Restaurant

SAN FRANCISCO - 3913 24TH ST (AT SANCHEZ ST)
TEL: 415.282.0344 HOURS: SU-TH 8-10; F-SA 8-11
Parking: street parking

"*...food is deeelish...good healthy children's menu...if it's not too crowded this place is great - especially the back of the restaurant or patio...seating around the walls of the restaurant is* *a long booth/bench with comfy pillows - perfect for a baby nap...staff doesn't mind when your child gets food all over...* **"**

Features		Criteria
Children's menu	✓	$$ .... Prices
Changing station	✗	❹ .... Speed of service
High chairs available	✓	❸ .... Stroller access

Singha Thai Cuisine

SAN FRANCISCO - 1666 MARKET ST (AT GOUGH ST)
TEL: 415.431.5421 HOURS: M-SA 11-3 5-10
Parking: street parking

The Grove

SAN FRANCISCO - 2016 FILLMORE ST (AT PINE ST)
TEL: 415.474.1419 HOURS: M-F 7-11; SA-SU 8-11
Parking: street parking
SAN FRANCISCO - 2250 CHESTNUT ST (AT DIVISADERO ST)
TEL: 415.474.4843 HOURS: M-F 7-11; SA-SU 8-11
Parking: street parking

The Ramp ★ ★ ★

www.ramprestaurant.com
SAN FRANCISCO - 855 CHINA BASIN ST (AT 3RD ST)
TEL: 415.621.2378 HOURS: M-F 11-3:30; SA-SU 8:30-7:30
Parking: lot in front of building

"*...a funky old place right on the water...nice kids menu...great outdoor seating...fun place to hang out in the sun...horrible bathrooms; you can't change a baby's diaper easily here...* **"**

Features		Criteria
Children's menu	✗	$$ .... Prices
Changing station	✗	❸ .... Speed of service
High chairs available	✓	❹ .... Stroller access

The Sea Breeze Cafe

SAN FRANCISCO - 3940 JUDAH ST (AT 44TH AVE)
TEL: 415.242 6022 HOURS: T-SA 11-4 5-9; SU 8-3
Parking: street parking

Ton Kiang ★ ★ ★

SAN FRANCISCO - 5821 GEARY BLVD (AT 22ND AVE)
TEL: 415.387.8273 HOURS: DAILY 10:30-10:30
Parking: street parking

"*...the best dim sum in town...love having food served immediately...the biggest downside is that they don't take reservations and the wait on weekends is very long...it can be a bit of a squeeze if you need to bring your stroller in...no changing table in the bathroom...parking is a nightmare...* **"**

Features

			Criteria
Children's menu	✗	$$	Prices
Changing station	✗	❹	Speed of service
High chairs available	✓	❸	Stroller access

Tyger's

SAN FRANCISCO - 2798 DIAMOND ST (AT CHENERY ST)
TEL: 415.239.4060 HOURS: DAILY 7-3:30
Parking: street parking

Via Vai

SAN FRANCISCO - 1715 UNION ST (AT GOUGH ST)
TEL: 415.441.2111 HOURS: SU-TH 11:30-2:30 5-9:30; F-SA 11:30-2:30
5-10:30
Parking: garage on Union St

Warming Hut Cafe

www.ggnpa.org

SAN FRANCISCO - PRESIDIO BUILDING 983 (AT END OF CRISSY
FIELD AT FT POINT PIER)
TEL: 415.561.3042 HOURS: DAILY 9-5
Parking: lot behind building

❝...after a walk or run with your child in the jogger, finish at the
Warming Hut and have the best latte in town...deeelish grilled
cheese, juice and other goodies for kids...spectacular view of the
Golden Gate bridge and lots of room to run around...little shop in
The Hut is great - unique gifts and books/toys for children...**❞**

Features

			Criteria
Children's menu	✗	$$	Prices
Changing station	✗	❹	Speed of service
High chairs available	✗	❺	Stroller access

Zao Noodle Bar

www.zaonoodle.com

SAN FRANCISCO - 2406 CALIFORNIA ST (AT FILLMORE ST)
TEL: 415.345.8088 HOURS: SU-TH 11-10; F-SA 11-11
Parking: lot on California St

SAN FRANCISCO - 3583 16TH ST (AT MARKET ST)
TEL: 415.864.2888 HOURS: SU-TH 11-10; F-SA 11-12AM
Parking: street parking

East Bay

Barclay's Restaurant & Pub

OAKLAND - 5940 COLLEGE AVE (AT KEITH AVE EXIT)
TEL: 510.654.1650 HOURS: M-SA 11-12; SU 10-12
Parking: street parking

Barney's Gourmet Hamburger

www.barneyshamburgers.com

BERKELEY - 1591 SOLANO AVE (AT TACOMA AVE)
TEL: 510.526.8185 HOURS: M-TH 11-9:30; F-SA 11-10; SU 11-9
Parking: street parking

BERKELEY - 1600 SHATTUCK AVE # 112 (AT CEDAR ST)
TEL: 510.849.2827 HOURS: M-TH 11-9:30; F-SA 11-10; SU 11-9
Parking: street parking

OAKLAND - 4162 PIEDMONT AVE (AT LINDA AVE)
TEL: 510.655.7180 HOURS: SU-TH 11-9:30; F-SA 11-10
Parking: street parking

OAKLAND - 5819 COLLEGE AVE (AT KEITH AVE)
TEL: 510.601.0444 HOURS: SU-TH 11-9:30; F-SA 11-10
Parking: street parking

❝...by far the best burgers, fries and salads around...always lots of families here...it's noisy enough that a wailing baby won't be noticed...booths have mirrors along the top that keeps older kids entertained...cheap yet generous portions...kids crayons and coloring books available...❞

Features		Criteria	
Children's menu	✓	$$	Prices
Changing station	✓	❹	Speed of service
High chairs available	✓	❸	Stroller access

Cactus Taqueria

BERKELEY - 1881 SOLANO AVE (AT THE ALAMEDA)
TEL: 510.528.1881 HOURS: DAILY 11-9
Parking: street parking

❝...healthy, good tasting Mexican food...great food, but it's a little crowded and the line can be long...decent variety that appeals to kids and adults...parking is tough...❞

Features		Criteria	
Children's menu	✗	$$	Prices
Changing station	✗	❸	Speed of service
High chairs available	✓	❸	Stroller access

California Pizza Kitchen ★★★★

www.californiapizzakitchen.com

WALNUT CREEK - 1120 BROADWAY PLZ (AT MT DIABLO BLVD)
TEL: 925.938.0720 HOURS: M-TH 11-10; F 11-11; SA 11-11; SU 11-10
Parking: lot near front of building

❝...the perfect place to go with kids...fast service...huge portions...completely kid-friendly staff...tons of great choices on the kid menu...crayons and games to play...clean highchairs...excellent mac and cheese for the kids...wait can be long at peak hours...❞

Features

Children's menu	✓
Changing station	✓
High chairs available	✓

Criteria

$$	Prices
❹	Speed of service
❹	Stroller access

Cancun

BERKELEY - 2134 ALLSTON WY (AT SHATTUCK AVE)
TEL: 510.549.0964 HOURS: M-TH 10-9:30; F-SA 10-10:30
Parking: street parking

Cato's Ale House ☆☆☆

www.mrcato.com

OAKLAND - 3891 PIEDMONT AVE (AT MONTELL ST)
TEL: 510.655.3349 HOURS: SU-W 11:30-10; TH-SA 11:30-11
Parking: street parking

❝...casual pub with great beer on tap...mellow atmosphere with nice booths - if you can snag one...sometimes the music can be loud, or if a big game is on it can get a little raucous...❞

Features

Children's menu	✗
Changing station	✗
High chairs available	✓

Criteria

$$$	Prices
❸	Speed of service
❷	Stroller access

Chevys Fresh Mex Restaurant ★★★★★

www.chevys.com

ALAMEDA - 2400 MARINER SQUARE DR (AT MARINER SQUARE LOOP)
TEL: 510.521.3768 HOURS: SU-TH 11-10:30; F-SA 11-11:30
Parking: lot in front of building

EMERYVILLE - 2000 POWELL ST # 200 (OFF HWY 80)
TEL: 510.653.8210 HOURS: SU-TH 11-10:30; F-SA 11-11:30

NEWARK - 5605 MOWRY SCHOOL RD (AT NEWPARK MALL)
TEL: 510.226.9080 HOURS: SU-TH 11-10:30; F-SA 11-11:30
Parking: mall has a lot

PLEASANT HILL - 650 ELLINWOOD WY (AT ROCK CREEK WY)
TEL: 925.685.6651 HOURS: SU-TH 11-10:30; F-SA 11-11:30
Parking: lot in front of building

PLEASANTON - 5877 OWENS DR (AT HACIENDA DR)
TEL: 925.416.0451 HOURS: SU-TH 11-10:30; F-SA 11-11:30
Parking: lot in front of building

RICHMOND - 3101 GARRITY WY (AT BLUME DR)
TEL: 510.222.9802 HOURS: SU-TH 11-10:30; F-SA 11-11:30
Parking: lot in front of building

SAN LEANDRO - 312 BAY FAIR MALL (AT HESPERIAN BLVD)
TEL: 510.276.0962 HOURS: SU-TH 11-10:30; F-SA 11-11:30
Parking: lot in front of building

SAN RAMON - 18080 SAN RAMON VALLEY RD (AT BOLLINGER
CANYON RD)
TEL: 925.327.1910 HOURS: SU-TH 11-10:30; F-SA 11-11:30
Parking: lot in front of building

UNION CITY - 31100 COURTHOUSE DR (OFF DYER ST)
TEL: 510.675.9620 HOURS: SU-TH 11-10:30; F-SA 11-11:30
Parking: lot in front of building

❝...a fun, reasonably priced place to eat...always a safe bet for a quick, tasty meal...lots of distractions for little ones such as the tortilla maker and balloons...totally kid-friendly - from the balloon at entry, to the crayons and kids' menu...usually pretty loud and busy so nobody minds if your little makes noise...the staff totally understand little children and are always quick and accommodating...changing stations aren't the greatest... ❞

Features

		Criteria	
Children's menu	✓	$$	Prices
Changing station	✓	❹	Speed of service
High chairs available	✓	❹	Stroller access

Compadres Bar & Grill   ☆ ☆ ☆ ☆

OAKLAND - 4239 PARK BLVD (AT WELLINGTON ST)
TEL: 510.482.3663 HOURS: M-F 11:30-10; SA-SU 9-10
Parking: street parking

❝...will accommodate large groups (five moms with strollers)...have high chairs and give balloons to the kids...the food isn't outstanding, but it's nice to get out.... ❞

Features

		Criteria	
Children's menu	✗	$$$	Prices
Changing station	✗	❸	Speed of service
High chairs available	✓	❹	Stroller access

Cornerstone Cafe

SAN LEANDRO - 600 DUTTON AVE (AT BANCROFT AVE)
TEL: 510.562.2535 HOURS: M-F 11-9; SA 8-9; SU 8-8
Parking: street parking

Crepevine

OAKLAND - 5600 COLLEGE AVE (AT KALES AVE)
TEL: 510.658.2026 HOURS: SU-TH 7:30-11; F-SA 7:30-12
Parking: street parking

Doug's Place

CASTRO VALLEY - 20871 REDWOOD RD (AT CASTRO VALLEY BLVD)
TEL: 510.538.9155 HOURS: DAILY 6:30-3
Parking: lot next to building

East Ocean Seafood Restaurant

ALAMEDA - 1713 WEBSTER ST (AT PACIFIC AVE)
TEL: 510.865.3381 HOURS: M-SU 10-9:30
Parking: lot behind building

Emery Bay Public Market

EMERYVILLE - 5800 SHELLMOUND ST (AT POWELL ST EXIT OFF 80)
TEL: 510.652.9300 HOURS: M-SA 7-9; SU 7-8
Parking: lot in front of market

❝...huge food court...not your typical Hot Dog On A Stick type fare...photo booth, ball jump, horsie rides, book store and ice cream...if you're not in the mood for fancy or uptight then this is the place...unfortunately, they only have two highchairs available and neither have safety belts...a bit too noisy for breastfeeding...**❞**

Features		Criteria	
Children's menu	✗	$	Prices
Changing station	✓	❹	Speed of service
High chairs available	✓	❺	Stroller access

Europa Hofbrau Deli & Pub

ORINDA - 64 MORAGA WY (AT CAMINO ENCINAS)
TEL: 925.254.7202 HOURS: M-SA 11-9; SU 11-8
Parking: street parking

Fatapples Restaurant

BERKELEY - 1346 MARTIN LUTHER KING JR WY (AT ROSE ST)
TEL: 510.526.2260 HOURS: SU-TH 7-9; F-SA 7-10
Parking: street parking

❝...basic and straightforward food...a great family restaurant that appeals to the fussy kid eater...very kid-friendly environment - they don't mind you lingering at your table...long wait on Saturdays and Sundays...**❞**

Features		Criteria	
Children's menu	✓	$$$	Prices
Changing station	✓	❸	Speed of service
High chairs available	✓	❸	Stroller access

Fresh Choice

www.freshchoice.com

CONCORD - 486 SUN VALLEY MALL (AT WILLOW PASS RD)
TEL: 925.671.7222 HOURS: SU-TH 11-9; F-SA 11-10
Parking: mall has a lot
PLEASANTON - 2453 STONERIDGE MALL RDTEL: 925.734.8186
HOURS: SU-TH 11-9; F-SA 11-10
Parking: lot parking

WALNUT CREEK - 1275 S MAIN ST (AT BOTELHO DR)
TEL: 925.938.1529 HOURS: SU-TH 11-9; F-SA 11-10
Parking: lot in front of building

...buffet-style restaurant, with fresh fruits, veggies, and potato bar...divided trays for kids and lots of high chairs and booster seats...usually lots of families dining, including breastfeeding mothers...it's self-serve, so you can spend as much time in there as necessary...the quality of food is always dependable and tastes great...prices are based on your kid's age with those under 3 eating free...

Features		Criteria
Children's menu	✗	$$ .... Prices
Changing station	✓	❹ .... Speed of service
High chairs available	✓	❹ .... Stroller access

Fuddruckers

★★★★

WALNUT CREEK - 1940 NORTH MAIN ST (AT YGNACIO VALLEY RD)
TEL: 925.943.1450 HOURS: SU-TH 11-10; F-SA 11-11
Parking: lot parking

...friendly burger joint...they have a small video area and the kids meals are great...kids get a free cookie too...space is a bit tight between tables...all-you-can-eat peanuts and popcorn, which makes waiting for your food much more tolerable especially for older children...

Features		Criteria
Children's menu	✓	$$ .... Prices
Changing station	✓	❸ .... Speed of service
High chairs available	✓	❹ .... Stroller access

Il Fornaio

www.ilfornaio.com

WALNUT CREEK - 1430 MT DIABLO BLVD (AT CONTRA COSTA BLVD)
TEL: 925.296.0100 HOURS: SU-TH 11-10; F-SA 11-11
Parking: valet parking

...scrumptious Italian food...not your typical child-friendly place...room next to tables for strollers...outdoor seating...a great restaurant to go with your baby, and still feels like a date...

Features

			Criteria
Children's menu	✗	$$$$	Prices
Changing station	✓	❸	Speed of service
High chairs available	✓	❸	Stroller access

Jimmy Bean's

www.jimmybeans.com

BERKELEY - 1290 6TH ST (AT GILMAN ST)
TEL: 510.528.3435 HOURS: M-F 6-4; SA-SU 8-4
Parking: street parking

Juan's Place

BERKELEY - 941 CARLETON ST (AT 9TH ST)
TEL: 510.845.6904 HOURS: M-F 11-10; SA-SU 2-10
Parking: street parking

Kensington Circus

KENSINGTON - 389 COLUSA AVE (AT THOUSAND OAKS BLVD)
TEL: 510.524.8814 HOURS: M-F 5:30-10; SA 9-10; SU 9-9
Parking: street parking

❝...truly one of the most relaxing places to go as a family...very fun place for mom and dad to enjoy a beer, visit with friends and hang out...always tons of kids there...toys all over the place...has great neighborhood feel... ❞

Features

			Criteria
Children's menu	✗	$$	Prices
Changing station	✓	❹	Speed of service
High chairs available	✓	❺	Stroller access

Kirin Chinese Restaurant

BERKELEY - 1767 SOLANO AVE (AT COLUSA AVE)
TEL: 510.524.1677 HOURS: DAILY 11:30-2:30 & 4-9
Parking: street parking

❝...good not-too-greasy food...roomy restaurant with easy stroller access...parking can be difficult on weekends... ❞

Features

			Criteria
Children's menu	✗	$$	Prices
Changing station	✗	❸	Speed of service
High chairs available	✓	❺	Stroller access

Lo Coco's Restaurant

OAKLAND - 4270 PIEDMONT AVE (AT ECHO AVE)
TEL: 510.652.6222 HOURS: TU-TH 4-10; F-SU 4-11
Parking: street parking

Long-life Veggie House ★★★★

BERKELEY - 2129 UNIVERSITY AVE (AT SHATTUCK AVE)
TEL: 510.845.6072 HOURS: M-TH 11:30-10; F-SU 11:30-10:30
Parking: street parking

"...*food is cheap and service is fast...good vegetarian Chinese...the staff loves children...* **"**

Features			Criteria
Children's menu	✗	$$	Prices
Changing station	✗	④	Speed of service
High chairs available	✓	③	Stroller access

Marie Callender's

CONCORD - 2090 DIAMOND BLVD (AT CONCORD AVE)
TEL: 925.827.4930 HOURS: M-TH 11-10; F-SA 11-11

Mel's Drive-In ★★★★

www.melsdrive-in.com
BERKELEY - 2240 SHATTUCK AVE (AT KITTREDGE ST)
TEL: 510.540.6351 HOURS: M-TH 9-11; F-SA 9-1AM; SU 9-11:30
Parking: garage on Kittredge

"...*easy place to take kids and very friendly...bright decor, music, pictures and most importantly a tasty chocolate malt, cheeseburger and fries...the kids meal that is served in a cardboard car is always a hit...prices are decent...lots of crayons and enough booster chairs to go around...large menu means something for everyone...* **"**

Features			Criteria
Children's menu	✓	$$	Prices
Changing station	✓	③	Speed of service
High chairs available	✓	④	Stroller access

Pasta Pomodoro ★★★★

www.pastapomodoro.com
EL CERRITO - 5040 EL CERRITO PLAZA, #E1 (CENTRAL AVE)
TEL: 510.225.0128 HOURS: SU-TH 11-10; F 11-11; SA 12-11
Parking: lot in front of building

OAKLAND - 5500 COLLEGE AVE (AT LAWTON)
TEL: 510.923.0900 HOURS: M-SA 11-11; SU 12-10
Parking: street parking

PLEASANT HILL - 45 CRESCENT DR (AT CONTRA COST)
TEL: 925.363.9641 HOURS: M-SA 11-11; SU 11-10
Parking: lot in front of building

SAN RAMON - 146 SUNSET DR (AT BOLLINGER CANYON)
TEL: 925.867.1407 HOURS: M-F 11-10; SA 11-11; SU 11-9
Parking: lot in front of building

"...*a great standard for those with active kids - quick service, a straight-forward kid-friendly menu, and enough noise and bustle that you don't stand out with a noisy infant or toddler...the wait* *staff automatically brings out the kids meals first, without being asked...prices are good, food is familiar and the atmosphere is comfy...they are used to having lots of moms and strollers in the restaurant...* **"**

Features

		Criteria	
Children's menu .... ✓	$$ .... Prices		
Changing station .... ✓	❹ .... Speed of service		
High chairs available .... ✓	❹ .... Stroller access		

Pete's Brass Rail & Car Wash

DANVILLE - 201 HARTZ AVE (AT E LINDA MESA AVE)
TEL: 925.820.8281 HOURS: M-SA 11-11; SU 11-8:30
Parking: lot behind building

Picante Cocina Mexicana ★★★★★

BERKELEY - 1328 6TH ST (AT GILMAN ST)
TEL: 510.525.3121 HOURS: M-TH 10-10; F-SA 10-11; SU 10-10
Parking: street parking

"...always fresh Mexican food and spiciness can be downplayed for kids...this place was made for parents with young children - incredibly fast service, very good food, great margaritas and lots of children everywhere...yummy food, large aisles for strollers and casual atmosphere make this a winner with our family...loud and inviting - no one will notice your child howling...* **"**

Features

		Criteria	
Children's menu .... ✓	$$ .... Prices		
Changing station .... ✓	❹ .... Speed of service		
High chairs available .... ✓	❹ .... Stroller access		

Portumex Restaurant

RICHMOND - 721 23RD ST (AT DOWNER AVE)
TEL: 510.237.7513 HOURS: TU-F 9-8:45; SA 8-8:45; SU 8-5:45
Parking: street parking

Red Tractor Cafe ★★★★

www.redtractor.com
OAKLAND - 5634 COLLEGE AVE (AT TAFT AVE)
TEL: 510.595.3500 HOURS: M-F 8-9; SA-SU 9-9
Parking: street parking

"...family-style-cooking...great for kids...tractor coloring place mats...milk cups with lids and straws...plenty of highchairs...meals served on Disney plates...bathroom has farm animal sounds, which is amusing to some kids and frightening to others...* **"**

Features

		Criteria	
Children's menu .... ✗	$$ .... Prices		
Changing station .... ✓	❹ .... Speed of service		
High chairs available .... ✓	❹ .... Stroller access		

Rick & Ann's Restaurant

www.rickandanns.com

BERKELEY - 2922 DOMINGO AVE (AT CLAREMONT AVE)
TEL: 510.649.8538 HOURS: DAILY 8-2:30; TU-SU 5:30-9:30
Parking: street parking

"...comfort food dressed up...many kid-friendly items on their menu in addition to a great kid's menu...excellent, tasty food for grownups and kids alike...relaxed environment...lots of cool decorations on the wall...tight squeeze for strollers and car seats...weekends are usually very crowded... **"**

Features		Criteria
Children's menu	✗	$$ .... Prices
Changing station	✗	❹ .... Speed of service
High chairs available	✓	❸ .... Stroller access

Sam's Log Cabin

ALBANY - 945 SAN PABLO AVE (AT SOLANO AVE)
TEL: 510.558.0494 HOURS: T-F 7-2; SA-SU 8-2
Parking: street parking

Skipolini's Pizza

WALNUT CREEK - 1535 GIAMMONA DR (AT LOCUST ST)
TEL: 925 .280.1100 HOURS: M-F 11:30-9:30; SA-SU 11:30-10:30
Parking: street and lot parking

Spettro

OAKLAND - 3355 LAKESHORE AVE (AT LAKE PARK AVE)
TEL: 510.465.8320 HOURS: DAILY 5PM-10
Parking: street parking

Sweet Tomatoes

www.sweettomatoes.com

FREMONT - 39370 PASEO PADRE PKWY (AT WALNUT AVE)
TEL: 510.494.0300 HOURS: SU-TH 11-9; F-SA 11-10
Parking: lot in front of building

PLEASANT HILL - 40 CRESCENT DR (AT MONUMENT BLVD)
TEL: 925.676.8493 HOURS: SU-TH 11-9; F-SA 11-10
Parking: mall has a lot

PLEASANTON - 4501 HOPYARD RD (AT STONERIDGE DR)
TEL: 925.463.9285 HOURS: SU-TH 11-9; F-SA 11-10
Parking: lot in front of building

"...all-you-can-eat salads, soups, bread, fruits, pizzas, muffins and ice cream...great place to bring children...wonderful selection of items for kids and a friendly breastfeeding environment... **"**

Features

		Criteria	
Children's menu	✗	$$ .... Prices	
Changing station	✓	❹ .... Speed of service	
High chairs available	✓	❹ .... Stroller access	

TGI Fridays

☆ ☆ ☆ ☆

www.tgifridays.com

OAKLAND - 450 WATER ST (AT JACK LONDON SQ)
TEL: 510.451.3834 HOURS: DAILY 11-12AM
Parking: lot on Broadway

❝...quick service...go ahead, make a mess, they don't care...free balloons...lots for kids to look at and always fast- paced and loud...**❞**

Features

		Criteria	
Children's menu	✓	$$$ .... Prices	
Changing station	✗	❸ .... Speed of service	
High chairs available	✓	❸ .... Stroller access	

Tomatina

☆ ☆ ☆

WALNUT CREEK - 1325 N MAIN ST (AT MT DIABLO BLVD)
TEL: 925.930.9999 HOURS: M-F 11-10; SA-SU 11:30-10
Parking: lot and street parking

❝...often busy...crayons and kids menu to color on...booth tables are huge...**❞**

Features

		Criteria	
Children's menu	✓	$$ .... Prices	
Changing station	✓	❹ .... Speed of service	
High chairs available	✓	❸ .... Stroller access	

Tomodachi

ALAMEDA - 1315 PARK ST (AT ENCINAL AVE)
TEL: 510.521.3298 HOURS: M-SA 11-2:30 5-10; SU 11-2:30 5-9:30
Parking: lot in front of building

Zza's Trattoria

OAKLAND - 552 GRAND AVE (AT EUCLID AVE)
TEL: 510.839.9124 HOURS: SU-TU 4:30-9; W-TH 10:30-9; F 10:30-10; SA 4:30-10
Parking: lot on Grand Ave

North Bay

Big Dipper

ST HELENA - 1336 OAK AVE (AT SPRING ST)
TEL: 707.963.2616 HOURS: M-F 11:30-5:30; SA 12-5
Parking: street parking

Bubbas Diner

SAN ANSELMO - 566 SAN ANSELMO AVE (AT MAGNOLIA AVE)
TEL: 415.459.6862 HOURS: M W-TH 9-2 5:30-9; SA-SU 8-2:30 5:30-9

California Pizza Kitchen

www.californiapizzakitchen.com
CORTE MADERA - 347 CORTE MADERA TOWN CTR (AT TAMALPAIS
DR)
TEL: 415.945.0401 HOURS: W-SA 11:30-10; SU-TU 11-9
Parking: mall has a lot

❝...the perfect place to go with kids...fast service...huge portions...completely kid-friendly staff...tons of great choices on the kid menu...crayons and games to play...clean highchairs...excellent mac and cheese for the kids...wait can be long at peak hours...❞

Features		Criteria	
Children's menu	✓	$$	Prices
Changing station	✓	❹	Speed of service
High chairs available	✓	❹	Stroller access

Cantina

MILL VALLEY - 651 E BLITHEDALE AVE (AT LOMITA DR)
TEL: 415.381.1070 HOURS: SU-TH 11:30-10; F-SA 11:30-11
Parking: lot in front of building

❝...great place to bring babies...fair amount of noise so no one will be disturbed by a crying baby...inexpensive, but good meals...a mom's group favorite...❞

Features		Criteria	
Children's menu	x	$$	Prices
Changing station	✓	❹	Speed of service
High chairs available	✓	❺	Stroller access

Chevys Fresh Mex Restaurant

www.chevys.com
GREENBRAE - 302 BON AIR CTR (OFF SIR FRANCIS DRAKE BLVD)
TEL: 415.461.3203 HOURS: SU-TH 11-10:30; F-SA 11-11:30
Parking: lot in front of building

NOVATO - 128 VINTAGE WY (AT ROWLAND BLVD)
TEL: 415.898.7345 HOURS: SU-TH 11-10:30; F-SA 11-11:30
Parking: lot in front of building

SANTA ROSA - 24 FOURTH ST (AT WILSON ST)
TEL: 707.571.1082 HOURS: SU-TH 11-10:30; F-SA 11-11:30
Parking: lot in front of building

VALLEJO - 157 PLAZA DR (AT ADMIRAL CALLAGHAN LN)
TEL: 707.644.1373 HOURS: SU-TH 11-10:30; F-SA 11-11:30
Parking: lot in front of building

"...a fun, reasonably priced place to eat...always a safe bet for a quick, tasty meal...lots of distractions for little ones such as the tortilla maker and balloons...totally kid-friendly - from the balloon at entry, to the crayons and kids' menu...usually pretty loud and busy so nobody minds if your little makes noise...the staff totally understand little children and are always quick and accommodating...changing stations aren't the greatest... **"**

Features

		Criteria
Children's menu	✓	
		$$ .... Prices
Changing station	✓	❹ .... Speed of service
High chairs available	✓	❹ .... Stroller access

D'Angelo Restaurant

MILL VALLEY - 22 MILLER AVE (AT THROCKMORTON AVE)
TEL: 415.388.2000 HOURS: M-F 11:30-12AM; SA-SU 10:30-12AM
Parking: lot behind building

Dipsea Cafe   ★ ★ ★ ★

www.dipseacafe.com

MILL VALLEY - 200 SHORELINE HWY (AT TENNESSEE VALLEY RD)
TEL: 415.381.0298 HOURS: DAILY 7-3
Parking: lot next to building

SAN RAFAEL - 2200 4TH ST (AT W CRESCENT DR)
TEL: 415.459.0700 HOURS: SU-M 7-3; TU-SA 7-9
Parking: street parking

"...they offer a somewhat eclectic menu...the best time to go on weekends is before 8am...crayons and doodle-mats for toddlers...a great kids menu...convenient, but somewhat pricey...great for parents since your kid is not the only one screaming...it gets very crowded on weekends, and service can be painfully slow... **"**

Features

		Criteria
Children's menu	✗	
		$$$$ .... Prices
Changing station	✗	❸ .... Speed of service
High chairs available	✓	❹ .... Stroller access

Double Rainbow Cafe

NOVATO - 112 VINTAGE WY # C3 (AT ROWLAND BLVD)
TEL: 415.898.8500 HOURS: M-SA 8-9; SU 10-9
Parking: lot in front of building

"...this isn't just about ice cream, they have a great sandwich menu and smoothies to boot...lots of foot traffic and bird watching to keep little ones happy...felt comfortable nursing...**"**

Features		Criteria
Children's menu .... ✗	$$$ .... Prices
Changing station .... ✗	❸ .... Speed of service
High chairs available .... ✓	❺ .... Stroller access

Easy Street Cafe

★ ★ ★ ★

SAN ANSELMO - 882 SIR FRANCIS DRAKE BLVD (AT SAN FRANCISCO BLVD)
TEL: 415.453.1984 HOURS: DAILY 6-9
Parking: street parking

"...dedicated play area for kids...totally kid-friendly...fresh food served fast, and what a variety...cool atmosphere with funky art and collectibles displayed...check out the early bird dinner special from 3-5pm...located near Memorial Park/Millennium Playground make this a popular place for kids...**"**

Features		Criteria
Children's menu .... ✗	$$ .... Prices
Changing station .... ✓	❹ .... Speed of service
High chairs available .... ✓	❹ .... Stroller access

Half Day Cafe

★ ★ ★ ★

KENTFIELD - 848 COLLEGE AVE (AT SIR FRANCIS DRAKE BLVD)
TEL: 415.459.0291 HOURS: DAILY 7-2:30
Parking: lot behind building

"...since breakfast is the fastest meal to get through we can actually bring our toddler...efficient staff attentive to kids' needs and parents...great atmosphere...variety of good food...**"**

Features		Criteria
Children's menu .... ✗	$$ .... Prices
Changing station .... ✓	❸ .... Speed of service
High chairs available .... ✓	❹ .... Stroller access

Hof Brau-Roast Haus

SAN RAFAEL - 276 NORTHGATE ONE (AT FREITAS PKWY)
TEL: 415.472.2233 HOURS: M-SA 11-9
Parking: lot in front of building

Joe's Taco Lounge ★★★★

MILL VALLEY - 382 MILLER AVE (AT MONTFORD AVE)
TEL: 415.383.8164 HOURS: M-TH 11:30-9; F-SA 11-10; SU 11-9
Parking: street parking

"...lively, fun place with a different twist on Mexican food...loud, lots of high chairs, very welcoming to babies and kids...no play area for kids...but the speed of service and quality of food make up for any these inconveniences...they understand a kid's meltdown... **"**

Features

		Criteria	
Children's menu	✓	$$	Prices
Changing station	✗	❹	Speed of service
High chairs available	✓	❸	Stroller access

Lark Creek Inn ★★★★

www.larkcreek.com

LARKSPUR - 234 MAGNOLIA AVE (AT MADRONE AVE)
TEL: 415.924.7766 HOURS: M-F 11:30-2 & 5:30-9; SA 5-10; SU 10-2 & 5-10
Parking: lot in front of building

"...good for parents who want to enjoy fine dining with their very young children...there usually are lots of babies and toddlers...the wait staff is very patient, accommodating and understanding...great place for a date night as well... **"**

Features

		Criteria	
Children's menu	✗	$$$$	Prices
Changing station	✓	❸	Speed of service
High chairs available	✓	❸	Stroller access

Mama's Royal Cafe

MILL VALLEY - 393 MILLER AVE (AT MONTFORD AVE)
TEL: 415.388.3261 HOURS: M-TH 7:30-2:30; F-SU 7:30-3:30
Parking: lot behind building

Marin Brewing Co ☆☆☆☆

www.marinbrewing.com

LARKSPUR - 1809 LARKSPUR LANDING CIR (AT OLD QUARRY RD S)
TEL: 415.461.4677 HOURS: DAILY 11:30-12AM
Parking: lot in front of building

"...nice safe place to dine outdoors with a small child...average food...great because it's loud and no one can hear your kid screaming... **"**

Features

		Criteria	
Children's menu	✓	$$	Prices
Changing station	✓	❸	Speed of service
High chairs available	✓	❹	Stroller access

Mary's Pizza Shack

www.maryspizzashack.com

PETALUMA - 359 E WASHINGTON ST (AT COPELAND ST)
TEL: 707.778.7200 HOURS: SU-TH 11-11; F-SA 11-12AM
Parking: lot in front of store

"...the menu is pretty basic, but tasty...sometimes crowded...staff is always friendly...food usually arrives pretty quickly...while waiting, kids are entertained watching the pizza makers, and tided over with free breadsticks... **"**

Features

		Criteria
Children's menu .... ✓	$$ .... Prices	
Changing station .... ✓	❹ .... Speed of service	
High chairs available .... ✓	❹ .... Stroller access	

Mc Near's Saloon & Dining House

www.mcnears.com

PETALUMA - 23 PETALUMA BLVD N (AT WESTERN AVE)
TEL: 707.765.2121 HOURS: M-F 11-9; SA-SU 8:30-9
Parking: street parking

"...the typical pub grub...a good choice with kids...full bar and outdoor seating...not the greatest changing tables...no one looks twice if you're nursing... **"**

Features

		Criteria
Children's menu .... ✗	$$$ .... Prices	
Changing station .... ✗	❸ .... Speed of service	
High chairs available .... ✓	❹ .... Stroller access	

Moylan's Brewery & Restaurant

www.moylans.com

NOVATO - 15 ROWLAND WY (AT BOTTOM OF ROWLAND BLVD)
TEL: 415.898.4677 HOURS: SU-TH 11:30-12AM; F-SA 11:30-1AM
Parking: lot in front of building

"...delicious food, high chairs that can be turned upside down to hold baby carriers and no strange looks when nursing...lots of kids...changing tables in both the men's and women's restrooms... **"**

Features

		Criteria
Children's menu .... ✗	$$ .... Prices	
Changing station .... ✓	❸ .... Speed of service	
High chairs available .... ✓	❹ .... Stroller access	

Muffin Mania

SAN RAFAEL - 2 BAYVIEW ST (AT WOODLAND AVE)
TEL: 415.485.1027 HOURS: M-F 5:30-3; SA 6-3; SU 6:30-12
Parking: street parking

Old Chicago Pizza

PETALUMA - 41 PETALUMA BLVD N (AT WESTERN AVE)
TEL: 707.763.3897 HOURS: M-TH 11:30-10:30; F-SA 11:30-11:30; SU 4-9:30
Parking: street parking

Pancho Villa's

FAIRFAX - 1625 SIR FRANCIS DRAKE BLVD (AT WILLOW AVE)
TEL: 415.459.0975 HOURS: DAILY 11-10
Parking: street parking

Pasta Pomodoro ★★★★

www.pastapomodoro.com
MILL VALLEY - STRAWBERRY VILLAGETEL: 415.388.1692 HOURS: M-TH 11-10; F-SA 11-11; SU 11-10
Parking: lot in front of building

SAN RAFAEL - 421 3RD ST (AT UNION ST)
TEL: 415.256.2401 HOURS: M-SA 11-10; SU 12-10
Parking: lot in front of building

VALLEJO - 163 PLAZA DR (AT ADMIRAL CALLAGHAN LN)
TEL: 707.557.6100 HOURS: M-TH 11-10; F-SA 11-11; SU 12-10
Parking: lot in front of building

"...a great standard for those with active kids - quick service, a straight-forward kid-friendly menu, and enough noise and bustle that you don't stand out with a noisy infant or toddler...the wait staff automatically brings out the kids meals first, without being asked...prices are good, food is familiar and the atmosphere is comfy...they are used to having lots of moms and strollers in the restaurant...**"**

Features
Children's menu .... ✓
Changing station .... ✓
High chairs available .... ✓

Criteria
$$ .... Prices
❹ .... Speed of service
❹ .... Stroller access

Piatti Restaurant

MILL VALLEY - 625 REDWOOD HWY (AT)
TEL: 415.380.2525 HOURS: DAILY 11:30-10
Parking: lot in front of building

Ross Valley Brewing Co ★★★★

www.rossvalleybrewing.com
FAIRFAX - 765 CENTER BLVD (AT MONO AVE)
TEL: 415.485.1005 HOURS: M-F 4-10; SA 12-11; SU 12-10
Parking: lot in front of building

"...a nice upscale brew pub with fabulous food...early Sunday evenings it turns into family central...bathrooms are a little inconvenient...**"**

Features

		Criteria	
Children's menu	✗	$$	Prices
Changing station	✓	❹	Speed of service
High chairs available	✓	❹	Stroller access

Shere Punjab Restaurant
☆☆☆☆

SAN RAFAEL - 1025 C ST (AT 5TH AVE)
TEL: 415.459.1320 HOURS: M-SA 11:30-2:30 & 5-10; SU 5-10
Parking: parking lot

❝...not your typical kids' restaurant, but you've got to check it out...good food, nice decor and staff that is very accommodating with children...excellent lunch buffet...❞

Features

		Criteria	
Children's menu	✗	$$	Prices
Changing station	✗	❹	Speed of service
High chairs available	✓	❹	Stroller access

Taco Jane's

SAN ANSELMO - 21 TAMALPAIS AVE (AT SAN ANSELMO AVE)
TEL: 415.454.6562 HOURS: M-F 11:30-3 & 5-9; SA-SU 11:30-9:30

Theresa & Johnny's
☆☆☆☆

SAN RAFAEL - 817 4TH ST (AT LINCOLN AVE)
TEL: 415.259.0182 HOURS: DAILY 8-3
Parking: street parking

❝...a very relaxed and comfortable environment...they even ask you to turn off your cell phone...no changing table in the bathroom...will prepare special "baby foods" when asked for something particular...breastfeeding friendly...❞

Features

		Criteria	
Children's menu	✗	$	Prices
Changing station	✗	❹	Speed of service
High chairs available	✓	❹	Stroller access

Waypoint Pizza

BELVEDERE TIBURON - 15 MAIN ST (AT BEACH RD)
TEL: 415.435.3440 HOURS: W-M 11:30-9:30
Parking: lot on Main St

Yankee Pier
★★★★

www.yankeepier.com
LARKSPUR - 286 MAGNOLIA AVE (AT ARCH ST)
TEL: 415.924.7676 HOURS: M-F 12-2:30 5-9; SA-SU 12-10
Parking: street parking; valet available

❝...Cape Cod style seafood...lots of toys to play with and sandboxes out front...have the new racks to set infant car seats in...do not take reservations, so there can be a wait...❞

Features

Children's menu .... ✗
Changing station .... ✓
High chairs available .... ✓

Criteria

$$$ .... Prices
❸ .... Speed of service
❸ .... Stroller access

Peninsula

Applewood 2 Go

MENLO PARK - 989 EL CAMINO REAL (AT OAK GROVE AVE)
TEL: 650.328.1556 HOURS: M-F 11-2 5-10
Parking: street parking

Aqui Cal-Mex Grill

SAN JOSE - 1145 LINCOLN AVE (AT WILLOW ST)
TEL: 408.995.0381 HOURS: SU-TH 11-9; F-SA 11-9:30
Parking: lot behind building

Chevys Fresh Mex Restaurant   ★★★★★

www.chevys.com

FOSTER CITY - 979 EDGEWATER BLVD # A (AT BEACH PARK BLVD)
TEL: 650.572.8441 HOURS: SU-TH 11-10:30; F-SA 11-11:30
Parking: lot in front of building

MOUNTAIN VIEW - 2116 W EL CAMINO REAL (AT S RENGSTORFF AVE)
TEL: 650.691.9955 HOURS: SU-TH 11-10:30; F-SA 11-11:30
Parking: lot in front of building

REDWOOD CITY - 2907 EL CAMINO REAL (AT SELBY LN)
TEL: 650.367.6892 HOURS: SU-TH 11-10:30; F-SA 11-11:30
Parking: lot in front of building

SAN JOSE - 1502 SARATOGA AVE (AT LAWRENCE EXPWY)
TEL: 408.871.9110 HOURS: SU-TH 11-10:30; F-SA 11-11:30
Parking: lot in front of building

SAN JOSE - 5305 ALMADEN EXPWY (AT CHYNOWETH AVE)
TEL: 408.266.1815 HOURS: SU-TH 11-10:30; F-SA 11-11:30
Parking: lot in front of building

SAN JOSE - 550 S WINCHESTER (AT MOORPARK AVE)
TEL: 408.241.0158 HOURS: SU-TH 11-10:30; F-SA 11-11:30
Parking: lot in front of building

SOUTH SAN FRANCISCO - 141 HICKEY BLVD (AT JUNIPERO SERRA BLVD)
TEL: 650.755.1617 HOURS: SU-TH 11-10:30; F-SA 11-11:30
Parking: lot in front of building

SUNNYVALE - 204 S MATHILDA AVE (AT W WASHINGTON AVE)
TEL: 408.737.7395 HOURS: SU-TH 11-10:30; F-SA 11-11:30
Parking: lot in front of building

❝...a fun, reasonably priced place to eat...always a safe bet for a quick, tasty meal...lots of distractions for little ones such as the tortilla maker and balloons...totally kid-friendly - from the balloon at entry, to the crayons and kids' menu...usually pretty loud and busy so nobody minds if your little makes noise...the staff totally understand little children and are always quick and accommodating...changing stations aren't the greatest... ❞

Features

Children's menu .... ✓
Changing station .... ✓
High chairs available .... ✓

Criteria

$$ .... Prices
❹ .... Speed of service
❹ .... Stroller access

Chili's Grill & Bar

www.chilis.com

SAN BRUNO - 899 EL CAMINO REAL (AT SAN BRUNO AVE W)
TEL: 650.952.2692 HOURS: M-TH 11-11; F-SA 11-12AM; SU 11-9:30
Parking: lot in front of building

Cucina Cucina Italian Cafe

www.cucinacucina.com

SAN JOSE - 1000 EL PASEO DE SARATOGA (AT CAMPBELL AVE)
TEL: 408.866.9222 HOURS: M-TH 11:30-10; F-SA 11:30-11
Parking: lot across the street

Fresh Choice   ★★★★

www.freshchoice.com

COLMA - 4927 JUNIPERO SERRA BLVD (AT SERRAMONTE BLVD)
TEL: 650.757.7892 HOURS: SU-TH 11-9; F-SA 11-10
Parking: mall has a lot

SAN JOSE - 1600 SARATOGA AVE (AT W CAMPBELL AVE)
TEL: 408.866.1491 HOURS: DAILY 11-9
Parking: mall has a lot

❝...buffet-style restaurant, with fresh fruits, veggies, and potato bar...divided trays for kids and lots of high chairs and booster seats...usually lots of families dining, including breastfeeding mothers...it's self-serve, so you can spend as much time in there as necessary...the quality of food is always dependable and tastes great...prices are based on your kid's age with those under 3 eating free...❞

Features

Children's menu .... ✓
Changing station .... ✓
High chairs available .... ✓

Criteria

$$ .... Prices
❹ .... Speed of service
❹ .... Stroller access

Left At Albuquerque   ☆☆☆

www.leftatalb.com

BURLINGAME - 1100 BURLINGAME AVE (AT CALIFORNIA DR)
TEL: 650.401.5700 HOURS: SU-TH 11:30-10; F-SA 11:30-11
Parking: lot across the street

Features

Children's menu .... ✗
Changing station .... ✓
High chairs available .... ✓

Criteria

$$$ .... Prices
❸ .... Speed of service
❸ .... Stroller access

Mimi's Cafe

www.mimiscafe.com

SAN MATEO - 2208 BRIDGEPOINTE PKWY (AT MARINERS ISLAND BLVD)
TEL: 650.574.8767 HOURS: DAILY 7-11
Parking: lot in front of building

"...they really enjoy children at Mimi's...the staff is wonderful...as soon as you're seated they provide cheerios, crackers and orange slices to keep the little ones busy...totally affordable..."

Features		Criteria	
Children's menu	✗	$$	Prices
Changing station	✓	❹	Speed of service
High chairs available	✓	❹	Stroller access

Pasta Pomodoro

www.pastapomodoro.com

MILPITAS - 181 RANCH DR (AT MCCARTHY BLVD)
TEL: 408.582.0160 HOURS: M-TH 11-10; F 11-11; SA 12-11; SU 12-9
Parking: lot in front of building

SAN BRUNO - 811 CHERRY AVE (AT SAN BRUNO AVE W)
TEL: 650.583.6622 HOURS: DAILY 11-10
Parking: lot in front of building

SAN JOSE - 1205 THE ALAMEDA (AT RACE ST)
TEL: 408.292.9929 HOURS: M-TH 11-10; F-SA 11-11; SU 12-10
Parking: lot behind building

SAN JOSE - 4898 SAN FELIPE RD (AT YERBA BUENA RD)
TEL: 408.532.0271 HOURS: M-TH 11-10; F-SA 11-11; SU 11-10
Parking: lot in front of building

SUNNYVALE - 300 W EL CAMINO REAL (AT S FRANCES ST)
TEL: 408.789.0037 HOURS: M-TH 11-10; F-SA 11-11; SU 12-10
Parking: lot in front building

"...a great standard for those with active kids - quick service, a straight-forward kid-friendly menu, and enough noise and bustle that you don't stand out with a noisy infant or toddler...the wait staff automatically brings out the kids meals first, without being asked...prices are good, food is familiar and the atmosphere is comfy...they are used to having lots of moms and strollers in the restaurant..."

Features		Criteria	
Children's menu	✓	$$	Prices
Changing station	✓	❹	Speed of service
High chairs available	✓	❹	Stroller access

Pizza My Heart

PALO ALTO - 220 UNIVERSITY AVE (AT EMERSON ST)
TEL: 650.327.9400 HOURS: SU-TH 11-12AM; FRI-SA 11-2AM
Parking: street parking

Key to abbreviations used in the indexes:

MC	maternity clothing
BB	baby basics & gear
BP	breast pump sales & rentals
PED	pediatricians
PRC	parenting resources & classes
NR	nanny referrals & baby sitters
DS	diaper delivery services
EX	exercise programs
HC	haircuts
PHOT	children's photographers
ACT	activities & playgroups
PG	playgrounds & parks
RES	child-friendly restaurants
SF	san francisco
EB	east bay
NB	north bay
P	peninsula
OL	online

San Jose

San Leandro

San Lorenzo

San Mateo

San Rafael

San Ramon

Santa Clara

Santa Rosa

Sausalito

St Helena

Sunnyvale

Union City

Vallejo

Walnut Creek

Nursery Furnishings

Baby Clothing

Baby/Toddler Shoes

Feeding Supplies

Diapers & Toiletries

Outing Equipment

Toys & Books

www.lilaguide.com

Activities – Toddlers

Activities – Parent Groups